LUDWIG VON MISES:

THE MAN AND HIS ECONOMICS

THE COLLECTED WORKS OF ISRAEL M. KIRZNER

ISRAEL M. KIRZNER

Ludwig von Mises: The Man and His Economics

Edited and with an Introduction by

PETER J. BOETTKE and FRÉDÉRIC SAUTET

LIBERTY FUND

This book is published by Liberty Fund, Inc., a foundation established to encourage study of the ideal of a society of free and responsible individuals.

𒂼𒄄

The cuneiform inscription that serves as our logo and as a design element in Liberty Fund books is the earliest-known written appearance of the word "freedom" (*amagi*), or "liberty." It is taken from a clay document written about 2300 B.C. in the Sumerian city-state of Lagash.

23 22 21 20 19 C 5 4 3 2 1
23 22 21 20 19 P 5 4 3 2 1

Library of Congress Cataloging-in-Publication Data

Names: Kirzner, Israel M., author. | Sautet, Frédéric E., editor. | Boettke, Peter J., editor.

Title: Ludwig von Mises: the man and his economics / Israel M. Kirzner ; edited and with an introduction by Peter J. Boettke and Frédéric Sautet.

Description: Carmel, Indiana : Liberty Fund Inc., 2019. | Series: The collected works of Israel M. Kirzner ; 10 | Includes index.

Identifiers: LCCN 2019002556 | ISBN 9780865978645 (hardback) | ISBN 9780865978652 (paperback)

Subjects: LCSH: Von Mises, Ludwig, 1881–1973. | Economists—Austria—Biography. | Austrian school of economics. | BISAC: BUSINESS & ECONOMICS / Economics / General. | BUSINESS & ECONOMICS / Economics / Theory.

Classification: LCC HB101.V66 K57 2019 | DDC 330.15/7—dc23

LC record available at https://lccn.loc.gov/2019002556

LIBERTY FUND, INC.
11301 North Meridian Street
Carmel, Indiana 46032-4564

B'EZRAS HASHEM

CONTENTS

The first volume of the Collected Works of Israel Kirzner contains his dissertation, *The Economic Point of View*, written under the guidance of Ludwig von Mises at New York University and defended in 1957. With the present volume, which completes the collection, we return to Mises through the publication of Kirzner's book that pays tribute to his mentor's life and work. One cannot overestimate the importance of Kirzner's encounter with Mises in the 1950s. They met while Kirzner was completing his coursework for the MBA. Following this encounter, Kirzner changed his career path, forsaking professional accountancy to become an academic economist.

Mises was the most significant free-market economist of the twentieth century and one of the greatest economists of all time. Although Carl Menger's influence helped him become an economist, it was under the tutelage of Eugen von Böhm-Bawerk that Mises completed his formative years and became one of the foremost specialists of monetary theory before World War I. Between the world wars, Mises taught as a *Privatdozent* at the University of Vienna and served as secretary at the Vienna Chamber of Commerce. Mises built, throughout his career, a comprehensive approach to economics and human action—praxeology—that encompasses the philosophical and sociological underpinnings of social science. "If economic theory, as the science of human action, has become a *system* at the hands of Mises," explains Kirzner, "it is so because his grasp of its praxeological character imposes on its propositions an epistemological rationale that in itself creates this systematic unity" (2009a; 164). After having fled Europe during World War II to come to the United States in order to avoid Nazi persecution, Mises started a seminar at New York University, which had a tremendous impact on the resurgence of Austrian economics in America. In his career, Mises not only presented the ideas of the Austrian tradition in a clearer and more encompassing manner than anyone before him; he also contributed to its development

---

1. Kirzner (2009b; 8). This is especially in reference to *Human Action*.

by deepening the insights of the Austrian school and producing a "spar-kling, fresh, fundamentally new interpretation of its central tenets."[1]

By Kirzner's own account, Mises's intellectual influence on his work is tremendous. Kirzner even claims that his own work is best seen as a clarification of Ludwig von Mises's oeuvre—all the elements were already contained in Mises's insights. Kirzner's work is, however, the foremost exemplar of the development of the Misesian—as well as Hayekian—research program. The entrepreneurial function was omnipresent in Mises's work but was not articulated in ways that most of the profession could understand and engage with. Kirzner provided a framework that puts the role of entrepreneurship at the center of modern market theory and our understanding of the price system. He opened up the closed approach of microeconomics and offered solutions that could not be envisaged within the traditional approach. This way, Kirzner successfully introduced Misesian ideas into contemporary scholarship. Kirzner's important influence on the field of entrepreneurship studies, for instance, also marks the introduction of Misesian insights into modern entrepreneurship research.

One may find the same analytical foundations in the works of both authors, and Kirzner implicitly recognizes this when he states: "Mises' economics, seen as the science of human action, must itself include understanding of the manner in which human beings become aware of the opportunities for gainful activity. For Mises, the verb 'to act' includes not only effective exploitation of all perceived net opportunities for gain, but also the *discovery* of those opportunities" (Kirzner 2001; 87). In his consistent development of the Misesian research program, Kirzner has fought against mechanistic representations of the market. Following Mises, he has continually argued that economists should move beyond the exclusive focus on equilibrium states of affairs and center their efforts instead upon explicating the principles of market processes. In Kirzner's view, to understand the system of capitalistic production the theorist must trace economic phenomena back to the purposes and plans of the individual decision makers and recognize the intertemporal coordinating role of capital markets. This utterly subjectivist approach is deeply rooted into Misesian praxeology.

Mises's influence on the revival of classical liberal ideas first in Europe but more importantly in the United States cannot be overstated. As Kirzner puts it: "Mises saw the denial of economics as an alarming threat to a free society and to Western civilization. It is economics that is able to demonstrate the social advantages of the unhampered market. The validity of these demonstrations rests heavily on precisely those insights into human action that positivist thought treats, in effect, as meaningless nonsense. What inspired Mises' vigorous and spirited crusade against the philosophic underpinnings of an economics not founded on human purposefulness was more than the scientist's passion for truth, it was his profound concern for the preservation of human freedom and dignity" (1978; vii).

This volume includes two sections. The first section contains Kirzner's book *Ludwig von Mises: The Man and His Economics*. It offers a treatment of Mises's life and it details his intellectual development and influence not only in economics—the development of Austrian economics in the last part of the twentieth century owes perhaps everything to Mises—but also in the classical liberal movement that emerged after World War II. Kirzner insists that his mentor, while a laissez-faire economist, built the praxeological approach upon the possibility and importance of *wertfrei* science, that is, the Weberian idea that science must be value free if it is to serve the truth. Reading through the volume, one can sense Kirzner's deep respect and admiration for his professor and mentor. As the foreword to *The Economic Point of View* attests, Mises thought very highly of his student's work and reciprocated such consideration. This mutual respect and admiration make the book all the more special, as one gets a glimpse into the feelings of two very private individuals.

Section two offers nine important articles by Israel Kirzner on Mises's life and work, which complement the book. The articles reflect on Mises's legacy in economics and focus on various aspects of his work, such as the roles of entrepreneurship, uncertainty, and subjectivism in economic science, as well as the importance of Mises's *Human Action* in intellectual history. It also includes Mises's obituary that Kirzner published in 1973. The volume concludes with a list of publications by Israel Kirzner and a general index for the entire series.

ACKNOWLEDGMENTS

We would first like to thank wholeheartedly Israel Kirzner for his unparalleled contribution to economic science. Kirzner's research program has deeply enriched the discipline and has shed light on some of economics' most difficult puzzles. Economists owe him an immense intellectual debt.

The publication of *The Collected Works of Israel M. Kirzner* would not be a reality without the participation of Liberty Fund, Inc. We are extremely grateful to Liberty Fund, and especially Emilio Pacheco, for making this project possible. To republish Kirzner's unique oeuvre has been on our minds since our time spent at New York University in the 1990s, where one of us was a professor (Peter) and the other a postdoc student (Frédéric). We are thrilled at the idea that current and future generations of economists and other scholars will have easy access to Kirzner's works.

Finally, we wish to thank Emily Washington for her invaluable help in the publication of this volume and Rosolino Candela for his critical work on Kirzner's bibliography.

Peter J. Boettke and Frédéric Sautet

REFERENCES

Kirzner, Israel M. 2009a. *The Economic Point of View*. Indianapolis, Ind.: Liberty Fund.

Kirzner, Israel M. 2009b. "*Human Action*, 1949: A Dramatic Episode in Intellectual History." *Freeman* 59 (September): 8–11.

Kirzner, Israel M. 2001. *Ludwig von Mises: The Man and His Economics*. Wilmington, Del.: ISI Books.

Mises, Ludwig von. 1978. *The Ultimate Foundation of Economic Science*. Kansas City, Kans.: Sheed, Andrews and McMeel.

LUDWIG VON MISES:

THE MAN AND HIS ECONOMICS

ABBREVIATIONS AND REFERENCES

All page references in the text are to the writings of Mises and his wife. When referring to his books, I use the following abbreviations. All other references are in the notes.

EFI   *Economic Freedom and Interventionism: An Anthology of Articles and Essays by Ludwig von Mises,* ed. Bettina Bien-Greaves (Irvington-on-Hudson: Foundation for Economic Education, 1990).

EP   *Economic Policy: Thoughts for Today and Tomorrow* (South Bend, Ind.: Regnery Gateway, 1979).

EPE   *Epistemological Problems of Economics* (Princeton, N.J.: Van Nostrand, 1960).

HA   *Human Action: A Treatise on Economics,* 3rd revised edition (Chicago: Henry Regnery, 1966).

HSAS   *The Historical Setting of the Austrian School of Economics* (New Rochelle, N.Y.: Arlington House, 1969).

LCT   *Liberalism in the Classical Tradition* (San Francisco: Foundation for Economic Education and Cobden Press, 1985).

MMC   *On the Manipulation of Money and Credit,* ed. Percy L. Greaves and trans. Bettina Bien-Greaves (Dobbs Ferry, N.Y.: Free Market Books, 1978).

MMMP   *Money, Method, and the Market Process: Essays by Ludwig von Mises,* ed. Richard M. Ebeling (Norwell, Mass.: Praxeology Press of the Ludwig von Mises Institute, and Kluwer Academic Publications, 1990).

MYWM   *My Years with Ludwig von Mises* (New Rochelle, N.Y.: Arlington House, 1976).

NR   *Notes and Recollections,* trans. Hans F. Sennholz (South Holland, Ill.: Libertarian Press, 1978).

S   *Socialism: An Economic and Sociological Analysis,* trans. J. Kahane (London: Jonathan Cape, 1936).

TH   *Theory and History: An Interpretation of Social and Economic Revolution* (New Haven: Yale University Press, 1957).

TMC   *The Theory of Money and Credit,* rev. edition (New Haven: Yale University Press, 1953).

UFES   *The Ultimate Foundation of Economic Science: An Essay on Method* (Princeton, N.J.: Van Nostrand, 1962).

This work is certainly not a full-length biography (nor even an intellectual biography) of Ludwig von Mises. What I have sought to present, in briefest outline, is the *story of Mises in his role of economist*. In attempting to provide this outline, I have faced certain difficulties which, not at all coincidentally, arose out of the very deep personal significance to me of telling this story. Ludwig von Mises was my revered teacher. Everything I have learned, taught, or written, in and on economics, derives, to greater or lesser extent, from what I learned close to a half-century ago in his classes and seminars at New York University, and from what I have learned during these past forty-six years from his published writings. Mises suffered severe professional rejection during the closing decades of his career. As my own understanding of economics has deepened over time, my awareness of this professional rejection has also deepened, in turn, the respect and affection with which I regard my teacher. And it is, of course, precisely this regard and affection which render it a virtual impossibility to hope that my story of Mises, the economist, can be a strictly impartial and objective one. Yet surely Mises, that stern exemplar of intellectual honesty, would have insisted that his story be told with complete candor and detachment. The standards of intellectual integrity which Mises represented are simply inconsistent with any hagiographic treatment.

I have done my best to present Mises and his economics without, on the one hand, concealing my own admiration for the subtlety and depth of Misesian economics, and, on the other hand, without failing to take note of the difficulties which other economists (and sometimes even Mises's own followers) have encountered in that work.

A number of scholars have explored various aspects of Mises's intellectual contributions and legacy. All students of Misesian economics must be grateful to Bettina Bien-Greaves for her remarkable two-volume *Mises: An Annotated Bibliography*, a veritable treasure house of information. Professor Richard Ebeling has devoted most of his scholarly career to the study of the life and work of Mises. He has contributed a number

Ludwig von Mises: The Man and His Economics was first published by ISI Books in 2001. © 2001 by Israel M. Kirzner. Reprinted by permission of ISI Books.

of superb introductions to several volumes of Mises's writings, which he also discovered and edited. Professor Ebeling's forthcoming full-length biography of Mises is eagerly awaited. Eamonn Butler has attempted an ambitious survey of Mises's overall intellectual contribution (from a somewhat different point of departure than that taken in the present work). Professor Karen Vaughn, in the course of her notable exploration of a broader, fascinating episode in intellectual history (*Austrian Economics in America: The Migration of a Tradition* [Cambridge: Cambridge University Press, 1994]), has dealt significantly (and critically) with important segments of Mises's career. The late Murray N. Rothbard, brilliant American disciple of Mises, has more than once presented his own appreciation of Mises's work. And Rothbard's own extraordinarily prolific published writings constitute—even where one feels compelled to disagree with aspects of those writings—a remarkable testimony to Mises's influence and inspiration. Others, too, (including, especially, scholars working with the Auburn University–based Ludwig von Mises Institute) have made significant additions to Mises scholarship. And I have no doubt that the years ahead will bring many more contributions to this fascinating area of intellectual history. It gives me great personal satisfaction to be able to add my own modest contribution to this literature.

I wish to thank Mr. Jeffrey O. Nelson, publisher of ISI Books, for suggesting this project to me and for encouraging me to pursue it. I am particularly grateful to my colleagues in the Austrian Economics Program at New York University, Professor Mario J. Rizzo and Dr. David Harper, for their contributions to this volume. Each of them gave me advice and encouragement during the writing of the work; each of them read a draft of the entire work and offered copious and valuable comments and suggestions. (Neither of them is in any way responsible for any remaining deficiencies in this work.) Grateful acknowledgment is due to the Sarah Scaife Foundation (and especially to Mr. Richard M. Larry) for its support of the Austrian Economics Program at New York University, under whose research auspices I have written this book. One of the central focal points of our research in this Austrian Economics Program at New York University has been the economic ideas of Ludwig von Mises. I take this opportunity to express my appreciation to my present and former colleagues in this program, Professor Mario J. Rizzo, Dr. David Harper, and Professor Peter J. Boettke (now continuing his prolific research in these same areas at George Mason University), and to those many others who, over the past quarter century, have made distinguished contributions to the revitalized interest in Misesian economics.

Ordinarily, when a scientist's career has ended, his work tends to lose its immediacy; it tends, as it were, to move aside, giving way to the subsequent contributions of others to his discipline. But, as the decades have slipped by since Mises's death in 1973, my own appreciation for his economic insights and understanding has only continued to mature. My recognition of Mises's scientific contributions, and my moral regard for the intellectual courage and integrity with which he carried on his work, have made this project a particularly rewarding one. I can only hope that my little book can help communicate to a new generation of readers some of that same scientific recognition and some of that same moral regard.

Israel M. Kirzner
September 2000

1. LUDWIG VON MISES, 1881–1973

The purpose of this short work is to provide a picture of Ludwig von Mises, the economist and social thinker. Such a picture must consist primarily of lines and brush strokes representing Mises's ideas, and explaining how these ideas differed importantly from those of his contemporaries. The subsequent chapters offer such accounts and explanations. But a picture consists of more than lines and strokes; it includes the canvas upon which these are imposed. The story of Mises, the intellectual and the scholar, cannot be appreciated unless it also includes brief attention to the human and historical context within which Mises's intellectual contributions emerged. This chapter seeks to give a brief survey of this human and historical context, a survey that will be brief not only because of space limitations, but also because many of the details of Mises's life, interesting though they may be for a full-length biography, are not, in fact, directly relevant to an appreciation of his intellectual stature.[1] I include in this chapter only those salient features of his biography (and of its historical background) which seem necessary in order for the development of Mises's economic and social ideas to be rendered coherent and understandable.

VIENNA: THE EARLY YEARS

Ludwig von Mises was born on September 29, 1881, in the city of Lemberg in the Austro-Hungarian Empire. His mother was Adele (Landau) von Mises; his father, Arthur Edler von Mises, a construction engineer in government service to the Ministry of Railroads, died at the age of forty-six (after a gall bladder operation) when Ludwig was a twenty-two-year-old university student. (Ludwig's only sibling to survive into adulthood was his younger brother Richard, who was to become a noted mathematician, Harvard professor, and probability theorist.) Although his birthplace was hundreds of miles away from the imperial capital, Mises was to spend some forty years of his life in Vienna. From the age of eleven he spent about eight years attending the Academic Gymnasium in Vienna, after which he became a student in the Faculty of Law and Political Sciences at

---

1. I understand that two separate full-length biographies of Mises are now being prepared by Professor Richard Ebeling and by Dr. J. Guido Hülsmann.

the University of Vienna. With an interruption of about one year's military service (at the conclusion of which he received his commission as lieutenant in a reserve artillery regiment), Mises spent about five years at the university, winning high university honors in the areas of juridical studies, social sciences, and history of law, and being awarded the degree of Doctor of Laws in 1906.

The bulk of Mises's work in economics up to this time was under the influence of teachers imbued directly or indirectly with the ideas of the German Historical School (about which more will be said in subsequent chapters), and Mises had, by the time he received his doctorate, already published several scholarly works in historical economics research. Mises was, however, already beginning to rebel against the methodological and ideological tenets of that school, presumably partly as a result of his reading Carl Menger's *Grundsätze* at the end of 1903[2]—an experience which, he later described, made an "economist" of him (NR, 33). It was apparently after receiving his doctorate that Mises came under the powerful personal influence of Eugen von Böhm-Bawerk (who, after retiring from prestigious service as Minister of Finance of the Austro-Hungarian Empire, began to conduct his famous seminar at the University of Vienna in 1905).[3] Mises attended Böhm-Bawerk's seminar for a number of years until he was himself admitted to the (unsalaried) rank of privatdozent, permitting him to lecture at the university, in 1913. It was during this period that his own systematic understanding of economics developed, along the lines pioneered by Menger (with whom he had extensive personal discussions (NR, 35) and Böhm-Bawerk, culminating in Mises's own pathbreaking 1912 work on monetary theory. This book established Mises as an important economic theorist in his own right, and was the foundation of his subsequent fame as a leading exponent of the "Austrian School."

After several years of engagement in various professional economic responsibilities, Mises obtained a position in 1909 at the Austrian Chamber of Commerce (a quasi-governmental body directly concerned with national commercial and industrial policy). It was his work in this

2. Carl Menger (1840–1921) was the founder of the Austrian School of Economics. His *Grundsätze der Volkswirtschaftslehre* (1871) was the book which initiated the Austrian tradition.

3. Eugen von Böhm-Bawerk (1851–1914) was one of the founding leaders of the Austrian School of Economics.

capacity which, especially after the end of World War I, thrust Mises squarely into the controversial public issues of his time and brought him into contact with many of the leading Austrian political, industrial, and financial personalities. Mises's career as economist thus developed, from the very beginning, as one combining academic research and university teaching with the very practical work of an economic public policy specialist at the center of ferocious political and policy debates.

The state of academic economics in Austria (and the rest of the continent) will be outlined in the chapter following this one. And it is not difficult to recognize the obvious relevance of Mises's earlier work in monetary economics for the public policy issues which reached the crisis point in the hyperinflations of the early twenties. Here we simply note the fact that Mises's early years as doctoral student, university lecturer, and public policy economist were years of social and political change and turmoil. The old courtly world of Imperial Vienna, center of the vast but crumbling Austro-Hungarian Empire, was giving way to a postwar milieu in which entirely new economic and political winds were to blow with an unprecedented ferocity.

Mises was himself, in his old age, to write about the political and ideological currents already at work in continental Europe around the turn of the century. There is no doubt that the views he expressed reflect his youthful impressions of the social context within which his lifelong convictions were forged. Mises saw the controversies that raged between the dominant German intellectuals in social science and the Austrian economists led by Menger, and subsequently Böhm-Bawerk, as having a significance extending far beyond the substance or methodology of economic theory. Most of the German professors, Mises wrote, "more or less eagerly made propaganda in their writings and in their courses for the policies of the Imperial Government: authoritarian conservatism, *Sozialpolitik,* protectionism, huge armaments, and aggressive nationalism" (HSAS, 23f). Mises saw the Mengerian School as the champion of liberalism, as the last intellectual source of hope for the preservation of freedom and civilization in the face of the dangers posed by statism and by Marxism. From his perspective at the outset of the last third of the twentieth century, Mises saw, in fact, a "straight line that leads from the work of the Historical School to Nazism," from "Schmoller's glorification of the Hohenzollern Electors and Kings, to Sombart's canonization of Adolf Hitler" (HSAS, 33–34). In memoirs written several decades earlier (1940), Mises also traced the cataclysmic twentieth-century events for which Marxism and Nazism have been responsible to the teachings of the German Historical School. He reports that Menger had (apparently well before the turn of the century) foreseen that the policies pursued by the European powers would "lead to a horrible war that will end with gruesome revolutions, with the extinction of European culture and the destruction of prosperity of all nations" (NR, 35). It was in this charged ideological atmosphere that Mises's own ideas developed and crystallized.

Mises himself experienced the hardships of war. During World War I he saw active service at the front in the Carpathians as a first lieutenant, but after getting typhoid in 1917 he was called back to Vienna to work in the economics division of the Department of War (MYWM, 25f). It was his work in that capacity, together with his reflections on the political turmoil which was to follow the conclusion of hostilities, which led him to publish his second book, *Nation, Staat und Wirtschaft*, in 1919. (The book was translated into English many years later by Professor Leland Yeager under the title *Nation, State and Economy*.) Mises was later to describe that work as "a scientific book with political design. It was an attempt at alienating the affections of the German and Austrian public from National-Socialist (*Nazi*) ideas which then had no special name, and recommending reconstruction by democratic-liberal policy" (NR, 66). This tone of the work captured the passion which was to characterize Mises's writings throughout his life. He saw the results of his scientific work as enormously significant for practical policy, if a civilized society was to be created and preserved.

VIENNA AFTER WORLD WAR I

During the years immediately following the war's end, Mises's stature as a Viennese intellectual came to be well established. Several aspects of his work during these years contributed to his prominence in the Vienna of the twenties. His 1919 book did not receive extensive attention. But his 1922 work *Die Gemeinwirtschaft* (published in English in 1936 as *Socialism: An Economic and Sociological Analysis*)—a work thoroughly out of step with both the strong political momentum toward socialism in Austria immediately after the war and the generally favorable attitude of intellectuals at that time toward socialism—placed Mises squarely in the eye of the storm of public debate. Expanding on a seminal 1920 article on the pure economics of socialist central planning, Mises laid out in this book not only his now-famous critique of the possibility of socialist economic calculation, but also his extensive economic and sociological critique of socialism in general. This work made Mises the archenemy of all those who saw Mises's ideal of a liberal (free-market) society as an old-fashioned reactionary ideology discredited by twentieth-century intellectual-progressive developments.

At the same time, Mises's rapidly expanding responsibilities at the Chamber of Commerce during these years of postwar turmoil involved him directly in the central political and policy issues of the day. Although formally only a staff member at the Chamber, in fact Mises's influence became national in scope. In Mises's own words (written some two decades later): "In the Chamber I created a position for myself. . . . My position was incomparably greater than that of any . . . Austrian who did not preside over one of the big political parties. I was the economist of the country" (NR, 73f). In his memoirs Mises describes how he persuaded the Marxist Otto Bauer to refrain from installing a Bolshevist regime in Vienna during the winter of 1918–19 (NR, 18f). But Mises's success was severely limited. "Supported only by a few friends I waged a hopeless fight. All I achieved was to delay the catastrophe. The fact that in the winter of 1918–19 Bolshevism did not take over and that the collapse of industry and banks did not occur in 1921, but in 1931, was in large part the result of my efforts" (NR, 74).[4]

It was during these early postwar years that Mises acquired the reputation of obstinacy and intransigence—character traits which more friendly observers would later interpret as the expression of Mises's consistency, incorruptibility, and intellectual (and political) courage.[5] Mises himself recognized and defended his "intransigence," seeing himself as intransigent only in matters of science. "I always drew a sharp distinction between my scientific and political activity. In science, compromises are treason to truth. In politics, compromises are unavoidable. . . . In the Austria of the postwar period I was the economic conscience" (NR, 75).

4. Although the claims made by Mises (in the quotations in this paragraph) may at first seem immodest, there are at least some grounds for accepting them at face value. See note 6 below.

5. See Jacques Rueff, "The Intransigence of Ludwig von Mises," chapter 1 in *On Freedom and Free Enterprise: Essays in Honor of Ludwig von Mises,* ed. M. Sennholz, rev. ed. (Irvington-on-Hudson, N.Y.: Foundation for Economic Education, 1994).

Mises was able to use his prestige as a specialist in monetary economics to help stem, to some extent, the threat of disastrous inflation in Austria during the early twenties. "If it had not been for our passionate agitation against the continuation of the deficit and inflation policy, the crown in early 1922 would have fallen to one-millionth or one-billionth of its gold parity of 1892. . . . This catastrophe was avoided. . . . The Austrian currency did not collapse like the German currency in 1923. . . . Nevertheless, the country for many years had to suffer from the destructive consequences of continuous inflation" (NR, 78).[6]

Looking back at Mises's activities during these early years of the twenties, it seems altogether remarkable that, at the same time as he was involved in such dramatic political and policy activity, he should have been able to find the time, the patience, and the peace of mind to write the scholarly works which poured from his pen. Moreover, Mises maintained his university affiliation during these years, lecturing and leading his university seminar. In addition he led his own famed *Privatseminar*, which met every two weeks in his Chamber office. (This seminar, to which we shall refer again in chapter 2, attracted some of the finest young Viennese intellectuals. Some of these were to become world famous economists, historians, sociologists, or philosophers. They included F. A. Hayek, G. Haberler, F. Machlup, E. Voegelin, Alfred Schutz, Felix Kaufmann.) It is no surprise to read that, at least to his friends, Mises was seen, already in those years, as "the greatest living mind in Austria" (MYWM, 22).

The truth is that, although Mises would have much preferred a full professorship at the university—a position that would have permitted him to engage entirely in research and teaching—this opportunity was consistently denied him. Mises, admitted to the university as lecturer ("Privatdozent") in 1913, received the title of Associate Professor ("ausserordentliche Professor") in 1918, but never did obtain a full university professorship. Hayek tells us that Mises blamed this on anti-Semitism;[7]

---

6. For confirmation of Mises's crucial role in stemming the Austrian inflation (and for personal information that one of the great disappointments of Mises's life was his not being called at that time to take over the finance ministry to stabilize the currency), see F. A. Hayek, *Hayek on Hayek: An Autobiographical Dialogue*, ed. S. Kresge and L. Wenar (London: Routledge, 1994), 70.

7. *Hayek on Hayek*, 59. See also Earlene Craver, "The Emigration of Austrian Economists," *History of Political Economy* 18 (spring 1987), 5.

but in his memoirs Mises makes no mention of any such "explanation." Instead, Mises writes: "I recognized rather early that as a classical liberal a full professorship at a university in German-speaking countries would always be denied me" (NR, 93). "A university professorship was closed to me inasmuch as the universities were searching for interventionists and socialists" (NR, 73). One of Mises's Vienna students, Dr. Fritz Kaufmann, referred to Mises's often being treated, in those years, with hostility. "This hostility was apparently the reason for the fact, otherwise hardly understandable, that he never became a full professor at the Vienna University, which he certainly would have deserved on the basis of his scientific and scholarly importance" (MYWM, 2nd ed., 202). Mises's influence at the university was limited, in particular, by the hostility of Hans Mayer (successor to the full professorship occupied earlier by Mayer's teacher, Friedrich von Wieser), who, at least in Mises's recollection, "occupied his time with . . . mischievous intrigues against me."

It was in late 1925 that Mises first met Margit Sereny-Herzfeld, whom he was to marry some thirteen years later. She had been widowed several years previously, had earlier pursued a successful career as an actress in Germany, and was the mother of two young children. In her published recollections of her life with Mises, Margit von Mises included several letters which Ludwig von Mises sent to her in the years after they met. Clearly Mises had fallen deeply in love, and in fact proposed marriage to her in 1926. Mrs. Mises explained that soon after their engagement, Mises "grew afraid of marriage, the bond it would mean, the change that children would bring to a quiet home, and the responsibilities that might distract him from his work." "Lu thought of the task he had set himself, the tremendous work that was ahead of him, all the writing he wanted to do." He faced "the choice between his work and duty to his intellectual ideals on the one hand, and a life of love and affection on the other" (MYWM, 27).

THE YEARS IN GENEVA

In her recollections (which she wrote in order "to reveal Ludwig von Mises as he really was: a great thinker, a great scholar, a great teacher— but still a lonely man with a great need for love and affection" [MYWM, 7]), Margit vividly describes the tense years in Vienna both prior and subsequent to the almost cataclysmic 1931 bankruptcy of the Credit Anstalt (a crash and the consequences of which Mises had predicted). She also opens up a window into Mises's human character and personality. These were turbulent years; Hitler's 1933 rise to power in Germany was to fatally endanger the independence of Austria.[8] Mises was fully aware of the near inevitability of an eventual Nazi takeover. He had no illusions concerning the danger to his own safety. And indeed, later, on the very night in 1938 when the Germans marched into Vienna, they entered the apartment where Mises had lived with his mother and drove away with his library, writings, and documents in thirty-eight cases (MYWM, 35). No doubt this awareness was partly the explanation for the circumstance that, when in 1934 he was offered an opportunity to join the faculty of the Graduate Institute of International Studies in Geneva, Switzerland, he immediately accepted the offer. His departure for Geneva in October 1934 ended a major chapter (or several chapters) in his life and career, but was to open an entirely new series. By all accounts Mises's six years at the "Institut" (as he often referred to it) in Geneva brought him satisfaction and peace. "For me," he would write in his memoirs, "it was a liberation to be removed from the political tasks I could not have escaped in Vienna. . . . Finally, I could devote myself completely and almost exclusively to scientific problems" (NR, 137). In his preface to *Human Action* (1949), Mises would describe the "serene atmosphere of this seat of learning," in which he was able to write a major treatise on economics. It is not difficult to understand why, in Margit von Mises's assessment, "[he] never had been so happy as he was in Geneva" (MYWM, 54).

And it was in Geneva in 1938, twelve years after first proposing marriage to her, that Ludwig von Mises married Margit Sereny-Herzfeld. The witnesses were Hans Kelsen, famous international legal authority, and Gottfried von Haberler, eminent economist at the League of Nations. Mises, whom his friends viewed as the epitome of confirmed bachelorhood,[9] had, after years of hesitation, finally married. If the first fifty-seven years of his life were largely years of loneliness, the last thirty-five were to be years of increasing reliance on the protective, loving care of his Margit. If his earlier hesitations had something to do with the fear that marriage might hamper his scientific work, it seems clear that his later work was to owe a very great debt indeed to the unswerving confidence, unstinting encouragement, and sustaining care with which Margit supported him

8. For Mises's own account of the political events of these years, see NR, chapter 15.

9. See MYWM, 41, for Kelsen's remark on this.

to the day of his death in 1973. Indeed, Mrs. Mises was to devote her years following Ludwig's death to the publication of his writings (as well as both of their memoirs). Margit was to write that, when they married, she knew that a successful marriage required that her husband's "work should be more important to [her] than anything [she] could do" (MYWM, 45). There is no doubt that it was this conviction which was to sustain Mises for the rest of his life, and beyond.

MISES'S CHARACTER AND PERSONALITY

In her memoirs Margit von Mises gives us, if not an impartial picture of her husband and of their marriage, at least a nuanced and remarkably candid view of his character and personality. Ludwig von Mises was a strong man who carefully controlled his emotions, but to Margit his affection was overpowering (MYWM, 44). And his commitment to his responsibilities was impressive. On one occasion in Geneva, he slipped and fell on the ice, hurting himself severely. Despite his injury (which a subsequent x-ray was to reveal as a fracture) and the terrible pain he must have experienced, he proceeded to deliver his scheduled lecture and to direct the following discussion (MYWM, 53f). Yet during the early years of their marriage (as well as during the Vienna years), Margit reveals, Mises was subject to frightening outbursts of temper. "His temper would flare up, mostly about a small, unimportant happening. He would lose control of himself . . . when it happened the first few times I was frightened to death." Gradually, she writes, she came to realize that these "terrible attacks" were really "a sign of depression," a hidden dissatisfaction and "the sign of a great, great need for love." These occurrences became less frequent after their marriage and disappeared completely after a few years (MYWM, 44). But that Mises's anger could continue to inspire fear is confirmed by his subsequent relationships with the former students of his Vienna days. Hayek has reported that "Mises was very resentful of any criticism by his pupils[10] and temporarily broke both with Machlup and Haberler because they criticized him."[11] Margit has described the episode in which (during a 1965 Mont Pelerin Society meeting)

10. In oral remarks Hayek once described (in the presence of this writer) his own trepidation when he first sent Mises a copy of his 1937 *Economica* paper, "Economics and Knowledge," in which he (somewhat obliquely) took issue with certain Misesian positions.

11. *Hayek on Hayek*, 72.

Machlup provoked his teacher's anger (MYWM, 145f). And Machlup has himself given an account of the episode, the outcome of which was that "for a number of years [Mises] refused to speak to [me]."[12] After Margit persuaded Ludwig to relent and was able to restore "the same friendly atmosphere that had existed in former years" (MYWM, 146), Machlup nevertheless "strictly avoided ever discussing again any questions of monetary policy with him or in his presence."[13] It is worthy of note that, in later years, several of these same pupils (including especially Machlup, Haberler, and certainly Hayek) consistently displayed remarkable personal loyalty and concern for Mises's well-being—in spite of any resentment that Mises may have at one time or another expressed toward them.

Despite the loyalty of his pupils, Ludwig von Mises was a man who inspired sharply divergent personal assessments. His strong doctrinal positions inspired persons hostile to those positions to see him as intransigent, extreme, and lacking in compassion. As Machlup was to put it several years after Mises's death, "[n]o wonder . . . that interventionists, monetary expansionists, socialists, egalitarians, and laborites disliked Mises, or even detested him."[14] And it was of course precisely Mises's strong doctrinal positions that led those supporting those positions to see him in a brilliantly favorable light. "With an indefatigable enthusiasm, and with courage and faith undaunted, he has never ceased to denounce the fallacious reasons and untruths offered to justify most of our new institutions," wrote one admirer.[15] In addition, however, to the substance of his doctrinal positions, it seems clear that the "intransigence" and passion with which Mises pursued his doctrinal positions (and perhaps the violent temper which Margit von Mises has described for us) contributed to the list of excuses used by those who chose to reject not only his teachings but also Mises as an individual—while his admirers saw only "his poise, his bearing, his European graciousness . . . his kindness and understanding to graduate students."[16] They marvelled that he had "at

---

12. Fritz Machlup, "Ludwig von Mises: A Scholar Who Would Not Compromise," in *Homage to Mises: The First Hundred Years,* ed. J. K. Andrews, Jr. (Hillsdale, Mich.: Hillsdale College Press, 1981), 25.

13. Ibid.

14. Ibid., 23.

15. Rueff, "Intransigence of Ludwig von Mises," 15.

16. W. H. Peterson, "Mises and Keynes," in *Homage to Mises,* 30.

his disposal a store of historical culture, the treasures of which are animated and illuminated by a form of humanity and Austrian wit rarely to be found on the surface of this globe."[17]

THE FIRST YEARS IN NEW YORK

The happiness and serenity of Mises's life in Geneva was sharply interrupted by World War II. Although neutral, Switzerland was not seen as providing any assurance for the safety of Mises, blacklisted by the Nazis, in a European continent overrun by the German armies. When France fell in June of 1940, Mises reluctantly agreed to his wife's insistence that they migrate to the U.S. (MYWM, 54). (Soon after arriving in the U.S., Mises himself wrote, somewhat cryptically, that he left his position at the *Institut* "because [he] could no longer face living in a country that considered [his] presence a political liability and a danger to its security" [MYWM, 138]). In a chapter in her memoirs entitled "Escape from Europe," Margit von Mises has provided us with a fascinating account of the month-long journey—parts of which were fraught with some danger—that took Ludwig and her from Geneva by bus, train, plane, and finally ship through France, Spain, and Portugal until, on August 2, 1940, they landed in the U.S.

Their physical safety was now assured, but this move was clearly a major setback to Ludwig von Mises's career. He was leaving a well-paid faculty position at a prestigious institution of higher learning, in a continent where his name was widely known in both academic and political circles, for a new country where—largely unknown, at an age close to sixty, and without complete familiarity with the language—his chances of resuming a successful academic career must surely have seemed slim. Although Mises entered the U.S. with a non-quota visa based on a hastily arranged invitation to take a six-month position as "lecturer and research associate professor" at the University of California, Berkeley, it seems doubtful if he ever expected that position to offer a permanent opportunity for him (MYWM, 55). In any event, soon after arriving in New York he "decided not to go to Berkeley. He felt that New York was the cultural center of the United States and it was here that he wanted to stay" (MYWM, 64). And, indeed, his first years in the United States were difficult ones, both professionally and financially. A number of Mises's friends from

17. W. H. Rappard, "On Reading von Mises," in *On Freedom and Free Enterprise*, 17.

Europe were helpful, and a number of his former students (including Alfred Schutz and Fritz Machlup) did their best to find a suitable academic position for their former mentor, but none such was ever offered to him. Mises gave guest lectures at Columbia, Harvard, and Princeton, but received no serious offers from any prestigious university. And it was not until 1945 that Mises was appointed to a "Visiting" Professorship at what was then a fledgling, hardly top-flight institution, New York University's Graduate School of Business Administration.

Clearly, apart from his age, Mises's unfashionable political and methodological positions in economics rendered him less than welcome in the front tiers of the U.S. economics profession. It would not have been surprising were Mises, after his arrival in the U.S., to have receded into a bitter, penurious old age, nourished only by memories of his former prominence. It is a tribute to his resilience, determination, and personal and intellectual courage that this was not the case. We may perhaps be tempted to raise our eyebrows at Margit von Mises's assertion that the twenty-five years beginning with the year 1943 "were the most productive and creative of [his] life" (MYWM, 89). But it is certainly the case that this period was one during which Mises built for himself a virtually new career, published a remarkable list of books and papers in the English language, won the friendship of a loyal group of new, American supporters, and inspired a number of American academic disciples who would, decades later, successfully spread his ideas to at least a significant minority of the economics profession around the world.

The several years between his arrival in the United States and his appointment at New York University were years of adjustment for Ludwig and Margit. In Margit's words, Mises "missed his work, his books, and his income"; his spirits, she writes, were at a low point (MYWM, 63). A reading of his memoirs (which he wrote during the first months after his arrival in New York) not only confirms this, but also brings to one's attention a certain tone of bitterness toward his academic and political foes of earlier years. Yet Mises did not permit any such antipathy to cloud his dealings with his new surroundings. By his wife's account of those years, Mises plunged vigorously into the New York scene, making new friends and contacting old European acquaintances, colleagues, or students. The West Side of New York's Manhattan was the area where Ludwig von Mises wished to live; its nearness to the theater district and to the New York Public Library meant much to him. A December 1940 grant from the Rockefeller Foundation to the National Bureau of Economic Research (NBER) to support Mises's work initiated an affiliation that was to last until 1945, and this provided a modest source of livelihood.

A small but growing number of American friends and admirers also developed, partly as a result of the enthusiasm and influence of Henry Hazlitt and Lawrence Fertig. Hazlitt was a prominent economic journalist, financial editor of the *New York Times,* who had become enormously impressed by the 1936 English edition of Mises's *Socialism.* This had led him to correspond with Mises in Geneva; he was to be a constant source of support for Mises in the years ahead. Hazlitt arranged for Mises to write a series of articles for the *Times,* and these 1942–43 articles caught the attention of key officers of the National Association of Manufacturers (NAM), leading to a series of assignments for Mises during the subsequent years. Lawrence Fertig had an influential weekly economic column in the *World Telegram;* he often mentioned Mises and his ideas in his columns (and in his frequent television appearances). In addition, beginning in 1952, Fertig was for many years a member of the New York University Board of Trustees (MYWM, 148). Margit von Mises writes of Hazlitt and Fertig that "they had recognized immediately that Lu was not a man interested in money for himself. So they both did for Lu what he could not do. They made sure that, financially, Lu got ground under his feet again" (MYWM, 90).

Perhaps as a result of his NAM connections, Mises was in 1943 brought into contact with Leonard Read, then General Manager of the Los Angeles Chamber of Commerce. Read was deeply impressed by Mises's strongly held convictions concerning the dangers of government intervention into the free market. In 1945, with the help of a number of influential and wealthy businessmen of vision, Read established the Irvington, New York–based Foundation for Economic Education (FEE). The Foundation's goal was educational, not political. Read and his colleagues wished to communicate the philosophy of free markets to the American public. Soon after its founding, Read made Mises a regular member of the FEE staff. Mises's association with FEE was to be a gratifying part of his work over subsequent decades. By late 1946, therefore, Mises had established himself in his new country, both personally and professionally. And in that year he acquired U.S. citizenship—something he valued greatly (MYWM, 70). He and Margit had, since 1942, occupied a comfortable West Side apartment where his study had a view of the

Hudson River. His personal library had arrived from Geneva. He held a visiting professorship at New York University and a staff position at FEE. These two positions enabled him to maintain both his teaching and his writing activities. Most important of all, perhaps, was that by 1946 he was in fact busy at work on his magnum opus, *Human Action*, the expanded, rewritten English version of the treatise he had published in Geneva in 1940, *Nationalökonomie*.

THE 1945–1973 YEARS

Human Action, published by Yale University Press, crystallized Mises's lifelong contributions to economic understanding. It was a major 889-page statement which systematically surveyed Mises's original ideas concerning economics, economic method, the market process, monetary and business cycle theory, and comparative economic systems (socialism and interventionism as contrasted with the market economy). But the work also included Mises's appreciation for the crucial significance of economic understanding for the preservation of freedom and civilization in human society. It was a work the size and intrinsic importance of which, despite the unpopularity and unfashionability of its positions, did not permit it to be entirely ignored. For those who valued Mises's passionate defense of free markets, the work was to become something of a manifesto. In more general terms, this work was to define Mises's role in the postwar economics profession and his place in postwar American social thought.

The truth is that the dynamics generated by changes in mainstream economics since the thirties, by Mises's migration to the U.S., and by his attempts to reestablish his career in his new surroundings, resulted in his occupying a position in American social discussion which subtly altered his image. During his Geneva years (and, with certain qualifications, also in his Vienna years), Mises was seen primarily as an academic economist whose contributions to the science were recognized, despite their controversial implications for social policy. But by the 1950s, after the publication of *Human Action*, Mises was almost completely ignored by the U.S. economics profession. The dominant changes in economic theorizing and economic methods (characterized by the explosive growth of mathematical economics and econometrics) since 1930—not to speak of changes in economic ideology—made Mises appear, to U.S. economists, thoroughly old-fashioned and out of step, both doctrinally and methodologically. (In subsequent chapters I shall suggest that the economics profession unfortunately failed to understand the economics which Mises was articulating.) The circle of friends and admirers who were attracted to Mises's insights and ideas were, in general, not academicians, but businessmen and professionals in law, medicine, and other fields.

In his New York University classes and seminars, Mises attracted over the years only a small handful of students prepared to follow Misesian scholarship in economic theory as a matter of science (although in the long run those students would make a not insignificant impact on late-twentieth-century perceptions of Austrian Economics). To the outside world, it appeared, Mises in the 1950s was not only a figure from an earlier era, but one whose ideas catered to the conservative prejudices and practical objectives of business interests. The very unpopularity and unfashionability of Mises's work within the economics "establishment" seemed to reinforce the impression that he had somehow changed the character of his work from contributions to economic science to ideologically charged apologetics for capitalism. The uncritical manner in which some of Mises's admirers fiercely defended his work must have strengthened this impression even further. Moreover, at least some of Mises's supporters probably did see Mises primarily as a social thinker who defended capitalism, rather than as the continuator of the Austrian tradition in pure economics. Indeed, it was during this period that the term "Austrian Economics" came to refer, for many of Mises's supporters, not so much to the subjectivist, Mengerian tradition in pure economics as to "economic argumentation in favor of laissez-faire public policy."

Whether he was or was not fully aware of the way in which he was now perceived, Mises proceeded imperturbably to teach his classes, conduct his seminars, and write his books, as if he was, so to speak, still the respected academician at his Geneva *Institut*. Though he passionately believed in the significance of his economics for public policy if a free, prosperous, and civilized society was to be preserved, Mises was utterly convinced that he was engaged in *wertfrei* (i.e., "value-free," a term to be discussed in later chapters) economic science. And he offered warm encouragement to his small number of close students, pointing them toward academic careers and nurturing their efforts at continuing the purely intellectual tradition of Austrian Economics.

Mises's admirers, and his New York University seminar audiences, included traditional conservatives who saw Mises's attacks on American liberalism (representing the ideology of interventionism) as making him one of their own. Other admirers were those who used his critique of excessive government as the foundation for a more radical intellectual case for pure anarchism. Mises presided over the somewhat uneasy alliance among his admirers with imperturbable calm. Rejecting anarchism, Mises embraced conservatism only to the extent that it offered support for his own staunchly held convictions concerning the desirability of classical liberalism. Mises articulated this view at his weekly New York University seminar, where he had not only students who were formally registered (as part of their work completing master's degrees in accounting, marketing, management, or finance), but also a number of non-registered regular seminar participants from outside the university.[18] Although this seminar did not include economists who could reach the stature of the participants in Mises's Vienna *Privatseminar* of the 1920s, it was from this seminar that Mises's influence toward the late-twentieth-century resurgence of Austrian Economics was to radiate outwards. Murray Rothbard, Hans Sennholz, George Reisman, and the present author, were all, at one time or another, participants in this seminar. Percy Greaves, Bettina Bien (later Bien-Greaves), who were subsequently active in translating, editing, and publishing important portions of Mises's work, were also regular participants for many years (as were a number of others). Yet even at New York University, Mises's academic colleagues did not treat him with the respect that might have been expected for a world-renowned senior scholar. He was viewed as being at least faintly embarrassing to the faculty; sometimes students were steered away from his courses.

In 1956, to mark the fiftieth anniversary of Mises's doctorate from the University of Vienna, a festschrift edited by Mary Sennholz was published in his honor. This volume reflects well the role which Mises had assumed in the United States. The distinguished contributors to the volume included internationally renowned European scholars such as Jacques Rueff, William E. Rappard, Bertrand de Jouvenel, Wilhelm Röpke, Friedrich Hayek, and Fritz Machlup. Younger American economists included F. A. Harper (later the founder of the Institute for Humane Studies, but at that time a staff member of FEE), Murray Rothbard, Louis Spadaro, and

18. See Hans F. Sennholz, "Postscript," to NR, 156ff; MYWM, chapter 9.

William Peterson. The South African scholars William H. Hutt and Ludwig M. Lachmann contributed to the volume; and the volume also included papers by non-academic friends and admirers such as Leonard Read, Henry Hazlitt, and Percy Greaves. Many of the contributors were members of the Mont Pelerin Society, the international society founded in 1947 by Hayek in order to promote scholarship and inquiry into classical-liberal values and ideas. Mises had been a founding member of the Society (although, as the years went by, he became increasingly disturbed by what he considered to be faulty views expressed at its periodic meetings by some of its newer members).

Clearly, Mises in the mid-1950s, at the age of seventy-five, was a world-renowned figure—even if one celebrated only by a relatively small (but prestigious) band of erstwhile European colleagues and former students, by a similarly small group of younger American economists, and by several other non-academic admirers. When, about fifteen years later, the Institute for Humane Studies published a two-volume festschrift in honor of Mises's ninetieth birthday, the list of contributors was much longer, but the make-up of that list was rather similar to that of the earlier volume. Mises's influence had certainly spread considerably—but it was confined to scholars and others around the world who, whatever their professional distinction in their own fields, did not, for the most part, stand high in the ranks of the professional economists of the time. All this will prove of considerable relevance in the later chapters of this volume, when we consider Mises more narrowly as economic theorist.

Besides his authorship of his massive treatise, *Human Action,* Mises produced a steady stream of books and articles during these American years. These included *Bureaucracy* (1944), *Omnipotent Government* (1944), *Planning for Freedom and Other Essays and Addresses* (1952; this volume includes the important paper, "Profit and Loss," first presented to a Mont Pelerin Society meeting), *The Anti-Capitalist Mentality* (1956), *Theory and History* (1957), and *The Ultimate Foundation of Economic Science: An Essay on Method* (1962). Many of Mises's books (including his major German-language books of the European days) were translated into a number of languages. Mises's influence as perhaps the foremost intellectual defender of pure capitalism spread around the world, and was especially felt in the countries of Central and South America, to a number of which Mises made lecture tours during his American years.

As Mises entered his ninth decade in the early sixties, he could look back on his two decades of life in the U.S. with quiet satisfaction. He had continued to write and publish on the themes he held to be of vital importance to human society; he had seen his influence, while negligible insofar as the mainstream of U.S. academic economics was concerned, spread to a modest but significant degree all over the world. He was still teaching at New York University, and still lecturing and writing for FEE. Indeed, in 1969, even the American Economic Association recognized the lifelong contributions to economic science of Ludwig von Mises, when, a short time before his eighty-eighth birthday, it named him a Distinguished Fellow. And it was on May 29, 1969, that Mises delivered his final seminar presentation at New York University (he kept up his seminars at FEE until 1972, at the age of ninety!) (MYWM, 169). There is every reason to believe that Mises's last years were happy ones. His health, mind, and stamina (apart from a deterioration in his hearing during his later years) were sound until about the last year of his life. The cold treatment which American academia and the professional economics establishment had given to him had never disturbed his equanimity. The honors he received from more friendly quarters during the last decades of his life (including several honorary degrees, a medal of honor from the Austrian government, a 200-guest dinner in honor of his eightieth birthday, and the festschrift in honor of his ninetieth birthday, which included seventy-one contributors) cannot but have contributed to his quiet satisfaction. Margit von Mises reports that after his ninetieth birthday Ludwig "read all the articles that were published about him in magazines and papers all over the world." He told her, "The only good thing about being a nonagenarian is that you are able to read your obituaries while you are still alive" (MYWM, 178f).

Ludwig von Mises died less than two weeks after his ninety-second birthday, on October 10, 1973. His wife Margit devoted the years after his death to publishing (and encouraging the publication of) hitherto unpublished writings of Mises, including his own memoirs (written upon his arrival in the U.S. and therefore covering only his earlier years), as well as her own *My Years with Ludwig von Mises*. In the decades after Mises's death, Bettina Bien-Greaves assembled a massive two-volume bibliography of Mises's writings (including many fascinating excerpts from book reviews concerning those writings), as well as a collection of shorter pieces by Mises. Richard Ebeling also edited a new collection of earlier papers by Mises. A memorial volume marking the hundredth anniversary of Mises's birth was edited by the present author. New editions and translations of Mises's books were published. In the coming chapters we will have the opportunity to define and explore the economic contributions of Ludwig von Mises, and to assess the extent and nature of his long-run impact on twentieth-century economic thought and beyond.

Margit von Mises aptly summed up her husband's character by quoting a passage which Mises himself wrote about Benjamin Anderson (an American twentieth-century economist and financial expert whom Mises much admired). The following excerpts from that passage do indeed precisely fit Mises himself. Both those who admired Mises fiercely, and those who detested the positions which he championed, can agree wholeheartedly that "[h]is most eminent qualities were his inflexible honesty, his unhesitating sincerity. . . . He never yielded. He always freely enunciated what he considered to be true. If he had been prepared to suppress or only to soften his criticism of popular, but obnoxious policies, the most influential positions and offices would have been offered to him. But he never compromised. This firmness marks him as one of the outstanding characters of this age" (MYWM, 181).

2. LUDWIG VON MISES, ECONOMIST

The purpose of this chapter is to provide an overview of the impact which Ludwig von Mises made on twentieth-century economics. The preceding chapter offered an account of Mises's life, and took note of the political and historical environments in which Mises lived; the present chapter seeks to offer, in broad outline, the story of the economics of Ludwig von Mises in the context of the history of modern economic thought. Subsequent chapters will take up some specific areas of economics to which Mises made contributions; this chapter considers these same contributions—but as making up a forest, rather than as trees, i.e., from a perspective wide enough to permit appreciation for the larger picture of Mises's place in the economics of his time.

THE STATE OF ECONOMICS AT THE OUTSET OF THE TWENTIETH CENTURY

Viewed from the perspective provided by the end of the twentieth century, the state of economics in the year 1900 (when Mises began his university studies) appears as that of a discipline standing at a critical crossroads in intellectual history. Classical economics—the economics of Ricardo and Mill—had been all but swept from the stage. In its place a number of contesting schools, with drastically contrasting sets of methodological and ideological agendas, were vying for professional dominance. The direction which twentieth-century economics would take was certainly not apparent. In fact, not all the candidate-directions were altogether clearly defined to the economists of that time.

On the continent, the most powerful school of economic thought was the German Historical School led by Gustav Schmoller. This school had rejected not only the centrality of the theoretical method in attaining economic knowledge; it had also, not coincidentally, rejected the Smithian conclusion that free markets can be relied upon to achieve the economic objectives to which, they maintained, "society" does or should aspire. The work which made up the economics of the Historical School consisted largely of historical and statistical studies of specific industries, locations, and times, interwoven with value-laden policy conclusions and prescriptions. To its adherents the work of this school was, unlike that of the "theoretical" school, "scientific" (because it was empirical). But to many observers, and particularly to Menger and his disciples in Vienna, the particular amalgam of science and ideology represented by the German Historical School offered a mix seen as politically disastrous, methodologically suspect, and substantively erroneous.

In Great Britain, the economics of Alfred Marshall was unquestionably dominant. Marshall's economics attempted to retain as much as possible from Ricardo and Mill while recognizing the relevance of the newer theoretical contributions represented by the theory of marginal utility (and its implications). Although most historians of economic thought credit the theory of diminishing marginal utility to the three (independent) pioneers of neoclassical economics—Jevons, Menger, and Walras—Marshall's economics tended to downplay the work of these pioneers, treating the ideas concerning marginal utility as largely his own elaborations and emphases supplied to round out the classical paradigm. The end-product was a body of theory centered around supply-and-demand concepts, which saw prices as determined through a subtle interplay of real (physical) cost elements (à la the classics) and purely subjective (marginal utility) elements. It was generally understood that this economics recognized the positive welfare implications of the market system. At the same time, Marshall paid lip service, at least, to the value of the historical work being done in German economics, and was thoroughly open to possibilities of social economic gain to be achieved through appropriate government interventions into otherwise free markets.

A third school of thought competing for professional attention at the turn of the century was the fledgling Walrasian School. The term "school" can be used only loosely in regard to this stream of thought; as of 1900, Walras had in fact not yet produced an identifiable group of adherents. Yet Walras's work represented a recognized approach to economics. Certainly its use of mathematical tools was distinctive. But ultimately its importance lay in its emphasis on the equilibrium construct, and, in particular, on the *general* equilibrium construct. Walras had taken a bird's-eye view of the entire market economy and offered a perspective which explains and accounts for market prices by seeing them as the crucial links in a vast network of smoothly interlocking individual decisions. Although Walras was prepared, on the basis of political value judgments, to sanction significant degrees of government intervention into markets, his general equilibrium system (and that of his subsequent successor at

Lausanne, Vilfredo Pareto) tended to support the broad neoclassical presumption in favor of the optimality of the market economy.

Especially on the European continent, Marxian economics was a perennial, if thoroughly unorthodox, contender for men's hearts and minds. By the turn of the century, Marxist thought—rooted in key classical modes of thinking but steeped in radical and indeed revolutionary contempt for, and intense hostility toward, capitalism—was perhaps the best known among various doctrinal denizens of the "underworld" of economics. The 1893 posthumous publication of the third volume of Marx's *Capital* provoked Böhm-Bawerk, the prominent Austrian economic theorist, to write a highly critical monograph pointing out serious theoretical problems in the Marxist system. This was to initiate (both within and without Böhm-Bawerk's famous University of Vienna seminar after 1905) a vigorous series of polemics pitting Marxist economics against more orthodox theories of value, distribution, and the business cycle.

The fifth (and final) stream of economic thought that we can identify as having existed in the year 1900 was, of course, the Austrian School. The birth of the school is routinely dated as 1871, the year Menger's *Grundsätze* was published. But although this work certainly launched the Austrian tradition, it was not until about a dozen years later, with the publication of significant works by Menger's younger colleagues and followers, Eugen von Böhm-Bawerk and Friedrich von Wieser, that this tradition became substantial enough to warrant being called a school. By the year 1900, the subjectivist economics of Menger, Böhm-Bawerk, and Wieser—an economics offering a predominantly theoretical content to the discipline—was widely known as an alternative not only to the German Historical School, but also to the economics of Alfred Marshall. The differences between the Mengerian School and the German Historical School had erupted, after Menger's 1883 pointed critique of the methodology of the latter, into the bitter *Methodenstreit* which raged during the closing decades of the nineteenth century. This acrimonious intellectual war, charged with all kinds of heated ideological overtones, largely poisoned the atmosphere of economic discussion on the continent. Menger and his followers, while indeed recognized professionally around the world as a distinct group by the 1890s, were, in terms of numbers and reputation, overwhelmingly outweighed by the German School. At the University of Vienna itself economics was by no means monolithically Mengerian. Several of the professors were in fact closely identified with the German School. And, as Mises noted in his 1940 memoirs, it was under the influence of these professors that he entered economic studies.

MISES AND ECONOMICS: THE EARLY YEARS

The year 1902 marked the appearance of Mises's first published work in economics. That work, a history of the 1772 to 1848 developments in the relationship between lord of the manor and peasant in Galicia (the part of the Austro-Hungarian Empire where Mises was born), was, as Mises has explained (NR, 6), written under Professor Karl Grünberg—himself an adherent of the Historical School.[1] But Mises has reported that at the end of the following year, he read Menger's *Grundsätze*. Clearly that work made a most significant impact on Mises. In his own words: "It was the reading of this book that made an 'economist' of me" (NR, 33). We can surmise that Menger's book taught Mises that there exist chains of economic causation that are generated systematically by the human preferences of market participants. No doubt it was this which impelled Mises to become a regular participant in Böhm-Bawerk's seminar in the years after he had been awarded his 1906 doctorate.

Böhm-Bawerk's seminar is famous both for the quality of its participants and the quality of their discussions. Schumpeter, whose first book (1908) created something of a sensation, was prominent among the seminar participants.[2] Others were the pro-Marxist economists Rudolph Hilferding, Otto Bauer, and Nikolai Bukharin. All of these were to make names for themselves in one way or another. It is easy to see why a substantial volume of seminar time was devoted to debates concerning Marxist theory (NR, 39f). Böhm-Bawerk had, as noted above, published a penetrating critique of central ideas in Marx's value theory, and Hilferding and Bauer were concerned to defend Marx from Böhm-Bawerk's "Austrian" criticisms. It is not surprising that, some years later, Bukharin

---

1. See *Hayek on Hayek*, 55, where Grünberg is described as "an economic historian who was a socialist and became later the founder of the famous Marxist-Freudian Frankfurt Institute of Social Research."

2. The relationship between Schumpeter and Mises, both personally and professionally, remained somewhat complicated throughout their careers. See further S. Boehm, "The Austrian Tradition: Schumpeter and Mises" (together with "Commentary" by the present writer), in *Neoclassical Economic Theory, 1870–1930*, ed. K. Hennings and W. Samuels (Boston, Dordrecht, London: Kluwer, 1990).

was to write that "it is well known that the most powerful opponent of Marxism is the Austrian School."[3] And it was, no doubt, his observation of the debates between Böhm-Bawerk and his Marxist challengers that helped lead Mises toward his broader analysis of socialism after the end of World War I.

Although we do not have any systematic records of the topics discussed in Böhm-Bawerk's seminar, they almost certainly included various controversial elements of Böhm-Bawerk's classic theories of capital and interest. No doubt a number of the chapters now collected as volume 3 of *Capital and Interest* emerged as a result of such seminar discussions. In some of these discussions, it seems clear from that volume, several seminar members, such as Schumpeter and Cuhel, stood out. Mises's name does not appear in that volume, but we need not doubt his lively participation in seminar debates. Mises has reported that the last two winter semesters during which he was able to attend the seminar (before he himself began lecturing at the university in 1913) were devoted (one gathers, entirely) to discussion of his own 1912 work, *The Theory of Money and Credit* (the original German title of which was *Theorie des Geldes und der Umlaufsmittel*) (NR, 40). During these discussions significant differences of opinion emerged between Mises and his eminent teacher (NR, 40, 59), and these differences were to be further developed in Mises's later work.[4]

THE THEORY OF MONEY AND CREDIT

Mises was barely thirty years old when he published this, his first book, *The Theory of Money and Credit*, which was to establish him as an important theorist in the Austrian tradition. Many of the reviews of this book in economic journals were quite negative. But professional opinion regarding the work changed rather rapidly. When Lionel Robbins introduced the 1934 English translation of this volume, he remarked that he knew

3. Nikolai Bukharin, "Introduction" [to the Russian edition, 1919] as translated in *The Economic Theory of the Leisure Class* (New York and London: Monthly Review Press, 1972), 9.

4. See chapter 5 in L. von Mises, *Epistemological Problems of Economics* (Princeton, N.J.: Van Nostrand, 1960). This book is the English translation of his *Grundprobleme der Nationalökonomie* (1933); this chapter was first published as a journal article in 1928.

"few works which convey a more profound impression of the logical unity and the power of modern economic analysis."[5] Especially after the hyperinflations of the early post–World War I years, the book became recognized as a prescient, authoritative work. As Robbins observed in 1934, Mises's book had in "continental circles long been regarded as the standard textbook on the subject."

Mises's work on the economics of money and banking began in a study of both monetary theory and the history of European currencies (NR, 43). In 1907 and 1908 he had published journal articles dealing with Austrian foreign exchange controls and with recent literature on money and banking. In 1909 he had published an English language paper in *Economic Journal* on the foreign exchange policy of the Austro-Hungarian Bank, and a German journal article expanding on the same topic (in Schmoller's "Jahrbuch"). These articles, Mises reported, "generated furious protest among the most powerful members of the Austrian inflation party" (NR, 44). It was in the fall of 1909 that Mises embarked on the writing of his book. Besides having the objective of continuing and systematizing his earlier critical ideas on the practical problems of currency and banking policy, Mises wrote his book in order to reject the then-dominant view that "the theory of money could be clearly separated from the total structure of economic problems" (NR, 56). Mises recognized that in order adequately to complete this latter objective it would be necessary to re-examine and restate the foundations of economic theory in the context of a barter economy. Even at this early stage in his research, Mises saw his work on the theory of money as merely a part of a more comprehensive theoretical undertaking (one that he would in fact complete only many years later). But, Mises later explained, he feared the imminent outbreak of "a great war," and hastened to complete his book, delivering the manuscript to the publisher early in 1912 (NR, 56). He was therefore forced to restrict himself, almost entirely, to "the narrow field of strictly monetary theory," leaving the broader questions of economic theory for later treatment.

5. See Lionel C. Robbins, "Introduction" (to the 1934 English edition), reprinted in the revised (1953) edition of *Ludwig von Mises, The Theory of Money and Credit* (New Haven: Yale University Press), 12. The translation was of the second (1924) German edition of the work.

Nonetheless, Mises's book did succeed in firmly rooting monetary theory (and, in particular, the theory of the value of money) in more general economic understanding (i.e., by offering an original, marginal-utility-based theory of the value of money).[6] There can be no doubt of the importance of this aspect of his work for the twentieth-century development of the basic ideas of the Austrian School of Economics. Presumably it was the publication of this book which led to Mises's 1913 admission to the faculty of law at the University of Vienna. And it was in this book that Mises briefly expounded what came later to be called the "Austrian" theory of the business cycle—the theory which was, twenty years later, as a result of Hayek's brilliant elaboration of it, to launch the latter's career at the London School of Economics.

MISES AND THE ECONOMICS OF SOCIALISM

As we have seen, Mises saw military service at the front in the Carpathians during World War I, and spent the last of the war years in the economics division of the Department of War in Vienna. Yet immediately after returning to civilian life, Mises plunged into his scientific work. Besides his 1919 book (the English title of which would be *Nation, State and Economy*), he published only one year later his famous paper on the economics of socialism, "Die Wirtschaftsrechnung im Sozialistischen Gemeinwesen."

With this paper, Mises initiated the celebrated interwar debate on the possibility of economic calculation. It seems likely that Mises did not see this article as offering any economic insights that were not already well known to the economically literate. He was directing his message at well-meaning proponents of socialism who were ignorant of the basic fundamentals of economic understanding. Nonetheless this article was to play an important role in the development of Mises's own understanding and expositions of economic theory. And it had the eventual effect of making Mises's name as an economist known in far wider professional circles, both in Europe and in the U.K., than might have followed simply from his prominence in the Austrian political economy and financial debates of the immediate postwar years.

Mises followed up his paper on the economics of socialism with a book-length study of socialism in all its dimensions (its subsequent English

6. For some elaboration of these statements see below, chapter 5.

translation was subtitled "An Economic and Sociological Analysis"). This book, published in 1922, included the virtually verbatim republication (as a chapter) of the earlier paper. It is quite clear that Mises considered the theoretical core of his critique of all forms of socialism (including interventionism) to be the primary argument in his 1920 paper. This argument was that rational central planning is a contradiction in terms—because, without the help of market prices for resources, socialist planners are simply unable to *calculate* economically. Since a socialist economy necessarily lacks a market in which independent agents competitively buy and sell economic resources, such an economy lacks any market *prices* for such resources. But without resource prices, would-be central planners, no matter how diligent and dedicated they may be, are simply unable to assess the extent to which use of a given resource for one specific purpose entails corresponding sacrifices in the myriad alternative lines of production (to which this resource *might* have been alternatively allocated). In other words, planners have no way of calculating the comparative urgency of competing potential uses for any particular unit of a resource. The pattern of resource allocation which the central planners finally adopt cannot, therefore, be considered the outcome of a rational plan. There is no assurance, nor even any systematic likelihood, that this adopted pattern of resource allocation achieves a volume, and a composition, of outputs which the central planners would deem to be preferable to all other possible alternatives.

Mises presented this lesson in economics as his critique of the possibility of socialist planning; it was a lesson implied by and derived from the economic theory of the market economy. What Mises was in effect teaching his readers was an appreciation of the manner in which market prices convey information to decision makers in a capitalist system, permitting their decisions to take mutual account of (and thus to become spontaneously coordinated with) the decisions being made by others. It was this lesson which constituted, for Mises, the core of economic science, and the very fountainhead of all economic understanding. Although Hayek would, a decade and a half later, present his own critique of the socialist economy in somewhat different language, there is every reason to conclude that, in supporting Mises in his critique, Hayek was subscribing to the same core economic understanding that inspired his mentor. In fact, Mises was, in his theoretical critique of socialist planning, laying out his Austrian theory of the market process in a way that would, eventually, clearly differentiate that theory from the mainstream microeconomic understanding of the manner in which the market economy works.

Mises's *Socialism* appeared ten years later in a second, revised edition (1932), and this second edition was translated into English in 1936. It was this later edition which attracted a great deal of attention, both from professional economists and intellectuals more generally. Much of this attention took the form of ideologically based attacks on the work; after all, the thirties were the years in which socialism was widely seen as both the moral and economic hope of the future. Nonetheless, professional economists could not but recognize the cogency of the theory upon which Mises based his critique. In a later chapter we shall see, in particular, how Oskar Lange and Abba P. Lerner, both professional economists with strong sympathies for socialism, attempted to deal with the theoretical challenge with which Mises had confronted them.

THE *PRIVATSEMINAR*

Besides the impact on the economics profession made by his published works, Mises made a less easily measured—but perhaps ultimately more important—impression on twentieth-century economics through his teaching at the University of Vienna and, separately from his university influence, through his famed *Privatseminar*. Mises had, upon his return from military service at the end of World War I, been promoted (from privatdozent) to the rank of "ausserordentlichen Professor."[7] While this gave him the title of professor, it was not an appointment to a professorial chair.

Nonetheless Mises did lecture at the university and also conducted a well-attended university seminar. But his most important influence was through the *Privatseminar* he held once every two weeks at his office in the Chamber of Commerce. A number of the participants in this seminar have published their reminiscences of it,[8] and Mises himself

7. Martha Steffy Browne, "Erinnerungen an das Mises-Privatseminar," in *Ludwig von Mises—seine Ideen und seine Wirkung* [this is the title of a special number of *Wirtschaftspolitische Blätter* 1981 (4)], 111.

8. Besides Martha Steffy Browne, Gottfried Haberler wrote a piece, "Mises' Private Seminar," in the above-cited number of *Wirtschaftspolitischer Blätter*. See also, the second edition of MYWM (Cedar Falls, Iowa: Center for Futures Education, 1984), appendix 1; also *Hayek on Hayek*, 71.

subsequently wrote about it with obvious pleasure. The seminar had no formal connection with the university. Its members participated by invitation; all were young scholars who had already obtained their doctorates. In Hayek's words, "during the final years of the Austrian School in Austria, it was the center not only for the Austrian School itself, but attracted students from all over the world. . . ."[9] Haberler has described it as one of the important elements of the intellectual life of Vienna during the years between 1920 and 1934. As was noted in chapter 1, the participants included a number of economists who were to become world famous in their profession, including Gottfried Haberler, Friedrich Hayek, Fritz Machlup, Oskar Morgenstern, and Paul Rosenstein-Rodan. But a number of scholars who were to become famous in other disciplines were also regular participants. Among these were Felix Kaufmann, a philosopher; Alfred Schutz, a sociologist; and Eric Voegelin, a philosopher of history. The topics discussed at the seminar ranged widely across the areas of "economic theory, economic policy, sociology or methodology."[10] As Martha Steffy Browne has observed: it is "an important fact which should be reported in future histories of economic thought that the contributions of members to future growth of economic thought was truly remarkable. Many of the seminar members joined the best universities in the U.S. and in England and participated in government projects in the U.S. and in basic work in [international organizations such as the World Bank]."[11]

The work being stimulated by the discussions in the *Privatseminar* of the twenties and early thirties must be appreciated within the broader context of contemporary developments in the Austrian tradition. Besides the circle of scholars that assembled around Mises, a second circle, centered around Hans Mayer, existed at the University of Vienna. Mayer, a disciple of Friedrich Wieser, had assumed (upon the latter's death in 1926) the professorial chair which Wieser had occupied at the University. Although, by all accounts, there was (to say the least!) little cordiality between Mises and Mayer, a number of the participants in the Mises seminar were at the same time members of the Mayer circle. (It was this fact

9. *Hayek on Hayek,* 71f.

10. Haberler, "Mises' Private Seminar," 123.

11. Browne, "Erinnerungen an das Mises-Privatseminar," 120.

that led Stephan Boehm to refer to the "inter-locking circles" in interwar Vienna economics.)[12] For the most part, it can be argued, the Austrian economics of the 1920s tended to follow up on the work of Böhm-Bawerk and Wieser, rather than that of Menger. As a result, the Austrian economics of the twenties tended to take on a character and offer a substance not at all radically different from what had developed as the broadly shared neoclassical economic consensus emerging from the Marshallian and Walrasian schools. When Lionel Robbins wrote *The Nature and Significance of Economic Science* in 1932, he drew freely from the Austrian writings of the twenties, introducing insights into British economics which had been absent from the Marshallian tradition (and also absent from the economics of Robbins's own teacher, Edwin Cannan). But Robbins made it clear that, in emphasizing Austrian insights concerning methodological individualism, the centrality of allocative, economizing choice, and the related importance of the opportunity cost concept, he was not requiring any revolution in British economics. "I venture to hope," he wrote, "that in one or two instances I have succeeded in giving expository force to certain principles not always clearly stated. But, in the main, my object has been to state, as simply as I could, propositions which are the common property of most modern economics."[13]

When, decades later, Fritz Machlup would attempt to pin down the defining tenets of Austrian economics, the list he offered hardly contained anything to which a mainstream mid-twentieth-century microeconomist might not have subscribed (if perhaps with a somewhat different emphasis).[14] Machlup was, in this respect, simply reflecting the atmosphere of Vienna economics of the twenties. The fact that, decades later, at a time of decline in the reputation of the Austrian tradition, mainstream economists could agree to Machlup's list, merely reflects the extent to which, partly as a result of Robbins's work, Austrian insights

12. Stephan Boehm, "Austrian Economics Between the Wars: Some Historiographical Problems," in *Austrian Economics: Tensions and New Directions*, ed. Bruce J. Caldwell and Stephan Boehm (Boston, Dordrecht, London: Kluwer, 1992), 6ff.

13. L. C. Robbins, *The Nature and Significance of Economic Science*, 2nd edition, (London: Macmillan, 1935), xv. This statement was from the preface to the first edition of the book, 1932.

14. See Fritz Machlup, "Austrian Economics" in *Encyclopedia of Economics*, ed. D. Greenwald (New York: McGraw-Hill, 1982).

had become successfully absorbed into the mainstream. Yet it seems fair to suggest, at the same time, that in spite of the degree of convergence between the Austrian economics of the twenties and the emerging mainstream neoclassical consensus, there were certain signs, even during the twenties and thirties, that Mises would steer Austrian economics onto a path that would eventually diverge sharply from that mainstream neoclassical consensus.

It was during the late twenties and early thirties that Mises wrote the methodological and foundational papers which he assembled in 1933 and published as *Grundprobleme der Nationalökonomie* (much later translated as *Epistemological Problems of Economics* [1960]). And at least some of these papers were, no doubt, discussed at his seminar. It is in these papers (as well as in certain passages in his earlier books of 1912 and 1922) that we find early statements of the positions which would later be systematically laid out in Mises's 1940 treatise, *Nationalökonomie* (and its subsequent expanded English-language counterpart, *Human Action*). These positions include Mises's concept of economics as the "science of human action," the role of a priorism in economic theory, the relation of theory to history, and his views on the limitations of mathematical methods in economics. (As we shall point out in some detail in subsequent chapters, these characteristically Misesian positions would set his work sharply apart from mainstream economics.) So it seems reasonable to assert that much that separates the Mises of *Human Action* from the general perspective of the Austrian economists of a quarter century earlier was in fact being developed, in Mises's thinking, during that very period, and was being discussed in his *Privatseminar*. On the one hand, the Austrian economics of the twenties was responsible for Lionel Robbins's work, which, while it introduced Austrian insights into British economics, was eventually to point that economics toward the standard neoclassical microeconomics of the post–World War II decades.[15] On the other hand, that same Austrian economics of the twenties was inspiring Mises toward a comprehensive revision of the basic foundations of economics, a revision that would eventually render his economics inconsistent with what was to emerge as the mainstream economics paradigm of the second half of the twentieth century. And it was largely these doctrinally

15. See V. C. Walsh, *Introduction to Contemporary Microeconomics* (New York: McGraw-Hill, 1970), 17.

radical features of Mises's system that would, in turn, inspire a late-twentieth-century revival of interest in the Austrian tradition.

MISES AT THE OUTSET OF THE THIRTIES

Mises's place in the economics profession would seem to have become firmly established by the end of the 1920s. He was the author of a number of books, including two major works (*Theory of Money and Credit* and *Socialism*) that would still be in print at the end of the century. His "influence, as teacher and mentor," was, mainly as a result of his *Privatseminar*, "enormous."[16] Nor was this influence confined to his own country. In Rothbard's words: "such were Mises' remarkable qualities as scholar and teacher that . . . his *Privatseminar* became the outstanding seminar and forum in all of Europe for discussion and research in economics and the social sciences."[17] In a tribute to Mises presented by Hayek in 1956 (in honor of the fiftieth anniversary of Mises's doctorate from the University of Vienna) he referred to the "profound impression" which Mises's *Socialism* had made on those who were young scholars, whether in England, Germany, Austria, or Sweden, during the twenties. That work, Hayek wrote, was on "political economy in the tradition of the great moral philosophers, a Montesquieu or Adam Smith, containing both acute knowledge and profound wisdom. I have little doubt that it will retain the position it has achieved in the history of political ideas. But there can be no doubt whatever about the effect on us who have been in our most impressible age. To none of us . . . was the world ever the same again. If Röpke stood here, or Robbins, or Ohlin . . . they would tell you the same story. . . ." (MYWM, 189). By 1930, Mises had published an additional stream of books and monographs, further amplifying his views on such phenomena as inflation, the trade cycle, the ideal of the (classically) liberal society and the dangers of interventionism. Virtually all his later positions on economic theory, economic methodology, and economic policy had been clearly articulated by 1930.

Yet the same Hayek who spoke so glowingly of the international impact of Mises's work on socialism was able to state that, as of 1931, "Mises was still a relatively minor figure confined to a particular field. . . .

16. Murray N. Rothbard, "Ludwig von Mises: The Dean of the Austrian School," in *15 Great Austrian Economists*, ed. R. G. Holcombe (Auburn, Ala.: Ludwig von Mises Institute, 1999), 159.

17. Ibid.

[B]y the early 1930s, Mises was internationally—so far as he was known at all, which was limited—known to people like Robbins as a man who had done a distinctive contribution to the theory of money, developing Menger and developing most effectively his criticism of socialism."[18] To be sure, this statement was an oral, off-the-cuff response to a rather persistent interviewer (and the statement continues, in fact, to include several inaccuracies concerning dates of later works of Mises). Yet the view expressed should not be declared flatly inconsistent with the more flattering view of Mises's influence expressed in Hayek's tribute quoted above. The simple truth is that, for all his renown in the German-speaking (and German-reading) segment of the economics profession, Mises's books and papers were virtually unknown to the vast majority of the international profession, for whom the only language of relevance was English. It was only in the thirties that, as a result of the initiatives of Lionel Robbins, the two major books of Mises were translated into English. These translations would establish Mises as an internationally known theorist in the U.K. (and, to a lesser extent, in the U.S.), perhaps with the help of the circumstance that he was known as the mentor of Friedrich Hayek, whose star rose phenomenally in British economics during the early thirties.[19]

It may be suggested that there was a special factor that was to help establish the prominent, international professional reputation that Mises had acquired by the end of the thirties in the economics profession. This factor was the widespread recognition by 1940 that Mises's views on economic method and economic policy, as well as on economic theory itself, were thoroughly out of step with the new ideas that were then asserting themselves. Distinctiveness, for better or for worse, helps promote recognition. Although most of Mises's later positions had already been clearly

---

18. *Hayek on Hayek*, 76.

19. Although several writers have claimed that Hayekian economics differs in crucial respects from that of Mises, this writer strongly disagrees. For a discussion of how, despite some significant differences between them, both Mises and Hayek understand the nature of the market process in basically the same non-neoclassical way, see Israel M. Kirzner, "Reflections on the Misesian Legacy in Economics," *Review of Austrian Economics* 9, no. 2 (1996): 143–54; reprinted as chapter 8 in Israel M. Kirzner, *The Driving Force of the Market: Essays in Austrian Economics* (London and New York: Routledge, 2000). There is every reason to recognize that one of Mises's most important influences upon twentieth-century economics consists in this "Misesian" character of Hayek's understanding of the market process.

articulated, at least in the German language, before 1930 (and certainly by 1933), these positions were not yet seen, either by Mises or by others, as setting Mises apart from his contemporaries. Mises's distinctiveness had *not* yet been firmly established by 1930. In fact it was in 1932 that Mises referred approvingly to a statement by Oskar Morgenstern that the major contemporary schools of economic thought, "the Austrian and the Anglo-American Schools and School of Lausanne . . . differ only in their mode of expressing the same fundamental idea and that they are divided more by their terminologies and by peculiarities of presentation than by the substance of their teachings" (EP, 214).

Mises himself was clearly not yet aware of how thoroughly his own views on the method and substance of economic theory differed from what was to emerge as the new mainstream consensus. Quite apart from the extraordinary influence which John Maynard Keynes was to exercise on the profession toward the end of the decade, those years of "High Theory" (as Shackle has called the thirties) placed mainstream price theory on a path pointing dramatically away from the direction that Mises was, more and more emphatically, to take in the years ahead. By 1930 the stage was set, as it were, for Mises to emerge with all the unique methodological and substantive distinctiveness that was to render him so unfashionable and so unpopular a figure in the post–World War II economics profession. It will be these elements of methodological and substantive distinctiveness that will occupy us during much of the rest of this book.

THE YEARS OF HIGH THEORY

A number of major developments in the method and substance of mainstream economics were to occur during the thirties. The growing communication of ideas in economics across national and linguistic barriers was drawing the followers of the major schools closer to one another and dissolving their distinctiveness. The growing emphasis on the use of mathematical tools in economics had the effect of crystallizing the centrality of the equilibrium concept in economics. This, in turn, tended to promote an understanding of the broad neoclassical teachings that had been common to the different schools, in terms of the perfectly competitive model.[20] (This tendency was encouraged rather than weakened by

20. On this see Frank M. Machovec, *Perfect Competition and the Transformation of Economics* (London and New York: Routledge, 1995).

the emergence of the doctrines of monopolistic and/or imperfect competition.) At the same time as these developments were occurring in the substance and method of mainstream theory, the profession was also undergoing something of a revolution in regard to the role of descriptive and applied economic theory. The emergence of econometrics (and the fashionability of the then-current epistemological doctrines of positivism)[21] tended to push the practice of economics further in directions uncongenial to those who, like Mises, saw the role of descriptive economics as emphatically secondary to the pure, universal truths of economic theory. And of course, the revolutionary impact of Keynesian theory, challenging as it did the relevance, if not the entire validity, of conventional neoclassical economics, was simply one more fatal and painful blow to the illusion which Mises may have had that his own economics was in fact close to the professionally shared consensus view of enlightened modern economists.

By the end of the thirties there could no longer be any doubt: Mises *was* thoroughly out of step with the brilliant, newly emerging economists of the thirties who were, each in his or her own way, remaking twentieth-century economics. Mises differed from his contemporaries both methodologically and substantively. Above all, he was, and was perceived to be, drastically out of step ideologically with the ethos reflected in the new varieties of economics. From the outset of World War II until his death, Mises would both be and feel isolated from the mainstream orthodoxy of his profession. It is of course true that for most of his career, Mises had been a voice representing unpopular economic policies, but for some time he could validly believe that he was representing, to relatively ignorant politicians and laymen, the settled doctrines emerging from "modern economics." After the end of the thirties, Mises was criticizing policies and doctrines espoused and championed by what, in the economics profession, were considered its most outstanding (and most "modern") theorists and practitioners.

It is a tribute to his intellectual integrity that Mises was, in the decades ahead, never to swerve from what he was convinced was the truth, no matter how unpopular that truth might be both in the public and the professional arenas. Quite apart from his ideological commitment to

21. A prominent example of this is Terence W. Hutchison's *The Significance and Basic Postulates of Economic Theory* (London: Macmillan, 1938).

classically liberal principles, Mises believed that the newer approaches did not appreciate the subtler nuances in the earlier neoclassical (and especially the Mengerian and Böhm-Bawerkian) orthodoxy. From this point on he would devote himself to deepening, and making more explicit, the foundations of this now unfashionable orthodoxy. His professional isolation was rendered all the more pronounced by the circumstance that it was precisely at this time, the start of the forties, that Mises migrated to the U.S. His lack of an academic position, his newness to the American professional scene, and his relative obscurity within that profession, cannot but have deepened his own sense of professional and intellectual isolation.

At the same time it seems fair to conclude, from a consideration of Mises's writings during the mid-thirties and onwards, that he seems to have failed to recognize the importance of the new work in economics being done during the thirties. While he of course recognized that the dominant economic doctrines were changing from those which represented for him the accepted conclusions of economic science, he apparently did not consider these newer doctrines as deserving careful, direct criticism. When Frank Knight wrote his review article on Mises's 1940 major treatise, *Nationalökonomie,* he correctly observed that the work "is highly controversial in substance and in tone, though the argument is directed toward positions, with very little debate or *Auseinandersetzung* with named authors."[22] It was as if Mises felt that if he could lay out his own view of economics, with sufficient care to its fundamentals, the newer work would be seen to be simply inadequate and unacceptable, without any need for detailed critiques.

The unfortunate result of this was that in the intellectual environment of postwar economics, Mises was seen not only as old-fashioned and out of step with modern developments, but as being in fact quite ignorant of these developments. This writer vividly recalls an oral remark made in the mid-fifties by a prominent U.S. economist (who happened to *agree* with Mises's policy positions on many issues): Mises, he remarked, had not had a new idea in twenty years. Mises, it was generally believed, had not advanced beyond the economics of the early thirties.

22. Frank H. Knight, "Professor Mises and the Theory of Capital," *Economica* 8 (November 1941): 409.

But this dismissive judgment was not only unfairly harsh; it is also demonstrably false. In his 1940 treatise, and especially in its 1949 English-language, substantially revised version (*Human Action*), Mises presented the orthodox Austrian ideas in a manner which constituted an almost dramatically fresh statement of that orthodoxy. Making good use of his years of peaceful concentration in Geneva, Mises was able to follow up his 1933 collection of methodological essays by constructing a grand, overarching epistemological and conceptual framework within which to present his Austrian orthodoxy as an integral part of a magnificent structure of social understanding. Whether one is or is not in agreement with this system, or with the Austrian orthodoxy which it incorporates, Mises's work offers a highly original and uniquely profound fundamental restatement of his own already well-developed economic doctrines.

Fundamentally, Mises's economics consists of the systematically developed logical implications of his *insights* into the nature of human decision making, and of the dynamics governing the processes of interaction among decisions. The tools of his economics were logical thinking and critical analysis, rather than algebraic or geometrical demonstrations. Unlike the newer economics of the thirties, Mises's economics never assessed market outcomes from a perspective of imagined omniscience, but instead always took into account the manner in which market processes both stimulate and are shaped by the *discoveries* made by imperfectly informed market participants. As we shall see, it is no accident that, in an era in which mainstream economics was led to call for massive arrays of government interventions in markets (in order to correct imagined shortcomings), Mises's economics led him to appreciate even more deeply the virtues of spontaneously inspired market processes.

It is unfortunate that Mises did not see fit to directly and specifically address, critically or otherwise, any of the newer work being done in the thirties. No doubt this failure contributed in some measure to his being professionally snubbed in the postwar years. At the same time Mises's attitude was not, perhaps, an entirely unreasonable one. This newer work was being done by writers ten or twenty years younger than he—writers who, in his opinion, brilliant though they might be, had simply not understood the true profundity and subtlety of the orthodoxy against which they were rebelling. It is possible that the fact that much of this newer work was being done in England by economists trained in the Marshallian tradition may have contributed to the disregard with which

Mises tended to treat them. There seems no doubt that Menger's disciples viewed British neoclassicism with a certain patronizing condescension. Whether or not there was any justification for this attitude, it would, as we have noticed, cost Mises dearly in terms of postwar reputation.

MISES AFTER WORLD WAR II

At the end of World War II, Mises was approaching his mid-sixties, an age which (at least at that time in the U.S.) was normally associated with professional retirement. Yet Mises was to continue for almost another quarter of a century to publish works in economics.

We have already noted in the preceding chapter that Mrs. Mises was to describe these years as "the most productive and creative of [his] life." Without accepting this overly expansive description, we must indeed recognize the importance of these years in the overall scientific contributions of Mises. Despite the professional isolation that was to characterize his postwar intellectual work, despite his being (unfairly) perceived as having somehow wandered from the path of the academic to that of the ideologically motivated apologist for capitalism, Mises in fact continued to pursue his own scientific agenda. And it would be precisely the work which he published in these postwar years, and his teaching and seminars at New York University, which would, in the fullness of time, eventually bear fruit in terms of long-term influence over the course of ideas.

We have noticed in the preceding chapter that Mises's magnum opus, his 1949 *Human Action,* was a work the sheer size and comprehensiveness of which did not permit it to be entirely ignored, even by a profession which considered Mises an old-fashioned relic of premodern economics. Without fully comprehending its scientific contribution, and while emphatically rejecting its policy pronouncements, the profession could yet sense the grandeur of Mises's structure of thought, and the exquisite consistency of its systematically constructed edifice. Yet the truth is that this work was much more than a treatise based on Mises's earlier work; it constituted a most significant advance in the economics of the Austrian tradition. This was not simply a comprehensive treatise in which Mises assembled and synthesized the many individual methodological and substantive contributions contained in his earlier writings. *Human Action* articulated an entirely fresh restatement of the foundations of Austrian economics in a manner that most definitively and with commanding clarity set that economics apart from the economic thought which had, by mid-century, swept the mainstream stage. It was most unfortunate that the profession failed to recognize this central element in *Human Action*. The profession missed entirely the subtle and consistent manner in which Mises presented his unique concept of purposeful human action in an open-ended world fraught with uncertainty, giving a reworking of the entire corpus of that early-twentieth-century neoclassical economics which *had* achieved professional consensus.

There is a certain drama in the circumstance that Mises offered this new articulation of the Mengerian legacy at a time when the Austrian tradition in economics appeared to have come to an end. By the end of the thirties, with the dispersal of the economists who made up the Mises circle in Vienna, and with the triumph of Keynesian economics in the years after 1936, the view in the economics profession was that what was valid in the Austrian tradition had been absorbed into the mainstream, and that what was not so absorbed was no longer to be held in high regard. In any event, it appeared that there simply *was* no longer any active Austrian school. When Mises published his *Human Action* in 1949 the profession considered it as perhaps the last gasp of a moribund tradition; it certainly failed to recognize it as a seminal, original work that for perhaps the first time spelled out with clarity and vigor the distinctive aspects of the Austrian tradition. This was a book which would, despite its unfashionability, eventually make its mark upon late-twentieth-century economic thought, bearing much of the responsibility for the late-century revival of the Austrian tradition.

After the publication of *Human Action,* Mises continued to write and publish. In 1951 he published "Profit and Loss." This paper presented features of Mises's theory of the entrepreneurial market process even more clearly than did *Human Action*. This was followed by two shorter books on themes that obviously fascinated Mises. In 1956 he published *The Anti-Capitalist Mentality,* a work in which Mises suggested sociological/psychological explanations for the puzzle (as it seemed to him) of why so wonderful a system as capitalism is so vilified, especially by intellectuals. If this work contained less of what can be described as strictly economic-scientific, his next work, *Theory and History* (1957), offered an austerely scientific treatment of the relationship between economic theory and history. This work builds on the methodological foundations laid carefully and extensively in *Human Action;* it develops themes already initiated in Mises's 1933 *Grundprobleme der Nationalökonomie* (a work which was in fact published in English translation in 1960). Mises published yet a further work on the methodological foundations of economics in 1962 (when he was already eighty years old), *The Ultimate Foundation of Economic Science: An Essay on Method*. And in 1969 he published a revealing and important forty-five-page monograph entitled *The Historical Setting of the Austrian School of Economics*, the English version of a work which had been published several years previously in a Spanish translation.

But the listing of these books does not fully reflect the activity with which Mises was writing and publishing. In the years between 1950 and 1970 Mises published many dozens of shorter articles in English and German (with many being translated into a number of other languages). Although it is true that these pieces were usually applied economics written for the intelligent layman, rather than for the economic specialist, they attest to Mises's alert and active professional work during these decades. Many of these shorter articles were assembled as books and published after Mises's death.

LUDWIG VON MISES AND TWENTIETH-CENTURY ECONOMICS: A RETROSPECTIVE ASSESSMENT

We shall, in the chapters ahead, be devoting attention to each of the areas in which Mises made significant contributions. In this chapter we have provided an outline or overview of his life's work as an economist. In concluding this chapter it is appropriate that we attempt to sum up that life's work and contrast it with the course that mainstream economics has taken during the twentieth century.

At the outset of this chapter we set forth the various schools of thought that were prominent in the economic profession at the start of the twentieth century. Mises's first works as an economic theorist were contributions to mainstream neoclassical economics as it was broadly understood and practiced at that time both on the continent and in the U.K. His work constituted a continuation of the Austrian tradition pioneered by Menger and Böhm-Bawerk. While some of the policy prescriptions that Mises drew from his theoretical work were certainly unfashionable at the time, it would be fair to describe the overall character of his work as original, yet solidly within the mainstream of contemporary professional theorizing.

But during the concluding decades of Mises's career his work was thoroughly at odds with mainstream economics, not only in substance and methodology, but in terms of policy implications. Mises's work had led him steadily in one direction—the direction which he saw as implicit in the Menger–Böhm-Bawerk tradition; mainstream economics, which had appeared so congenial to the Austrian tradition at the start of the century, had taken an entirely different direction. The years in which these crucial, diverging steps were taken—by Mises on the one hand, and by mainstream economists on the other—were primarily the decades between 1920 and 1950.

During these decades, which encompass the remarkably vigorous doctrinal developments of the interwar years, mainstream economics took a turn that led it to prize technical mathematical technique over conceptual clarity and depth, to value empirical predictability over theoretical "Verstehen," to rank the reliability of well-intentioned proactive and regulatory government economic policy ahead of that of the regularities to be expected from the free market's spontaneous invisible hand. It was precisely in these decades during which Mises completed his own system, a system consistently broadening the applicability of the principles laid down by Menger and Böhm-Bawerk and consistently deepening their epistemological foundations. The economic system that he articulated during those decades offered a comprehensive view of the capitalist system, a view which differed in just about every conceivable respect from the view provided by the mainstream economics which dominated the immediate postwar economics profession. As a result, Mises's work in economics during the concluding decades of his career was seen by the profession at large as obscurantist doctrine, evidence of an obstinate refusal to accept the advances achieved by economics in its most fruitful years.

It is noteworthy that, when the century ended more than a quarter century after Mises's death, the perception in the economics profession concerning his economics had changed to a significant, if modest, degree. While Mises's methodological position was still treated as unacceptable, his substantive doctrinal positions, as well as his practical policy recommendations, had come to be treated with far more respect and interest than they had enjoyed during his own lifetime. The consistency and integrity with which Mises pursued his scientific work, what Jacques Rueff termed his "intransigence,"[23] had, by the close of the twentieth century, turned the perception of his work from contemptuously dismissed

23. See the citation above, chapter 1, note 5.

obscurantism into a respected—if unconventional and even somewhat eccentric—point of view.

Perhaps the central element in Mises's point of view, the element which has recently been successful in capturing the interest of younger economists, is his radical *subjectivism,* the insight that economic phenomena express the way in which economic *agents* see the world. Many years ago, in an oft-quoted passage, Hayek put his finger on this central element. Hayek remarked that "it is probably no exaggeration to say that every important advance in economic theory during the last hundred years was a further step in the consistent application of subjectivism."[24] In a note, Hayek observes that this development of subjectivism "has probably been carried out most consistently by L. v. Mises. . . . Probably all the characteristic features of his theories, from his theory of money (so much ahead of his time in 1912!) to what he calls his *a priorism,* his views about mathematical economics in general and the measurement of economic phenomena in particular, and his criticism of planning all follow . . . from this central position."[25]

This subjectivist point of view is, in fact, stimulating the curiosity and attention of many younger economists who have found themselves to a greater or lesser degree repelled by what they see as the aridity and unrealism of the mainstream tradition in which the profession is still for the greater part enveloped. It is to this curiosity and attention that we can attribute the resurgence of interest in the Austrian (and in particular to the Misesian) tradition in economics, which has, somewhat surprisingly, occurred in the economics profession during the past two decades.

24. F. A. Hayek, *The Counter-Revolution of Science: Studies on the Abuse of Reason* (Glencoe: Free Press, 1955), 31.

25. Ibid., 209f.

3. THE NATURE OF ECONOMIC INQUIRY

The remaining chapters in this book focus more specifically on several key aspects of Mises's economics. We take up first his strongly held and highly unfashionable ideas on economic method. For Mises this aspect of his work was of the highest importance. Yet it is in this area of his contributions that Mises has found fewest followers. The purpose of this chapter is not to convince the reader of the validity of Mises's methodological positions. Rather, its purpose is simply to set forth as clearly as possible what it was that Mises so strongly believed, why he considered his positions to be so critically important for the substance of his work in economics, and why those positions have seemed so strange, not only to mainstream economists intent on disparaging Misesian economics *in toto*, but also to economists who have enthusiastically endorsed that economics.

That Mises believed his methodological views to be of critical importance for his economics is clear not only from his explicit statements (e.g., he doubted "whether it is possible to separate the analysis of epistemological problems from the treatment of the substantive issues of the science concerned"), but also from the volume of attention which he paid to this area, especially in his later years. Of the three full-length new books which Mises published after his 1949 *Human Action,* two dealt primarily with matters of method and epistemology (TH and UFES). In addition, part 1 of *Human Action,* covering some 140 pages (about one-sixth of the entire book), is devoted entirely to the epistemological foundations of Mises's system. A number of Mises's earlier papers of the twenties and early thirties, collected in his 1933 *Grundprobleme der Nationalökonomie* (and translated much later under the title *Epistemological Problems of Economics*) were early—but remarkably well-articulated—statements of Mises's positions. In addition, several of Mises's very first papers written and published in the U.S. dealt with these same issues.[1]

---

1. "Social Science and Natural Science," *Journal of Social Philosophy and Jurisprudence* 7, no. 3 (April 1942); "The Treatment of 'Irrationality' in the Social Sciences," *Philosophy and Phenomenological Research* 4, no. 4 (June 1944). Both these papers have been republished in MMMP.

Indeed, this degree of attention might at first seem quite surprising. After all, Mises, especially during the 1920s, was a very down-to-earth, policy-oriented and applied economist. His work would seem to be sharply removed from that of the pure theorist, and even more sharply removed from that of the philosopher of knowledge concerned with the epistemological foundations of economics. If Mises did focus so much of his attention upon questions of epistemology and method, it is, I shall suggest, because he came to be convinced that the vitally important lessons which economics can teach are likely to be dismissed on methodological grounds by those representing special interests. Again and again during the history of economics over the past two centuries, its results have been rejected by those who either failed to understand, or who refused to understand, the basis upon which those results came to be scientifically established. "Political parties which passionately rejected all the practical conclusions to which the results of economic thought inevitably lead, but were unable to raise any tenable objections against their truth and correctness, shifted the argument to the fields of epistemology and methodology" (TH, 2). Perhaps the most effective way of conveying Mises's views on the epistemology and methodology of economics is to begin by recognizing the *intellectually revolutionary* character which Mises attributed to economics within the range of the scientific disciplines known to man.

THE INTELLECTUALLY REVOLUTIONARY
CHARACTER OF ECONOMICS

Mises saw the emergence of economic understanding in the eighteenth and early-nineteenth centuries as introducing a genuinely revolutionary new insight into man's understanding of the conditions within which society exists. He expressed this belief in words of striking and almost dramatic directness. "The development of economics . . . from Cantillon and Hume to Bentham and Ricardo *did more to transform human thinking than any other scientific theory before or since*" (EPE, 3; emphasis supplied). Until the emergence of economic thought in the eighteenth century, it was taken for granted that anyone (or any government) wishing to change features of the social landscape was limited only by the laws of physical nature on the one hand and by the strength of will (and the brute force available to enforce, if needed, that will) on the other. "With good men and strong governments everything was considered feasible" (MMMP, 3).

But with the advent of economic science, "Now it was learned that in the social realm too there is something operative which power and force are unable to alter and to which they must adjust themselves if they hope to achieve success, in precisely the same way as they must take into account the laws of nature" (EPE, 3).[2]

Thus, the idea that there exist in society "laws" which operate regardless of the will of the rulers was a genuinely revolutionary idea. "People came to realize with astonishment that human actions were open to investigation from other points of view than that of moral judgment. They were compelled to recognize a regularity which they compared to that with which they were already familiar in the field of the natural sciences" (MMMP, 3f). Mises would claim that, from the very beginning, the source of the new economic understanding was a mode of inquiry stemming from and unique to the *human* character of the phenomena with which the new discipline was dealing. Attempts to discredit the (often unwelcome) policy implications which flowed from the new understanding therefore tended to take the form of discrediting the mode of inquiry central to this new discipline by insisting on rejecting all modes of inquiry other than those long established in the natural sciences. For Mises, then, correctly identifying and appreciating the appropriate mode of inquiry for the discipline of economics is a task vitally important if the practical usefulness of this discipline is not to be smothered and lost through the epistemological and methodological confusions sown by its enemies. It had, after all, only been by transcending the epistemological model of the natural sciences that the eighteenth-century pioneers had succeeded in revealing the regularities that prevail in the market economy. Unless the legitimacy of (and in fact the strict need for) this methodological approach is acknowledged, the essential contributions of economic science have been, Mises argued, tragically and disastrously jeopardized.

MISES AND METHODOLOGICAL DUALISM

The bedrock conviction upon which Mises built his epistemological system was the insight that "in spite of the unity of the logical structure of

---

2. Mises considered the idea of economic law to be the great contribution of the classical economists. He attached particular importance to what he called the Ricardian "Law of Association" [see HA, 159–64], a generalization of what is more commonly termed the "Law of Comparative Advantage."

our thought, we are compelled to have recourse to two separate spheres of scientific cognition: the science of nature and the science of human action. . . . We approach the subject matter of the natural sciences from without. The result of our observations is the establishment of functional relations of dependence. . . . In the sciences of human action, on the other hand, we comprehend phenomena from within. Because we are human beings, we are in a position to grasp the meaning of human action, that is, the meaning that the actor has attached to his action" (EPE, 130). Because "we do not know how external facts—physical and physiological—produce in a human mind definite thoughts and volitions resulting in concrete acts, we have to face an insurmountable *methodological dualism.* . . . Reason and experience show us two separate realms: the external world of physical, chemical, and physiological phenomena and the internal world of thought, feeling, valuation, and purposeful action. No bridge connects—as far as we can see today—these two spheres" (HA, 18; italics in original).

Mises's insistence on the sharp difference between the epistemological character of the "sciences of human action" and that of the natural sciences is, of course, by no means a radical or "extreme" position. The great American economist Frank H. Knight, the revered progenitor of the Chicago School, emphatically espoused a closely similar point of view.[3] Friedrich A. Hayek wrote an entire book, *The Counter-Revolution of Science: Studies on the Abuse of Reason* (1955) primarily devoted to the criticism of "scientism"—the mechanical and uncritical application of the methods of the natural sciences to the field of the "social sciences." Yet the manner in which Mises pursued and developed his methodological dualism led him to formulate certain methodological and epistemological assertions with which few others have felt entirely comfortable. It seems plausible to suggest that the admittedly extreme character of these latter Misesian positions had much to do with the doctrinal opponents against whom he was, directly or indirectly, doing battle—on behalf of what Mises held to be the settled propositions of economic science. Mises was indeed convinced that these doctrinal opponents must be treated as the intellectual enemies of economics.

3. See his "'What is Truth' in Economics?" *Journal of Political Economy* 48, no. 1 (Feb. 1940), reprinted as chapter 7 in F. H. Knight, *On the History and Method of Economics: Selected Essays* (Chicago: University of Chicago Press, 1956).

THE ENEMIES OF ECONOMICS
I. THE HISTORICISTS

The German Historical School dominated continental economics during the last three decades of the nineteenth century. As noted in chapter 2, a bitter methodological controversy erupted between this school, led by Gustav Schmoller, and the small group of Austrian economists following the lead of Carl Menger. The flames generated by this controversy did not die down until well into the twentieth century. For Mises the doctrines propagated by the Historical School constituted a direct denial of those regularities in social phenomena which he believed to be demonstrated by economic reasoning. The roots of this denial, Mises was convinced, were to be found in the school's historicism, its belief that economic knowledge must be sought *primarily* in the specific factual context surrounding the particular situations or episodes being investigated. Such a point of view explained the contemptuous rejection by the school's leading exponents of the claims made by the Austrians regarding the universality of economic law, transcending the particularities of time and space.

What rendered the controversy between the Historical School and the Austrian School particularly fascinating, perhaps, was the circumstance that both schools appreciated the subjective dimension of social phenomena. It was of course Menger who, in almost revolutionary fashion, stood classical economic theory on its head by insisting on the subjective character of economic phenomena and on the primacy of individual choice. But the German Historical School, too, recognized that social phenomena cannot be understood apart from human motives and interests. Late-nineteenth-century German philosophers such as Windelband and Rickert had done battle with those wishing to reconstruct historical scholarship on strictly positive lines (i.e., by rejecting all reference to such non-observables as human purposes). They had pointed out, contra the positivists, that the phenomena with which the social sciences (including history) deal are fundamentally different from the subject matter of the natural sciences. Unlike the latter, social phenomena are characterized by *meaning*, by the human purposefulness from which they arise. Members of the German Historical School recognized the validity of these insights. "Nevertheless," Mises wrote in 1933, Windelband, Rickert, and their followers failed "to conceive of the possibility of universally valid knowledge in the sphere of human action. In their view the domain of social science comprises only history and the historical method. They regarded the findings of economics and historical investigation in the same light as the Historical School" (EPE, 5). In other words, to use Roger Koppl's felicitous phrasing, the "historicists offered subjectivism without science."[4]

From Mises's perspective, the propensity of the German Historical School to deny the universality of the conclusions of economic theory led the school to deny the essential contributions of economics. For Mises, therefore, the statist policies supported by the Historical School (policies at variance with the normative conclusions which can be reasonably derived from standard economic theory) stamped the school as an enemy of economics—despite its recognition of the subjectivist and cultural elements in social and economic phenomena.

For Mises, on the other hand, as for all the Austrian School, the subjectivism of economic theorizing, rigorously and consistently pursued, yields understanding of law-like regularities within economic society. Mises found it essential to emphasize the universality of these regularities, a universality which consigns empirical knowledge of the *specific* situations (which may instantiate such regularities) to a distinctly inferior level of significance. Mises insisted on *both* subjectivism *and* science.

THE ENEMIES OF ECONOMICS
II. THE POSITIVISTS

After the end of World War I, Austrian economics did not have to contend seriously with the German Historical School, whose influence had by then drastically declined. But a new group of doctrinal opponents emerged. In fact, these opponents emerged in Vienna itself. They were the logical positivists of the Vienna Circle, led by Otto Neurath, Rudolph Carnap, Moritz Schlick, and others. These writers, being "determined to exorcise metaphysical speculation from scientific theorizing" formulated "strongly empiricist tenets."[5] In economics this campaign took the form of excluding any insights based upon

---

4. Roger Koppl, "Alfred Schutz and F. A. Hayek as Misesian Methodologists," (paper delivered to workshop on "Spontaneous Orders: Austrian Economics, Philosophy and Aesthetics," Copenhagen School of Business, November 1998), 4.

5. F. Machlup, *Methodology of Economics and Other Social Sciences* (New York: Academic Press, 1978), ix.

introspection and insisting on "operationalism" in selecting elements of reality for scientific discussion.[6] The extreme empiricism of this approach in effect excluded all subjectivist insights from legitimate discussion—offering a challenge to the very foundations of the Mengerian research program. The positivist position rejected attention to human purposefulness and such concepts as marginal utility, except insofar as they could be held to be manifested in observed regularities (in which case it is the latter observed regularities which become the foundation for subsequent theorizing).

By midcentury the fashionability of positivist epistemology had declined from its earlier prominence in philosophical discussion. Economists, however (always having a tendency to grasp the philosophically fashionable tenets of earlier decades), would continue to pursue the empiricist method with great determination for several decades longer.[7] For Mises, and many others, such positivist economics, closing its eyes to subjectivist insights, meant deliberate refusal to see what is readily visible to the mind's eye. Frank Knight was pungent in his reaction to the positivists' refusal to recognize that realm of reality which is constituted by "interests and motivations." It is true, he wrote, that the existence of this realm cannot be established in a way that can meet the positivist standard of testability. However, if "anyone denies that men have interests . . . economics and all its works will simply be to such a person what the world of color is to the blind man. But there would be a difference: a man who is physically, ocularly blind may still be rated of normal intelligence and in his right mind."[8] Certainly for Mises, too, the positivists, necessarily blind to what he (agreeing in this case with Knight) considered to be economics "and all its works," were not simply philosophically mistaken but the enemies of economics.

6. "Operationalism" was a notion first advanced by Percy Bridgman in 1927. The doctrine eventually had great influence on midcentury mainstream economics; see for example, P. A. Samuelson, *Foundations of Economic Analysis* (Cambridge: Harvard University Press, 1947); R. G. Lipsey and P. O. Steiner, *Economics* (New York: Harper and Row, 1966).

7. An important methodological work on these lines was Terence W. Hutchison, *The Significance and Basic Postulates of Economic Theory* (London: Macmillan, 1938).

8. Knight, *On the History and Method of Economics*, 160.

MISES'S METHODOLOGICAL DEFENSE

Mises saw the central teachings of economics as constituted by its understanding of the systematic operation of the force of dynamic competition in free markets. The entrepreneurial-competitive market process operates systematically to ensure a tendency toward that allocation of society's resources—and that steady advance in society's awareness of its resource and technological potential—which reflects consumer rankings of preference and consumer awareness of the expanding possibilities of fulfilling preferences hitherto unattainable. These systematic tendencies make up the so-called "laws" of economics. Awareness of these "laws" on the part of governments can help avoid disastrous policies that might unwittingly run afoul of these systematic tendencies. Yet these "laws" are not easily discernible to the eye of the historian or statistician. The German Historical School, for all its wealth of historical scholarship, failed to observe the systematic operation of these laws. Nor did it seem likely that statistical or econometric analysis (unless, indeed, such analysis itself was based on insights grounded in abstract economic theorizing) would be able to detect the operation of these laws in a manner sufficiently clear as to be able to convince the positivist skeptic. Only abstract economic theorizing, recognizing the nature and operation of human purposefulness, and recognizing the nature and thrust of human entrepreneurial resourcefulness, is able to identify the systematic tendencies which shape the entrepreneurial-competitive market process. Mises believed, therefore, that it was his scientific duty to identify with clarity the epistemological and methodological foundations of economic theory, and to point out the epistemological and methodological fallacies that, in his view, marred the economics which midcentury positivist and other schools of thought were attempting, with great technical virtuosity, to establish as the basis for professional thought.

MISES AND THE A PRIORI: THE EXTREMIST?

Mises took methodological dualism to its most consistent possible conclusions. Not only do the phenomena of human action pertain to a dimension beyond that which relates to the "external world of physical, chemical, and physiological phenomena": along this dimension of human action the phenomena of the external world play no essential role whatsoever. To be sure, human action is undertaken, for the greater part, to attain objectives that are part of the external world. Moreover, such action is undertaken through the deployment of tools and means which are part of the external world. But our understanding of the systematic consequences of human actions as they interact in the world does not in any way depend on the particularities of these objectives, or on the means deployed toward their attainment. Whether members of society compete in the market for food or for books, whether prospective producers must gain command of ploughs or of the services of violin maestros, the general laws of competition and the manner in which prices are hammered out are the same. Understanding these laws in no way depends on one's specific knowledge of those aspects of the external world that are relevant to the objectives of market participants, or to the tools that they employ in their attempts to achieve these objectives.

The source of our understanding of these laws is our direct awareness of the purposefulness of human action, and of the way in which action is systematically modified by encountering changed arrays of contextual circumstances. This, for Mises, meant that our knowledge of the conclusions of economic theory is a priori. Of course, when it comes to the *application* of these conclusions for the analysis of some specific real-world event, such as a natural disaster affecting a source of supply of some important raw material, or a piece of legislation placing a ceiling on a particular price, Mises did not need to be instructed on the relevance of and central role played by empirical facts. But, he would insist, there is a crucial epistemological gulf separating our knowledge of the general laws of economic causation and our knowledge of how those general laws are exemplified in specific situations. It is the former knowledge, Mises insisted, that in no way depends on empirical information.

Mises's insistence on the a priori character of economic science was viewed as rather odd, even by scholars otherwise sympathetic to his views on economics. This insistence was treated by others as nothing less than an outrageous challenge to the very scientific character of economics. In the 1938 words of one prominent economist, an adherent of logical positivism, "a proposition which can never *conceivably* be shown to be true or false . . . can *never* be of any use to a scientist."[9] In more recent times Mark Blaug has referred (in a passage that has been cited with some frequency) to Mises's "later writings on the foundations of economic

9. T. W. Hutchison, *Significance and Basic Postulates*, 152–53.

science" as being "so cranky and idiosyncratic that we can only wonder that they have been taken seriously by anyone."[10] More moderate disagreement with Mises's position has been expressed by his disciple Fritz Machlup[11] and by Bruce Caldwell.[12] Perhaps the most significant (and perhaps also the least frequently noticed) critic of Mises's "extreme" a priorism was Friedrich A. Hayek.

Hayek is often viewed as a follower of Mises (although he was never his formal student at the University of Vienna). Hayek has himself referred to Mises as the person "from whom . . . I have probably learnt more than from any other man."[13] And in Hayek's own discussions of methodological issues (particularly in *The Counter-Revolution of Science*) he refers to Mises in terms of considerable praise and demonstrates broad agreement with Mises's central positions. Yet in his famous 1937 paper "Economics and Knowledge," Hayek took pains to dissociate himself from a view of economics which sees it as nothing more than an exercise in pure logic ("the logic of choice").[14] Without mentioning Mises by name, Hayek was clearly, if gently, pointing out to his mentor that the propositions of economic theory "can be turned into propositions which tell us anything about causation in the real world only in so far as we are able to fill those formal propositions with definite statements about how knowledge is acquired and communicated."[15]

In other words, Hayek was arguing that the a priori logic of choice can succeed in describing positions of societal equilibrium, and the

10. M. Blaug, *The Methodology of Economics, or How Economists Explain* (Cambridge: Cambridge University Press, 1980), 93. See ibid. where Blaug approvingly cites a similar blast by Paul Samuelson.

11. See Fritz Machlup, "The Problem of Verification in Economics," *Southern Economic Journal* 22 (July 1955): 1–21.

12. Bruce Caldwell, *Beyond Positivism: Economic Methodology in the Twentieth Century* (London: George Allen and Unwin, 1982), 118–35.

13. *Hayek on Hayek*, 68.

14. F. A. Hayek, "Economics and Knowledge," *Economica* n.s., 4 (February 1937): 33–54; reprinted in *Hayek, Individualism and Economic Order* (London: Routledge and Kegan Paul, 1949), chapter 2.

15. *Hayek, Individualism and Economic Order*, 33. In oral remarks years later, Hayek emphasized that his paper had the intent of identifying the limited role of a priori reasoning in economics.

conditions that must be fulfilled in such equilibrium states, but that such logical exercises cannot predict, explain, or describe the process of equilibration that might in fact bring about the attainment of any equilibrium state. For insight into the processes of equilibration we require concrete empirical information concerning the acquisition and communication of knowledge. This is so because (as Hayek was at the time of the writing of that paper beginning to recognize and to emphasize) the equilibrium state implies complete relevant mutual information on the part of market participants. Disequilibrium implies gaps in such completeness of information. A process of equilibration must therefore be a process of learning. Pure logic cannot, Hayek was convinced, predict the nature of such learning processes; only empirical knowledge can provide the economist with insight into the processes of learning which must make up any processes of equilibration that do in fact occur.

Now Hayek once expressed to a small group, including this writer, his surprise that, on receiving and reading this 1937 paper, Mises expressed his warm admiration for it. Hayek had, with trepidation it seems, expected Mises to express his sharp displeasure at Hayek's thesis expressing his reservations regarding the pure a priorism of economic theory. Hayek was puzzled that Mises had apparently failed to recognize, in Hayek's diplomatic language, his definite disagreement with Mises's views on a priorism.

I would suggest the following explanation, one that can not only solve the puzzle that Hayek saw in Mises's reaction to his paper, but can also help us understand why, unlike Hayek, Mises did not believe it necessary to consider empirical research on learning behavior in markets in order to understand market processes of equilibration. Mises really did believe that the same a priori insights which permit us to understand how individuals behave in market situations permit us also to understand—at least at the most general level—those powerful tendencies toward equilibration which markets generate. The key to all this seems to lie in the important distinction that sets apart the foundation concept of *human action* (in Mises's system) from that of allocative, or maximizing, choice (in mainstream neoclassical microeconomics).

Following on Lionel Robbins's 1932 *Nature and Significance of Economic Science*, mainstream microeconomics took as its analytical unit the act of maximizing choice (under the constraint of scarcity). With ends and means taken as given, the agent—whether consumer, producer, or factory owner—allocates his given means in such a way as to maximize the achievement of his most valued ends. All the explanations and predictions of microeconomic theory (insofar as it is the Logic of Choice) consist, then, of working out (a) at the level of the individual, what constrained maximization will imply in terms of buying, selling, and/or production decisions, and (b) at the societal level, what sets of prices will permit and inspire all individuals to carry out their planned maximizing decisions without disappointment or regret. It is because the individual decision, as mainstream economics thus understands it, is based on given knowledge or expectations (and contains no internal devices for spontaneous revision of such knowledge and expectations) that mainstream economics is unable to account for spontaneous processes of equilibration (which, as noted above, consist in processes of learning). Hayek, working within such a mainstream, Robbinsian framework (in which decision making is conceived within the framework of given and known arrays of ends and means), thus saw processes of equilibration as necessarily involving facts of the learning process that must be recognized as *outside* the realm of economic logic. But Mises, who had a view of human decision making that differed significantly from that of Robbins, saw things differently.

For Mises, the analytical unit is *not* the act of choice within a given ends-means framework. For Mises the unit of analysis is *human action,* a concept which includes the *identification of the very ends-means framework* within which efficient decision making must be exercised. And it is here that Mises's economics, seen as the science of human action, must itself include understanding of the manner in which human beings become aware of the opportunities for gainful activity. For Mises, the verb "to act" includes not only effective exploitation of all perceived net opportunities for gain, but also the *discovery* of those opportunities. The logic of economics reveals not only what men will do in specific situations of perceived possible gain, but also the circumstance that men will tend to discover opportunities for gain generated by earlier errors by market participants (errors expressed in their failure to perceive existing price differentials). In other words, in explaining the source of profit opportunities in the entrepreneurial errors made at any given moment, economics is, *in that very explanation,* also identifying the scope of the tendency of real-world entrepreneurs to discover and exploit pure profit opportunities. The equilibrating process is seen as implied, in the general sense, in the very notion of human action. To be sure, in order to track the specific path of an equilibrating process more is required than the a priori logic of human action. But to articulate the central theorems of economics (which depend crucially, but only in a most general way, upon equilibrating tendencies) nothing more is needed than the pure logic of human action.

It seems reasonable to see Mises's reaction to Hayek's 1937 paper (a reaction which Hayek found puzzling) as reflecting (a) Mises's (apparently mistaken) belief that Hayek shared Mises's own view of things (as described here above), so that (b) he interpreted Hayek's references to the need for empirical knowledge regarding processes of learning as relating only to the applied level—that is, to the task of identifying which specific path of equilibration is likely to be manifested in the real world under given initial conditions.

MISES AND THE A PRIORI: NOT SO EXTREME!

As I have noted, Mises's views on the a priori character of economic theorizing are rooted in the primordial concept of "human action," of human agents being perceived as purposeful individuals who are alert to opportunities that might prove beneficial to them. This writer once asked Mises how a person can know that human beings other than himself are indeed purposeful. How can we know that one is not the only purposeful human agent in existence? How can a priori reasoning generate the knowledge that society is made up of rational, goal-seeking persons? Mises's answer surprised me greatly: it may perhaps soften the image of Ludwig von Mises as an *extreme* a priorist. Mises answered my query by saying, in effect, that we become aware of the existence of other human agents by observation.[16] It is observation that convinces us not to be solipsists. It is observation that convinces us that the human race is a race of rational, purposeful, alert human beings.

If we take this oral response of Mises seriously, it becomes clear that Mises's a priorism must be understood as being rather less extreme than it is often believed to have been. Mises was not maintaining that an isolated economic thinker can explain what occurs in market society without leaving his cell. At the very least he must establish—on the basis of empirical investigation, it turns out—that a market society made up of

16. Professor Rizzo has drawn my attention to the section in HA, 23–27, entitled "The Alter Ego," which seems to reflect this perspective.

purposefully acting human beings does in fact exist. Once, however, one has, on the basis of such empirical observation, convinced oneself that society *is* made up of purposeful human agents, one can *then,* in Mises's view, develop through deductive reasoning those chains of economic theorizing (based on introspective understanding of what it *means* to be a purposeful, rational, human being) that make up the core of economics.

MISES AND *WERTFREIHEIT*: ONLY A SUPERFICIAL PARADOX

For Mises, economics is a science; its pursuit calls for strict adherence to the canons of scientific investigation generally. Among the foremost of these canons, in Mises's judgment, is that of *wertfreiheit.* "[T]he scientific character of [an] investigation," he remarked in 1933 (as if this is a matter that is self-understood) "precludes all standards and judgments of value" (EPE, 36). "What is impermissible . . . is the obliteration of the boundary between scientific explanation and political value judgment" (EPE, 37). In this regard Mises was following the path laid down most emphatically by the eminent sociologist Max Weber (who had strongly attacked lapses from *wertfreiheit* in the economics of the German Historical School—despite his own roots in that school).[17] Clearly, Mises believed that a distinct separation of a scholar's economic analysis from his personal judgments of value was *possible* (something which many later philosophers have questioned). He also believed, as had Max Weber, that a genuinely practiced policy of *wertfreiheit* was absolutely *essential* for economists, if their views were to have salutary influence and to command the respect ordinarily accorded to scientific pronouncements. Mises concluded his magnum opus, *Human Action,* with a strong defense of the doctrine of *wertfreiheit* in science generally and in economics in particular. There can be no doubt that for Mises this doctrine was a central pillar in his praxeological system. And here is where the *apparent* paradox in Mises obtrudes.

No one who reads Mises can doubt that he was, even when developing propositions of economic science, writing with enormous *passion.* After several pages in which he carefully articulated the above statement expounding the *wertfreiheit* doctrine, Mises concluded his 885-page

---

17. See Joseph A. Schumpeter, *History of Economic Analysis* (New York: Oxford University Press, 1954), 804f.

treatise with the following stirring sentences: "The body of economic knowledge is an essential element in the structure of human civilization; it is the foundation upon which modern industrialism and all the moral, intellectual and therapeutical achievements of the last centuries have been built. It rests with men whether they will make proper use of the rich treasure with which this knowledge provides them or whether they will leave it unused. But if they fail to take the best advantage of it and disregard its teachings and warnings, they will not annul economics; they will stamp out society and the human race" (HA, 885). Anyone reading these sentences can understand the passion with which Mises fought for what he believed to be economic truth; he believed that the very survival of the human race depends upon the recognition and application of that truth. But at the same time it may seem difficult to reconcile Mises's passionate advocacy of the free economy with his insistence on the value-neutrality of the economist. Even so devoted a disciple of Mises as the late Fritz Machlup apparently found such a reconciliation too difficult to achieve.

In a 1955 review of the English translation of a well-known 1930 (German-language) book by the prominent economist Gunnar Myrdal,[18] Machlup expressed this as follows. Myrdal's book was largely a series of criticisms of economists for injecting political presuppositions and ideals into their supposedly scientific discussions. In this regard, however, Myrdal gave the Austrian School a generally positive assessment. "[I]n Austria, economics has never had direct political aims. . . ."[19] Machlup expressed surprise at this positive assessment. "How did the anti-interventionist writings of the Austrian von Mises escape Myrdal's attention?"[20] But a more careful reading of Mises should convince us that, at least in principle, there is no inconsistency in Mises's position. Although we will leave a fuller exploration of this issue for chapter 6, we offer here one brief observation that relates especially to the topic of the present chapter.

18. Gunnar Myrdal, *The Political Element in the Development of Economic Theory* (Cambridge, Mass.: Harvard University Press, 1954). Machlup's review was in *American Economic Review* (December 1955).

19. Myrdal, 128.

20. See the republished text of Machlup's review in his *Methodology of Economics and Other Social Sciences*, 478.

Certainly, Mises maintained the value-neutrality of economic science itself. Yet he also understood and emphasized that *any* human activity, scientific investigation not excluded, is engaged in under the motivating power of ultimate human values. One may engage in scientific investigation for the sake of fame, for the sake of material success, or for the sake of satisfying one's passion to know the truth. No matter what the motivation may be, the scientific investigation, if indeed it is to be a scientific undertaking, must itself be engaged in a manner detached from any value which may be motivating the investigation. As Mises put it, the "objectivity of bacteriology as a branch of biology is not in the least vitiated by the fact that the researchers in this field regard their task as a struggle against the viruses responsible for conditions harmful to the human organism" (EPE, 36). For Mises, a prime motivation for economic investigation is the goal of promoting the very survival of the human race. This motivation indeed accounts for the passion with which Mises fought for what he considered sound economics. It did not, however, necessarily jeopardize the impartial objectivity with which his investigations themselves were conducted.

4. THE ECONOMICS OF THE MARKET PROCESS

By far the longest of the seven sections of Mises's monumental *Human Action* is part 4, entitled "Catallactics or Economics of the Market Society." Taking up approximately one half of the entire work, part 4 covers the entire array of topics that relate to the economics of a market society, including the role of money and the phenomenon of the trade cycle. We will take up these latter topics in chapter 5. In the present chapter, we focus on Mises's broad understanding of the *market process*. It is this aspect of Mises's economics which provides the foundation for his entire system of economics. And it is in this portion of his economics that Mises differed most importantly and fundamentally from his neoclassical (as distinct from his Keynesian) contemporaries. It will be important, therefore, to begin with what came to appear, during the early decades of the twentieth century, as the shared neoclassical understanding of the market society.

NEOCLASSICAL ECONOMICS AND THE MARKET ECONOMY

The various schools of economic theory that flourished around the turn of the century, and which are generally included under the broad umbrella of neoclassical economics, came to understand the market economy in a way which is still the core perspective within modern (non-Austrian) microeconomics. This perspective came to see the phenomena of the market as the determinate expression of (a) individual decisions made in rational, utility-maximizing or profit-maximizing fashion, and (b) a pattern of *interaction* among these rational, individual decisions, such that *all* of them can be simultaneously and successfully executed without disappointment and without regret. The roots of this perspective can be seen, in principle, in Menger's *Grundsätze,* as well as in Walras's *Elements.* As Austrian economics developed in the decade immediately following World War I, the followers of Menger's tradition indeed tended to believe that their economics was, at least in substance (as distinct from the technique of its exposition), not significantly different from that of the Walrasian tradition.

It was to be the Austrian-influenced work of Lionel Robbins that, in his 1932 book, would introduce this continental perspective to the British (and thus eventually to the Anglo-American) mainstream. It thus became easy for the Austrians of the 1920s gradually to fall into the habit of seeing their theory of market prices as being primarily the theory of *equilibrium* price. It was the Austrian Ewald Schams whom Lionel Robbins cited as the apparent originator of the term "comparative statics."[1] As neoclassical economics progressed, it indeed became gradually identified as almost exclusively concerned with equilibrium analysis (and especially with the equilibrium economics of the perfectly competitive model—of which more will be discussed later in this chapter). A concentration on equilibrium tends to divert analytical attention away from the *process* of equilibration. In Frank Machovec's opinion, the course of neoclassical economics during the first four decades of this century indeed saw its transformation from a theory of process to one of (perfectly competitive) equilibrium.[2] Mises never accepted, nor did he play a role in, any such transformation.

MISES AND THE MARKET PROCESS

"What distinguishes the Austrian School and will lend it immortal fame is precisely the fact that it created a theory of economic action and not of economic equilibrium or non-action" (NR, 36). Writing this in 1940 (shortly after the publication of his *Nationalökonomie*), Mises recognized that economic thought cannot do without the idea of equilibrium, but maintained that the Austrian School "is always aware of the purely instrumental nature of such an idea" (NR, 36). The core of economic understanding, for Mises, does not consist in the elucidation of the conditions required to be fulfilled in the state of equilibrium; the core of economic understanding consists, instead, in revealing the systematic character of the market process—a process set in motion precisely by the circumstance that the conditions for equilibrium have *not* been fulfilled. "The market," Mises wrote in 1949, "is not a place, a thing, or a collective entity. The market is a *process,* actuated by the interplay of the actions of the various individuals cooperating under the division of labor" (HA, 257; emphasis supplied).

1. See Lionel C. Robbins, *The Nature and Significance of Economic Science,* 2nd edition (London: Macmillan, 1935), 101. See however J. A. Schumpeter, *History of Economic Analysis* (Oxford and New York: Oxford University Press, 1954), 965, for a different attribution.

2. See Frank M. Machovec, *Perfect Competition and the Transformation of Economics* (London and New York: Routledge, 1995).

THE ENTREPRENEURIAL CHARACTER
OF THE MISESIAN MARKET PROCESS

The prime active element in the Misesian market process is the profit-motivated activity of entrepreneurs. "The driving force of the market, the element tending toward unceasing innovation and improvement, is provided by the restlessness of the promoter and his eagerness to make profits as large as possible" (HA, 255). "The driving force of the market process is provided . . . by the promoting and speculating entrepreneurs" (HA, 328). The entrepreneur is the person who acts in the face of uncertainty; in the imaginary, settled world of the equilibrium state, without uncertainty, there is no scope for entrepreneurial activity (HA, 252–53). More narrowly, Mises observed, the term "entrepreneur" is used in economics to refer to those "who have more initiative, more venturesomeness, and a quicker eye than the crowd, the pushing and promoting pioneers of economic improvement" (HA, 255). (When Mises uses the word "promoter," he wishes to draw our attention to this narrower subset of the broader category of entrepreneurship.) The entrepreneurial function is the correction of "maladjustments" in market prices and decisions. When an entrepreneur is able to grasp pure profit by buying factors of production at prices below those of the products they generate, he has discovered, and moved to correct, such a maladjustment. The maladjustment consisted in the fact that the factor prices were "from the point of view of the future state of the market . . . too low."[3] Entrepreneurial profit and loss "are generated by success or failure in adjusting the course of production activities to the most urgent wants of the consumers."[4]

There is, in the Misesian view of things, a one-to-one correspondence between (a) maladjustments in the market, reflecting earlier entrepreneurial "errors" (i.e., failures to anticipate the true conditions of—and the true potential arising out of—resource supply and consumer demand), and (b) opportunities for profit that are likely to alert potential entrepreneurs to act, in the face of the ineradicable uncertainty of the future, in ways consistent with the correction of those

---

3. Ludwig von Mises, "Profit and Loss," in *Planning for Freedom and Other Essays and Addresses,* 2nd edition (South Holland, Ill.: Libertarian Press, 1962), 109.

4. Ibid.

maladjustments. The market process, then, consists of continual discoveries (and "corrections") of such maladjustments/pure-profit opportunities by entrepreneurial market participants. These discoveries are being continually pointed in new directions by the never-ceasing flood of exogenous changes (such as autonomous changes in consumer preferences, autonomous changes in resource supply conditions, and autonomous changes in technological possibilities). To see and to describe the continuous market process of entrepreneurial discoveries as *equilibrating* in character is to be both illuminating and possibly misleading at the same time. It is misleading to see this process as equilibrating, not only because the continual flood of exogenous changes renders the attainment of equilibrium utterly unthinkable, but also because that flood of change virtually ensures that the direction of innovative entrepreneurial decisions at any given moment is likely *not* to be consistent with the patterns of potential adjustment implicit in the exogenous changes about to occur *after* that given moment.

Yet, at the same time, there *is* an illuminating quality to the Misesian insight that the innovative moves of entrepreneurs within any given period constitute a systematic "corrective" (and thus "equilibrative") series of steps *from the perspective of the entrepreneurial insights of that period.* Those insights have (at least in the judgments of the relevant entrepreneurs) revealed existing "maladjustments" among earlier market decisions; these discoveries have triggered entrepreneurial moves, the effect of which, *absent further unanticipated change,* will be to correct the earlier maladjustments. The insight that the absence of unanticipated change is itself something *not* to be anticipated does not erase the valuable character of the insight that, in a well-defined sense, these discoveries have set in motion equilibrating, corrective, entrepreneurial adjustments. The valuable character of this insight lies in its illuminating clarification of the definite sense in which the entrepreneur-driven market process is *not* a free-floating series of random changes, but rather is, at each and every instant, a process operating under powerful forces which continually produce outcomes that are, if not "determinate" (as they certainly are not!), at least systematically and benignly inspired by error-correcting incentives. Seen from the Misesian perspective, the ceaseless agitation of the market becomes "understandable" as the continuous flow of corrective discoveries, linked to the current and anticipated conditions (of resource supply, consumer demand, and technological knowledge) by powerful tendencies of entrepreneurs to discover what it is in their interest to discover.[5]

THE DYNAMICALLY COMPETITIVE CHARACTER
OF THE MISESIAN MARKET PROCESS

Although Mises himself did not emphasize this aspect of his system, the present writer has found it useful to point out that if the Misesian market process is an entrepreneurial one, it is, by that very token, also a dynamically *competitive* process.[6] Mises referred to what he called "catallactic competition" as being "one of the characteristic features of the market economy" (HA, 275). In this regard Mises had in mind the incentives operating upon competing producers to seek improved ways of serving the consumer. What creates these incentives is the awareness of producers that others are free to enter their "territories" and compete for their customers' allegiance. What is needed in order to ensure freedom of what Mises called "catallactic competition"[7] is simply the absence of artificial barriers to entry that might restrict entrepreneurial entry into a field in which improvements for consumer satisfaction might be held to be possible and worthwhile. The point is that dynamically competitive entry into a market *means* entrepreneurial entry, so that to recognize the entrepreneurial character of the Misesian market process is to recognize its dynamically competitive character.

What we have referred to as *dynamic* competition (and we have used this term as equivalent to Mises's "catallactic" competition) differs, it must be emphasized, from the concept of competition used in mainstream neoclassical textbooks for the past six or seven decades.

---

5. This section has not emphasized the role of entrepreneurial innovation in the Misesian market process. Certainly Mises recognized the importance of innovation in the market process, and its entrepreneurial character. (See, for example, HA, 511–12). Unlike Schumpeter, however, Mises did not place innovation, as such, at the heart of his analysis of the market. For further discussion of the relationship between Misesian entrepreneurship and Schumpeterian (innovative) entrepreneurship, see this writer's *The Driving Force of the Market: Essays in Austrian Economics* (London and New York: Routledge, 2000), chapter 13.

6. See Israel M. Kirzner, *Competition and Entrepreneurship* (Chicago: University of Chicago Press, 1973).

7. "Catallactics" is the term Mises adopted (from the nineteenth-century economist Richard Whately) to describe the study of exchanges.

Mainstream neoclassical textbooks, following especially upon the ideas of Frank H. Knight, have identified competition, in its most "perfect" form, as referring to a particular *equilibrium* or *state of affairs*. In this state of affairs, the imagined universality of information and knowledge, and the imagined extremely large number of market participants, combine with other elements to ensure that, at each and every instant, each potential seller (buyer) is confronted with a perfectly elastic demand (supply) curve. In other words, the state of perfect competition is one in which (a) the market price has *already* (before the model of perfect competition has had a chance to "perform") somehow been set at the equilibrium level (and each market participant is too insignificant to be able to make any change in that price), and in which (b) each market participant (correctly) sees himself as able to carry out all his selling (or buying) decisions at the market price without disappointment and without regret. Mises must have found this model of perfect competition not only wildly unrealistic (something never denied by neoclassical economists), but also analytically obfuscating. He seems to have deliberately ignored this model in all his writing on the role of competition in markets.

Thus, while the perfectly competitive state (being an equilibrium situation) cannot possibly provide scope for the Misesian entrepreneur, the dynamically competitive process (in which, for Mises, the consumers assign success and failure among the competing producers) is *essentially* entrepreneurial. An act of competitive entry is necessarily entrepreneurial; it expresses the implicit conviction of the entering competitor that profits can be won by directing some particular resources away from their current destinations toward the production of a particular product, which they expect to be able to sell at a profit. The entrepreneurial market process thus consists of an endless series of entrepreneurial steps, each of which constitutes an act of "entry." The generally understood benign character of "competition" thus consists, in the Misesian perspective, in its permitting and stimulating a continual flow of entrepreneurial ventures. These ventures introduce new products and new methods of production, but they also introduce new prices into the market, for both resources and products. These new prices explore possibilities for attracting resources to where they can be most productive, as judged by consumers; they explore possibilities for making products available to consumers at lower costs to them.

The sense in which Mises believed that consumers are well served by the market process depends on the *competitive* character of this process, that is, on the extent to which the institutions of the market permit and encourage entrepreneurs to enter sectors of the market where they believe they can win profit. For the Misesian market process, "competition" means simply an institutional framework characterized by *freedom of entrepreneurial entry,* or, equivalently, the absence of privileges granted to incumbents, which serve as artificial barriers to entry.

MISES AND MAINSTREAM PRICE THEORY

All this adds up to a significant difference between the Misesian understanding of the market process and the mainstream neoclassical theory of competitive price. The latter theory sees prices as emerging spontaneously out of the imagined conditions of perfectly competitive supply and demand. These prices are, at each and every instant, equilibrium prices. The task of the pure theory of price is seen as fully accomplished by the identification of the conditions that must be fulfilled—at the level of the consumer, at the level of the producer, and at the level of the resource owner—in order for all decisions to be able to be carried out simultaneously without disappointment and without regret. From this perspective, this price theory is helpful in understanding the real world because the *predictions* of the model are in fact approximately fulfilled in the real world (even though, it is of course conceded, the real world does *not* exemplify the *assumptions* of the perfectly competitive equilibrium model). In other words, mainstream theory applies its competitive model to the real world by treating that world as having, at each and every moment, attained the equilibrium state. For Mises, the nature and applicability of market process theory is entirely different.

For Mises, the identification of what might be the equilibrium price (given the current state of supply and demand) is of distinctly secondary importance. (Mises at one point refers to the drawing of supply and demand diagrams as possibly helpful for teaching purposes, but as not really helpful in understanding the essential analytics of market price determination [HA, 333].) What is important for Mises is to understand the dynamic process continually at work in markets, operating to identify where resource or product prices are "too high" or "too low," and operating to "correct" them by attracting appropriate entrepreneurial discoveries.[8] The diagrams which dominate the microeconomics text-books have virtually no place in the Misesian system. These diagrams identify optimal decisions for various market participants (including, especially, producing firms) under a variety of assumed demand and cost situations. They throw no light on the dynamics through which these relevant demand and cost situations, as they confront the various decision makers, are themselves being changed in the course of the market process.

Where the mainstream theory of price has, because it is an equilibrium theory, squeezed the entrepreneurial role out of existence, Misesian theory places that role at the very center of the analytics of the process.

One very important result of these differences between the Misesian theory of the market process and the mainstream neoclassical theory of price, is that these two approaches have two entirely different perspectives on the meaning and significance of *monopoly* in the working of markets. (As we shall see in a later chapter, a direct implication of these different perspectives is that they generate two entirely contrasting views on the appropriate public policy in regard to the phenomenon of monopoly.)[9]

THE PLACE OF MONOPOLY IN THE MISESIAN SYSTEM

I.

In mainstream neoclassical economics, the idea of monopoly has come to mean a market in which a seller has a certain control over his price, reflected in his being confronted by a demand curve for his product that is less than perfectly elastic (i.e., not horizontal but downward sloping). In such a market the monopolist can, by limiting the quantity he offers

---

8. The Misesian process of entrepreneurial discovery is to be sharply distinguished from the modern neoclassical economics of search, pioneered by G. J. Stigler's 1962 paper, "The Economics of Information," *Journal of Political Economy* 69 (June 1962). In the economics of search, agents are assumed, at the very outset of analysis, to know exactly what it is they are looking for and what the costs and benefits of the search will be (at least in probabilistic terms). Search is then a deliberate, cost-benefit-controlled, production-of-information process. By contrast, Misesian entrepreneurial discovery is serendipitous, expressing the flash of entrepreneurial insight and recognition that "senses" (without deliberate, cost-benefit-calculated search) where opportunities are to be found.

9. See particularly below, chapter 6.

for sale, choose his price (whereas in the perfectly competitive market each seller finds the price somehow set automatically by "the market"; he is powerless to sell at any other price). Mainstream price theory then focuses on the differences that separate the price and output decision of the monopolist from the aggregate price and output outcomes of perfectly competitive industries, and on the evaluation of these differences from the perspective of their social welfare implications. To the extent that a seller is indeed a monopolist, his price is *not* determined by competition, but by his own profit-maximizing calculation.

For Mises, however, the notion of monopoly, as we shall see, is rather different. We can perhaps best grasp this difference by pondering the following statement by Mises: "It would be a serious blunder to deduce from the antithesis between monopoly price and competitive price that the monopoly price is the outgrowth of the absence of competition. There is always catallactic competition on the market. Catallactic competition is no less a factor in the determination of monopoly prices than it is in the determination of competitive prices" (HA, 278). At first glance this seems puzzling. Surely, if monopoly is in some sense the antithesis of competition, competition can hardly be a determining factor in generating monopoly price. The solution to this puzzle lies in Mises's understanding of what competition is (and in his consequently quite unusual definition of what monopoly means).

Mises believed that the dynamic process of entrepreneurial competition is *always* at work in the market. So long as there *is* a market, it necessarily consists, for Mises, in the scope it offers for the dynamic competitive process to proceed. There is, in this dynamic process of competition, nothing to ensure that market participants have no control over price (that they be seen as "price-takers"). On the contrary, a most important dimension along which dynamic competition proceeds is that of price; market participants compete with each other by offering to sell (or buy) at lower (or higher) prices than others. Thus, monopoly cannot be defined in terms of the less-than-perfect elasticity of the demand curve faced by the monopolist. Instead, it must be defined in terms of the obstacles to entry that protect the monopolist from the competition of others. In the absence of governmentally granted monopoly privileges, Mises found only one source of such obstacles to entry to be possible: *the possibility that one seller controls the entire supply of a particular scarce resource that is of great importance to a particular branch of production.* The conditions of competition surrounding this branch of production are now *different* from what they would be in the absence of the resource monopoly. Competition is not absent; the resource monopoly has forced the competitive process into different channels, as it were. From the space defined by the scope of the scarce monopolized resource, the force of the competitive process has been pushed outside, but the process continues to exercise determining power over the monopolist's prices.

It is still this competitive process, and only this competitive process, which is at work in helping determine the price that the monopolist producer will select. Just as the competitive process nudges a competitive producer to select his price (based on his entrepreneurial judgment concerning his alternative opportunities), so the competitive process nudges the monopolist producer to select his price in similar fashion. "The shape of the demand curve that . . . directs the monopolist's conduct is determined by the competition of all other commodities competing for the buyers' dollars. . . . On the market every commodity competes with all other commodities" (HA, 278). Now, mainstream theorists would recognize that the monopolist's demand curve is determined by happenings in other industries. But they would prefer to say that, *given* the monopolist's demand curve, its very shape dictates that the manner in which he selects his price is simply *not* competitive. Mises, on the other hand, alive as he was to the dynamic character of competition, sees the monopolist as at all times engaged in active entrepreneurial competition (with producers in other industries) for the consumer dollar, in a manner not different, in principle, from the manner in which competing producers compete actively in *any* competitive market.

The obvious question which presents itself, then, is precisely how a monopolized industry differs from a competitive industry, in the Misesian view of things. In both kinds of industry, we have seen, each producer-seller exercises *some* degree of control over price. In both kinds of industry, prices are determined, in large part, by the activities of competitors (in the same or in other industries). What positive differences separate the two kinds of industries? Is there any sense in which, for Mises, the monopolized industry can be pronounced economically "bad," or socially "inefficient"? To answer these questions we must first offer a brief digression concerning "consumer sovereignty," and its role in Mises's system of economic thought.

THE DOCTRINE OF CONSUMER SOVEREIGNTY

Although the Misesian theory of the competitive market process is a positive one, in that it simply describes and explains what occurs in a free market, the theory does lead indirectly to possible policy implications. For Mises, one possible link between his theory and policy was the concept of consumer sovereignty. In a brief section of *Human Action* (a section entitled "The Sovereignty of the Consumers"), Mises explained this concept. In the market, he argued, while it is the entrepreneur-producers who directly control production and "are at the helm and steer the ship," they are not supreme; the "captain is the consumer" (HA, 270). "A wealthy man can preserve his wealth only by continuing to serve the consumers in the most efficient way." Owners of material factors of production can prosper from the value represented by their assets only by placing those assets at the service of consumers in the ways preferred by consumers. It is by his decisions to buy and to refrain from buying that the consumer controls the pattern of production. The competition of entrepreneurs for profit leads them to seek more and more accurately to anticipate consumer preferences, and to move energetically, efficiently, and imaginatively to seek ways of catering to those preferences. In particular, as long as scarcity governs human society, competition for entrepreneurial profit expresses consumer sovereignty by tending to ensure that every ounce of potential resources is employed to further consumer satisfaction. Consumer sovereignty "forbids" the possibility of idle, wasted resources.

It is reasonable to interpret Mises's emphasis upon the notion of consumer sovereignty as expressing a profoundly Mengerian insight.[10] Menger had pioneered the theory of market prices as governed, both at the product level and at the resource level, by the demand of the consumer. The valuations of consumers (given the configuration of resource availability) determine the values of resources of production. Mises was simply pursuing this insight to its logical conclusion. He pointed out that market outcomes, the allocation of society's resources, are under the ultimate control of consumers. The consumers are sovereign.

---

10. On this see Israel M. Kirzner, "Mises and His Understanding of the Capitalist System," *Cato Journal* 19, no. 2 (fall 1999), reprinted as chapter 9 in Israel M. Kirzner, *The Driving Force of the Market.*

Certainly, so stated, this doctrine is a positive one; it is, by itself, *wert-frei*. Whether one is made happy or unhappy by the thought that consumers ultimately dictate the course of production, the *fact* of consumer sovereignty stands. But it is easy to see the implications of this doctrine for public policy in an environment in which public opinion favors consumer supremacy. As we shall see in chapter 6, it is certainly this which underlay much of Mises's lifelong convictions concerning the economic desirability of free markets. For present purposes, however, it is not necessary to proceed beyond the purely positive doctrine of consumer sovereignty. We shall see that it is from the perspective of this doctrine that Mises's views on the consequences of monopoly become clear.

THE PLACE OF MONOPOLY IN THE MISESIAN SYSTEM
II.

We must remember that for Mises the defining feature of the monopolist is his exclusive control over some important scarce resource. Because no one else can produce the product (for which this resource is a necessary ingredient), the owner of this monopolized resource *may* find it in his own interest to *destroy* part of his supply of this resource—if doing so would allow him to raise its price to a level that will maximize the revenue he can obtain from his resource. This *need* not be the case. It may *not* be possible to enhance revenue by withholding some of the resource from production. But where it is the case that the price of a resource has been raised through the deliberate withholding of supply from the market, Mises used the term "monopoly price." He saw this case as one which, while certainly possible, is extremely unlikely and rather unimportant from a practical point of view. (It is also virtually impossible to establish such a case empirically, since we are never in a position to know objectively whether the nonutilization of a monopolized resource was indeed motivated by the objective of enhancing revenue—it could have been motivated by the monopolist's speculation concerning a future price rise, or by his own desire not to use his resource for industrial purposes but instead to enjoy it in his capacity as consumer.)

For Mises, the monopoly price case is a unique situation ordinarily not able to occur in a market economy. Where a monopoly price has occurred, this means that the monopoly owner of the resource has successfully defied the preferences of consumers. He has been able to extract value from his assets, *not* by putting them at the service of the consuming public, but, to the contrary, by withholding them from such service. In the Misesian system such a possibility was fascinating (if unlikely); it meant that the doctrine of consumer sovereignty was, in one possible respect, not universally validated. Where the market economy generally imposes a *harmony* of interests among resource owners and consumers, monopoly resource ownership offers the possibility of a *conflict* of interests.

We should emphasize that, in enunciating this theory of monopoly, Mises was *not* drawing policy conclusions supporting state action against monopolies. His doctrine was stated at the positive level. (Indeed, the Misesian system strongly suggests the inappropriateness of the antitrust policies that Western capitalist countries adopted during the first decades of the twentieth century and earlier.)

For anyone familiar with the mainstream neoclassical theory of monopoly, Mises's theory cannot fail to appear quite strange. But its strangeness arises entirely from the profound differences, noted earlier, that separate the Misesian theory of the market from the mainstream neoclassical theory.[11]

For the mainstream theory, the theory of monopoly begins with a downward sloping demand curve confronting the monopolist producer. With a degree of control thus available to the monopolist producer, he selects the price which maximizes his net gain ("profit," in textbook terminology) by (a) producing a quantity which is lower than would have been produced were this monopolist somehow replaced by a perfectly competitive industry, and (b) charging a price shown to be higher than his marginal cost of production. The uniqueness of monopoly, in the mainstream neoclassical view, lies in these two implications of the downward sloping demand curve facing the monopolist producer.

But for Mises, *every* producer, even under (dynamically) competitive conditions, has a degree of entrepreneurial "control" over price (at least insofar as we can talk of "control" in the face of the radical uncertainty of an open-ended world). The question that Mises would pose for neoclassical theory would be: "what is it that (in the absence of governmentally granted privileges) protects the monopolist's profits from being whittled away by new entrants?" The answer, Mises would say, must lie in an implicitly postulated unique ownership over a scarce resource. The

---

11. For further discussion of this writer's critique of alternative readings of the Misesian position, see chapter 12 in the writer's *Driving Force of the Market.*

interesting implication for Mises, then, follows in the possibility that such monopoly ownership of a resource may lead to some of its supply being deliberately withheld from satisfaction of consumer preferences. The emphasis is not on the monopolist as producer (possibly, as a result, producing less than might otherwise have been produced), but on the monopolist resource owner, who may be motivated to act along lines that conflict with the interests of the consumer—a possibility never, in the Misesian system, otherwise arising under free market conditions.

THE PRICING OF FACTORS OF PRODUCTION

In mainstream neoclassical price theory, the prices of resource services (such as labor and the use of land) are seen as determined in markets which are parallel to the markets for the products which these resources produce. Just as supply and demand determine product prices in competitive markets, so too do supply and demand determine resource prices in competitive markets. Where the market demand curve for products is derived from marginal utility, the market demand curve for resources is derived from marginal productivity. It is this mainstream neoclassical insight that informs the textbook chapters on the so-called "marginal productivity theory of distribution" (largely based on the century-old work of the U.S. economist John Bates Clark). Mises would have, in regard to factor pricing, few new points of disagreement with the mainstream theory beyond those we have discussed with regard to the market process in general. In other words, Mises would of course be impatient with a strictly equilibrium theory of factor prices; and he would be impatient with the notions of perfect competition implicit in much of the mainstream theory. But, subject to the modifications implicit in these objections, he would in principle accept the Clarkian notion of "derived demand."

In this, indeed, Mises would simply be following the route, outlined in Carl Menger's 1871 work, in which the prices of resources ("higher order goods") are seen as derived by the market from the prices (themselves the expression of consumer valuations) of the consumer goods ("goods of lowest order"). Although Mises rarely used the term "marginal productivity" (HA, 597), he certainly accepted the general neoclassical insight that the wage which an employer of labor will offer is based on that employer's assessment of the additional revenue expected to be forthcoming from the laborer's productive efforts. What Mises emphasized, possibly more than is the case in mainstream neoclassical theory, is what he somewhat awkwardly referred to as the "connexity of prices" (HA, 391f). Following on Menger's insights concerning the linkages between the markets and prices of higher order goods and those of lower order goods, Mises saw the panorama of prices (of all resources and of all products) as linked in a dynamic competitive market process. Because one factor—labor—is necessary for every kind of production, and because in general the efforts of a laborer can be directed to a variety of different kinds of output, the connexity of prices emerges. It is this which "integrates the pricing into a whole in which all gears work on one another. It makes the market a concatenation of mutually interdependent phenomena" (HA, 392). Clearly this perspective shares certain features with the Walrasian general equilibrium perspective (in contrast to the Marshallian emphasis on the single industry). But the dynamic, competitive-entrepreneurial market process insights that inform the Misesian perspective clearly mark that perspective as a Mengerian (and quintessentially Austrian), rather than Walrasian, point of view.

THE MARKET PRICES THAT PREVAIL AT A GIVEN MOMENT

This chapter has emphasized Mises's view of the market process as one which, through steps of entrepreneurial discovery, tends to correct "maladjustments" (brought about by earlier entrepreneurial failure correctly to anticipate changing developments). In this view of things the market prices at any given instant are *"false"* prices (HA, 338; italics in original). It is because of their falsity that they are necessarily disequilibrium prices. It is the market through which profit-seeking entrepreneurs systematically tend to modify these prices, tending to ensure that they be replaced by prices which more closely and "truthfully" reflect the underlying preferences of consumers. But, while this is indeed the central theme in Mises's theory of the market process, there is also another, at first glance almost antithetical, theme in Mises's theory. This theme is the sense in which the real-world market prices at any given moment are seen by Mises as the right prices, the "equilibrium" prices, the "market-clearing" prices. Government interference in these prices necessarily *worsens* matters.[12] We offer here a brief explanation of this second Misesian theme,

---

12. This latter theme has been valuably emphasized by Joseph T. Salerno; see especially his "Mises and Hayek Dehomogenized," *Review of Austrian Economics* 6, no. 2, 113–46. For this writer's discussion, see further in *The Driving Force of the Market,* chapter 9.

in order both to show its consistency with the first theme we have been emphasizing and to show its importance in Mises's overall understanding of the market economy.

When Mises described the real-world market prices at any given instant as reflecting an "equilibrium of demand and supply" (HA, 762), he did not mean the demand-supply equilibrium of the mainstream neoclassical textbooks. The latter equilibrium state is one in which *all* participants (and all potential participants) in a specific market *have become aware of that price* which is capable of clearing the market, and *have correctly anticipated* that this market-clearing price would indeed prevail in the market. Equilibrium presumes complete and accurate mutual anticipation by each market participant of the actions of all other participants. There are *no* relevant "maladjustments" in the neoclassical equilibrium state. Obviously, Mises did *not* refer to the real-world prices at any given moment in any such omniscient context. Rather Mises was referring to what he called the "plain state of rest." In the Misesian plain state of rest all possible transactions *between those who have become aware of the possibility of such mutually beneficial transactions* have been completed. In Mises's scheme, this plain state of rest "comes to pass" in the real world "again and again." "At any instant all those transactions take place which the parties are ready to enter into at the realizable prices" (HA, 244). Clearly, these prices are "equilibrium" prices only in the very narrow sense that, *given current knowledge* on the part of market participants, these prices have permitted all known possibilities for exchange transactions to be realized. In no way are these prices—"false" as we have seen Mises to believe them to be—equilibrium prices in the sense of accurately expressing all conceivable mutually beneficial exchanges between market participants.

The reason why Mises nonetheless attached great significance to the spontaneous market prices at any instant, despite their "falsity," is quite straightforward. It has to do with the idea of *consumer sovereignty,* an idea which we have seen Mises to emphasize as central in understanding markets. For Mises the market prices at any given instant are, despite their falsity, the prices *completely* dictated by the sovereignty of the consumer—in the following somewhat special sense. These prices express the bids and offers of all market participants, and as such reflect the entrepreneurial judgment, as of that moment, of the brightest and most alert individuals, *in the light of what they believe will most effectively cater to the preferences of the consumer.* It is of course true that many of these bids and offers will have been made mistakenly, that is, will have been based on erroneous entrepreneurial judgment. But even these mistakes have been made under the pressure of consumer sovereignty. After all, "sovereignty" does not necessarily imply that all actions taken are "correct," in the sense of fulfilling the sovereign's will; it merely implies that all actions taken are taken with utmost seriousness and deliberation, *in order* to fulfil the sovereign's will. In this sense Mises saw the free market as *continuously* expressive of consumer sovereignty. From this perspective, well-meaning government interventions offering obstacles to the free movement of market prices constitute, *even where they are undertaken in order to correct alleged market failures of one kind or another,* an interference with the constant tendency of the free market to respect the sovereignty of consumers.

MISES AND THE MARKET PROCESS

As we shall see in subsequent chapters, these ideas of Mises concerning the dynamically competitive-entrepreneurial market process, and concerning its consequent fulfillment of the notion of consumer sovereignty, were fundamental to his economics. In some respects (as in the simple analysis of government price-fixing), this perspective led Mises in paths hardly different from those pursued by mainstream neoclassical economists. In others (as in the assessment of "antitrust" policies believed to enhance the competitiveness of the market), Mises's perspective led him sharply to disagree with the mainstream. In all his economics, however, Mises consistently adhered to his own Mengerian and Austrian understanding of how the market works.

5. MONETARY THEORY, CYCLE THEORY, AND THE RATE OF INTEREST

Mises's first book was *The Theory of Money and Credit* (1912). In addressing the field of monetary theory in that work, Mises applied the principles of the Austrian School as developed particularly by Menger and by Böhm-Bawerk—but in ways which went beyond the positions taken by his teachers. In Mises's own words: "The systems of Menger and Böhm-Bawerk were no longer wholly satisfactory to me. I was ready to proceed further on the road these old masters had discovered. But I could not use their treatment of those problems with which the monetary theorist must begin" (NR, 56). Mises's 1912 book followed some six years of study by Mises of monetary, currency, and banking issues, and had been preceded by several journal articles dealing with these topics. These topics were to take up a good deal of Mises's professional attention in the coming decades, and to result in several shorter, German-language works published in the twenties.[1] Mises returned, finally, to these same theoretical and applied issues in his 1949 *Human Action* (following on a similar treatment in his 1940 *Nationalökonomie*).

In this chapter, we will attempt to outline Mises's contributions to monetary theory. We will also examine Mises's important role in developing what came to be known as the Austrian Theory of the Trade Cycle. (Mises's work in this regard was in fact first put forward in the concluding chapters of his 1912 book on monetary theory, as an aspect of the advanced theory of money.) We will conclude with a brief survey of Mises's views on the nature of capital and interest (topics which, in Mises's overall system of economics, had at least tangential relevance to his views on the theory of the trade cycle).

---

1. See the three longer essays translated by Bettina Bien-Greaves and published under the editorship of Percy L. Greaves as the volume, Ludwig von Mises, *On the Manipulation of Money and Credit* (Dobbs Ferry, N.Y.: Free Market Books, 1978). The more important of these essays was first published as a monograph, *Geldwertstabilisierung und Konjunkturpolitik* (Jena: Gustav Fischer, 1928).

A. *Monetary Theory*

At the time of his 1912 book, much of Mises's monetary theory must have seemed novel, if not revolutionary. And if, as we shall see, his ideas required him to reject certain positions taken by his Austrian mentors, they constituted even more radical departures from the doctrines that were then dominant in the German monetary literature. In Mises's own retrospective account of the strongly negative reception accorded to his book in Germany, one can sense the defiant pride that Mises took in having decisively undermined the monetary doctrines generally accepted at the time of his youthful effort. "Men such as Knapp, Bendixen, Liefmann, Diehl, Adolf Wagner and Bortkiewicz," Mises wrote in 1940, "who then were celebrated in Germany as 'monetary theorists' are no longer considered authorities." Clearly it was Mises's book which contributed significantly to the change in professional opinions. So successful was the book in this regard, indeed, that certain key elements in Mises's approach no longer appear today as fresh and as original as they must have appeared in 1912 and in the immediately following years. A fair treatment of Mises's contributions to economics must not, however, ignore the degree to which they pioneered in changing the climate of professional opinion—even to the point where they may seem, to today's readers, to be comfortably familiar.

THE RADICAL CHARACTER OF MISES'S APPROACH

Mises has given us his own retrospective (1940) assessment of the radical purpose of his 1912 book. "According to prevailing opinion at that time, the theory of money could be clearly separated from the total structure of economic problems . . . ; in a certain respect it was an independent discipline. . . . It was my intention to reveal this position as erroneous and restore the theory of money to its appropriate position as an integral part of the science of economics" (NR, 56).

To achieve this objective, Mises found it necessary to attack several strands of the conventional monetary-theoretic wisdom of his time. These included: (a) the dominant view that the Austrian theory of marginal utility was inapplicable to the theory of the value of money; (b) the dominant view that money can be treated as "neutral" (i.e., that changes in the supply of money lead to changes in the purchasing power of money, but do not generate significant substantive changes in the ("real") structure of an economy; (c) the view (dominant in the German literature) that the state (i.e., the government) fills a role, in regard to the economic functions of money, categorically different from its role in regard to commercial transactions generally.

While each of these strands of then-conventional wisdom relates to a separate and distinct aspect of monetary theory, Mises's strongly dissenting positions on all three derived from a single taproot: his conviction that monetary theory must be recognized "as an integral part of the science of economics."

THE VALUE OF MONEY

At the time that Mises wrote his book, the dominant theory believed to account for the purchasing power of money was the Quantity Theory. Originating in sixteenth-century empirical observations and the insights of Bodin and Davanzati, the theory had had its ups and downs in professional opinion. By the start of the twentieth century the theory was fairly widely upheld, but the term "Quantity Theory of Money" had become quite elastic, covering a number of rather different versions.[2] As we shall see, Mises recognized the kernel of truth in these various versions of the Quantity Theory (and indeed defended the theory against a number of the objections of its critics). But his own positive theory explaining the way in which the purchasing power (the "value") of money is determined must be understood against the background of the Fisherine version of the Quantity Theory, a version which he vigorously attacked for what he considered its "mechanical" character (TMC, 144).[3] Mises was referring especially to Irving Fisher's 1911 book (with H. G. Brown), *The Purchasing Power of Money*. (Schumpeter remarked that ever since the publication of that book "Fisher has been classed as a sponsor of a particularly rigid form of quantity theory.")[4] The nub of this "mechanical," "rigid" version of the theory was, in Mises's words, its "conclusion that variations in the ratio between the quantity of money and the demand for it lead to

2. On this see J. A. Schumpeter, *History of Economic Analysis* (New York: Oxford University Press, 1954), part 4, chapter 8 (and especially section 5).

3. This work was a new edition of the English translation (first published in 1934) of the second (1924) German-language edition of Mises's (1912) work, *Theorie des Geldes und der Umlaufsmittel*.

4. J. A. Schumpeter, *History of Economic Analysis*, 1083.

proportionate variations in the objective exchange-value of money" (TMC, 144). Mises devoted considerable space to refuting this conclusion; he found it difficult to understand how economists familiar with the subjective theory of value could have fallen into the error it represented. The only explanation he could put forward had to do with their failure to integrate monetary theory with economic theory generally (a failure the correction of which was, as we have noted, a principal objective of Mises's book). "One thing only can explain how Fisher is able to maintain his mechanical Quantity Theory. To him the Quantity Theory seems a doctrine peculiar to the value of money; in fact, he contrasts it outright with the laws of value of other economic goods" (TMC, 144).

The challenge which Mises set for himself was in fact to show that the theoretical explanation for the value of money is, in principle, exactly the *same* explanation (i.e., the subjective theory of value) that economists (at least since the marginal utility revolution of the early 1870s) used to account for *all* commodity market values. Mises recognized that he faced a formidable challenge. Until the appearance of his own work, he observed, "the subjective school" (by which he meant in particular the Austrians) had not succeeded in "developing a complete theory of the value of money on the basis of the subjective theory of value and its peculiar doctrine of marginal utility" (TMC, 114).

Perhaps the best known argument which had hitherto been advanced in order to claim that the standard marginal utility theory of value could *not* be used to account for the value of money was the "circularity" argument. Mises cited Helfferich (author of a well-known, German-language 1903 monetary treatise) on this point. Helfferich noted that marginal utility theory explains the exchange-value (i.e., the market prices) of goods by reference to the degree of utility that potential consumers attach to these goods. A similar explanation for the exchange-value (i.e., the purchasing power) of a unit of money would then have to proceed by reference to the degree of utility that potential users of money attach to that unit. But the utility attached to a unit of money is nothing else but "the amount of consumable goods that can be obtained in exchange for it. . . . The marginal utility of money . . . *presupposes* a certain exchange-value of the money; so the latter cannot be derived from the former" (TMC, 119–20; emphasis supplied). The marginal utility of a loaf of bread is independent of the price of bread. The marginal utility of a dollar is meaningful only in terms of the purchasing power of the dollar. To explain the purchasing power of the dollar by reference to its marginal utility is to fall into a circularity trap.

Now this circularity argument has been totally dismissed by some modern writers (notably by Don Patinkin, an eminent midcentury monetary theorist).[5] Mises, however, took the argument seriously and developed what came to be a well-known solution to the circularity problem. For purposes of present discussion it is not really important to explain what Patinkin's reasoning for his dismissal was, and why Mises would not have accepted that reasoning. (This is all the more so since this would involve us in "Austrian" considerations basically unrelated to Mises's contributions to monetary theory.)[6] For us, it is sufficient to note that, at the time Mises wrote his book, the circularity argument was treated with great respect. Mises, in advancing his own solution (his "regression theorem") for this problem, was addressing an important issue in the monetary-theoretic debates of his time. For Mises, perhaps the even more important implication of his regression theorem was his ability, with the use of this theorem, to integrate the theory of the value of money into the main body of value theory as developed by the subjective economics of the Austrian School.

MISES'S REGRESSION THEOREM

Mises's solution to the circularity problem proceeded by distinguishing sharply between (a) the purchasing power of money as it enters into the marginal utility considerations of prospective demanders of money, and (b) the purchasing power of money (emerging out of the marginal-utility-driven choices of such prospective demanders) that we are seeking to explain. The circularity problem exists only if one fails to recognize this distinction (so that a marginal utility explanation of the purchasing

5. See Don Patinkin, *Money, Interest and Prices: An Integration of Monetary and Value Theory*, 2nd edition (New York: Harper and Row, 1965), 573ff, n. D.

6. For relevant literature see: (a) Murray N. Rothbard, "The Austrian Theory of Money," in *The Foundations of Modern Austrian Economics*, ed. Edwin G. Dolan (Kansas City: Sheed and Ward, 1976), 170f; (b) Karen I. Vaughn, "Critical Discussion of the Four Papers," in *The Economics of Ludwig von Mises: Toward a Critical Reappraisal*, ed. L. Moss (Kansas City: Sheed and Ward, 1976), 103; (c) Leland Yeager, *The Fluttering Veil; Essays on Monetary Disequilibrium* (Indianapolis: Liberty Fund, 1997), 152f.

power of money would *appear* to involve a circularity). "The difficulty is, however, merely apparent. The purchasing power which we explain . . . is not the same purchasing power the height of which determines . . . demand. The problem is . . . the determination of the purchasing power of the immediate future. . . . For the solution of this problem we refer to the purchasing power of the immediate past. . . . These are two distinct magnitudes. It is erroneous to object to our theorem . . . that it moves in a vicious circle" (HA, 408f).

The purchasing power that informs the decisions of potential individual demanders of money is the purchasing power that they *expect* to reside in units of money that they may acquire. Mises postulated that this *expected* purchasing power will generally be assumed to be what it has in fact been in the immediate *past*. As a result of the interaction between innumerable individual market participants, each basing his marginal utility calculations on the *past* purchasing power of money, the market generates—at each moment—a new market value for money—that is, a new purchasing power of money, which may well be (but of course need not be) at a different level than that of the past purchasing power which informed the individual calculations.

Mises recognized, of course, that this seems to push us back into an endless historical regression. Each day's purchasing power of money is determined, it would seem, by that of the preceding day. This would seem to be an endless sequence of "explanations," and thus a sequence unable to provide us with an independent starting point to serve as an explanatory element. But Mises maintained that this historical regression was not endless. Building on Menger's theory of how the institution of money can be understood to have emerged spontaneously out of prehistoric barter markets (TMC, 30–34), Mises points out that the historical regression which he has outlined for us need (and can) proceed back only to the moment when the monetary commodity first came to be valued, to some extent at least, as a common medium of exchange. Up until that point in time the market value of this commodity was determined entirely by marginal utility considerations that did *not* include (and were thus entirely independent of) purchasing power considerations. "At this point yesterday's exchange value is exclusively determined by the non-monetary . . . demand which is displayed only by those who want to use this good for other employments than that of a medium of exchange" (HA, 409).

Mises had thus succeeded in using the Austrian School's marginal utility theory of value to explain the determination of the value of money. And it is here that Mises found a place for what he considered the kernel of truth in the Quantity Theory of the value of money. "[T]he idea that a connexion exists between the variations in the value of money on the one hand and variations in the relations between the demand for money and the supply of it on the other hand, . . . constitutes the core of truth in the [Quantity] theory . . ." (TMC, 130). His main objections to the more mechanical versions of the Quantity Theory were closely related to his objections to widespread views concerning the desirability and possibility of "neutral" money.

THE CONCEPT OF NEUTRAL MONEY

The term "neutral money" was not in general professional use when Mises wrote his 1912 book, and he did not couch his criticisms of the Quantity Theory explicitly in terms of this idea. (Hayek attributes the term itself to Wicksell, who used it "more or less incidentally, and without the intention to introduce it as a technical term.")[7] Friedrich Lutz credits Hayek's writings of the early thirties as being "largely responsible for its adoption . . . as a technical term by economists in the English-speaking world."[8] There is no doubt, however, that Mises's criticisms in 1912 (which are fundamentally identical with those with which, in his 1949 *Human Action,* he *did* explicitly attack the neutral money idea) were directed at the *idea,* if not the term, of neutral money. The idea of neutral money was closely bound up with the view of the theory of money as conceivable separately from the theory of the market economy in general.[9] It was the idea that, in a general equilibrium system, exchange can be conceived of as occurring through the medium of a *numeraire,* a system in which there are no cash holdings. The "'money' of this system is not a medium of exchange; it is not money at all; it is merely a *numeraire,* an

7. Friedrich A. Hayek, *Prices and Production,* 2nd edition (London: Routledge, 1935), 129.

8. F. A. Lutz, "On Neutral Money," in *Roads To Freedom: Essays in Honor of Friedrich A. von Hayek,* E. Streissler, G. Haberler, F. A. Lutz, and F. Machlup (London: Routledge and Kegan Paul, 1969), 105.

9. See Lutz, for the ambiguities surrounding the precise definition of the term.

ethereal and undetermined unit of accounting of that vague and indefinable character which the fancy of some economists . . . have attributed to money" (HA, 249). This view of money's neutrality held that the theory of exchange "can be elaborated under the assumption that there is direct exchange [i.e., barter] only. . . . It was not believed that [the introduction of money into the theory] could alter anything essential in the structure of economic teachings. The main task of economics was conceived as the study of direct exchange" (HA, 202).

We have already noted Mises's criticism of Fisher (and Brown) for believing that "variations in the ratio between the quantity of money and the demand for it lead to proportionate variations in the objective exchange-value of money." Mises's objections rested on his insight that money, like all economic goods in the real world, enters into the realm of market exchange as a *dynamic factor*. As early as 1912 he wrote: "All those who ascribe to variations in the quantity of money an inverse proportionate effect on the value of the monetary unit are applying to dynamic conditions a method of analysis that is only suitable for static condition" (TMC, 145). Three and a half decades later he expressed his critique of the idea of neutral money in similar terms: "Money is necessarily a 'dynamic factor'; there is no room left for money in a 'static' system" (HA, 249). It is the "spurious idea of the supposed neutrality of money" that is responsible for the "notion of the 'level' of prices that rises or falls proportionately with the increase or decrease in the quantity of money in circulation. It was not realized that changes in the quantity of money can never affect the prices of all goods and services at the same time and to the same extent" (HA, 398f).

Not only did Mises criticize the idea of any money in fact being neutral. He also attacked the idea that there is something desirable in the supposed neutrality of money. The idea of neutral money (changes in the quantity of which can be supposed not to affect the structure of prices and quantities in the "real" sector) is a chimera. "Money, without a driving force of its own would not, as people assume, be a perfect money; it would not be money at all" (HA, 418). There is nothing perfect about a supposedly neutral money. In a world of action and change, neutrality is simply impossible. "It is therefore neither strange nor vicious that in a frame of . . . a changing world money is neither neutral nor stable in purchasing power. . . . Money is an element of action and consequently of change" (HA, 419). In this critique of the neutral money idea, Mises

is consistently applying the dynamic-theoretic perspective for the understanding of market processes, which we outlined in chapter 4, to the
monetary aspects of those processes. His monetary theory categorically
refuses to recognize any gulf separating the theory of money from the
economic theory of markets in general. The circumstance that the market process consists of series of exchanges, virtually all of which involve
a commonly used medium of exchange, makes it crucially important to
recognize how its use vitally and actively affects the pattern and structure
of production and exchange decisions made. The integration of monetary
theory into general economic theory grows out of our understanding that
the idea of neutral money is empirically irrelevant and analytically obfuscating. All this is closely related to Mises's rejection of one of the most
popular elements in the monetary theory of his time, the so-called State
Theory of Money.

THE STATE THEORY OF MONEY

One of the most influential books on money during the years when
Mises was writing his own *Theorie des Geldes und der Umlaufsmittel* was a
work by an eminent German economist of the Historical School, Georg
Friedrich Knapp. *Die Staatliche Theorie des Geldes* appeared in 1905 and
enjoyed remarkable success.[10] Although certainly not the first to advance
such a theory, "Knapp's exposition was extremely effective. His forceful
dogmatism and his original conceptualization of his theory impressed
laymen and those economists who were laymen in economic theory."[11]
His thesis was a simple one: "Money is the Creature of Law."[12] The institution of money was essentially an invention of the state; and it is the
state which determines which commodity is to serve as money. Now
Menger had already, in effect, rejected Knapp's theory. Both in his 1871
Grundsätze and in an 1892 encyclopedia article titled "Geld"[13] (and also
elsewhere), Menger had developed the theme that money "is one of the
spontaneous, unconscious, unplanned social discoveries, which are not

---

10. On the success of this work, see Mises, TMC, 465; J. A. Schumpeter, *History of
Economic Analysis,* 1091.

11. Schumpeter, *History of Economic Analysis,* 1091. For an admiring characteriza-
tion of Knapp as an economic historian, see ibid., 811n.

12. Ibid., 1091.

13. In the *Handwörterbuch der Staatswissenschaften.*

inventions of the State or products of a legislative act, as Knapp was to emphasize."[14] (In fact Mises reports that, when he used to raise Knapp's work in conversation with Menger, the latter used to refer to it in most contemptuous terms, and to express derisive dismay at its popularity in Germany [NR, 35].)[15] One implication of Knapp's theory had rather obvious political resonance. As Schumpeter put it: "[M]any people and especially politicians at that time welcomed a theory that seemed to offer a basis for the growing popularity of state-managed money." Moreover, as Schumpeter noted, "during the First World War [Knapp's theory] was in fact widely used to 'prove' that the inflation of the currency had nothing to do with soaring prices."[16] In Mises's terminology, Knapp's theory of money was an "acatallactic" theory, one that "cannot be built into any system that deals realistically with the processes of economic activity." It is, Mises asserted, "utterly impossible to employ [acatallactic theories] as foundations for a theory of exchange" (TMC, 461).[17]

In refuting Knapp's theory, therefore, Mises was not merely reaffirming Menger's rejection of this *genre* of monetary theories, he was rejecting the idea that monetary phenomena can be separated analytically from the general phenomena of market exchanges. We have seen in chapter 3 that Mises emphasized the insight, provided by the development of a science of economics, that there are regularities ("laws") in economic phenomena to which governments must pay heed, and to which they must adjust their policies. The rejection of economics by politicians and others seeking to declare the absolute power of the government in achieving its economic objectives for society, we saw, had much to do with the realization that economics teaches the inevitable limits to such power. Mises's rejection of the State Theory of Money was a consistent extension of this Misesian perspective on the tension between economic science and absolute political power. The dichotomy (conceded, in effect, even by

---

14. T. W. Hutchison, *A Review of Economic Doctrines, 1870–1929* (Oxford: Clarendon Press, 1953), 143.

15. For similar later assessments of Knapp's theory, see Schumpeter, 1090, and M. L. Burstein, *Modern Monetary Theory* (New York: St. Martin's Press, 1986), 3 (where Knapp is described as having "exercised great, mostly pernicious, influence").

16. Schumpeter, ibid.

17. This is part of an appendix added to the 1924, 2nd edition, of the book.

economists of the Austrian School up to that time) between the monetary sector (and monetary theory) and the real exchange economy (and general economic theory)—a dichotomy against which Mises was battling in his 1912 work—was virtually an acknowledgment of the absolute power of the state in the monetary area. Mises was explicit in refusing to recognize this or any other such exception.

"The position of the State in the market," he wrote, "differs in no way from that of any other parties to commercial transactions. . . . If it wishes to alter any of the exchange-ratios established in the market, it can only do this through the market's own mechanism. . . . [It] cannot set aside the laws of the pricing process" (TMC, 68). Mises cited famous examples of the inevitable "failure of authoritative interference with the market" (TMC, 68). He proceeded immediately to the consistent conclusion: "The concept of money as a creature of Law and the State is clearly untenable. . . . To ascribe to the State the power of dictating the laws of exchange, is to ignore the fundamental principle of money-using society" (TMC, 69). In other words, just as governments must adjust to the laws of the market (so that they must be aware that attempts to fix prices will have inevitable—and unwelcome—consequences), so too must governments be aware that the laws of the market apply to monetary phenomena as well (so that, for example, they realize that attempts to achieve their own economic objectives for society by printing more money will have inevitable, market-generated consequences that, indeed, can be disastrously unwelcome).

B. *Trade Cycle Theory*

We have noted Mises's decisive rejection of the notion of "neutral money." One direct manifestation of this rejection was Mises's pioneering work in what came to be known as the Austrian (or, sometimes, the Mises-Hayek) Theory of the Trade Cycle. Mises's contribution was first advanced, in no more than several pages, in the closing chapters of his 1912 work on monetary theory. Consistent development of his foundational ideas on money as an integral element in the exchange economy led Mises to offer an outline of the way in which changes in the supply of money can lead (in fact, in Mises's view, must *inevitably* lead) to structural aberrations in the pattern of production and exchanges, the inevitable corrections to which by the market must express themselves as what we know as the crisis and depression phases of the trade cycle.

Mises developed these ideas further in his 1928 monograph (translated under the title *Monetary Stabilization and Cyclical Policy*) and in his later treatises (*Nationalökonomie*, 1940, and *Human Action*, 1949).

It must be acknowledged that certain ambiguities surround the relation between Mises's contribution to the theory of the trade cycle, and antecedent ideas which Mises cited from both the British Currency School, developed before the middle of the nineteenth century, and the great Swedish economist Knut Wicksell around the turn of the century. Ambiguities also surround the relation between Mises's contribution to the more fully articulated (and much better known) theory of Hayek which the latter developed in the early 1930s. Sometimes Mises himself seemed to downplay his own role in the "Austrian" theory,[18] even questioning the appropriateness of the "Austrian" label in the light of the antecedent British and Swedish ideas. But, in his 1940 memoirs, in referring to the theory of business cycle phenomena, he wrote: "I am honored that it was named the Austrian Trade Cycle Theory" (NR, 61).

Hayek's first (1925) published reference to the "Austrian" theory of the cycle cites only one source, Mises's 1924 edition of his 1912 book. (In his 1984 introduction to the publication of English translations of a number of his papers of the 1920s, Hayek singles out that first published reference of his and refers to "what I thought was a theory of Ludwig von Mises that was familiar to us in the Vienna circle.")[19] In his *Monetary Theory and the Trade Cycle* (1933; a translation and revision of the German *Geldtheorie und Konjunkturtheorie* published in 1929), Hayek cites

---

18. See Mises, *Money, Method and the Market Process*, 77, 86; Mises, preface to "Monetary Stabilization and Cyclical Policy [1929]" in *On the Manipulation of Money and Credit*, 59, 115. See especially also the following statement in Ludwig von Mises, *The Historical Setting of the Austrian School of Economics* (New Rochelle, N.Y.: Arlington House, 1969), 41: "The interpretation of the causes . . . of the trade cycle which the present writer provided, first in his *Theory of Money and Credit* . . . was called by some authors the Austrian Theory of the Trade Cycle. Like all such national labels, this too is objectionable. The Circulation Credit Theory is a continuation, enlargement, and generalization of ideas first developed by the British Currency School and of some additions to them by later economists, among them also the Swede, Knut Wicksell."

19. F. A. Hayek, *Money, Capital, and Fluctuations; Early Essays*, ed. Roy McCloughry (Chicago: University of Chicago Press, 1984), 2.

Mises extensively. Yet the preface to the first edition (1931) of his *Prices and Production* did not, surprisingly, mention Mises among his acknowledgments to intellectual predecessors. Hayek seemed, in his preface to the second (1934) edition of the same work, to go out of his way to add Mises to his list of intellectual predecessors. Apparently, Hayek (at least in the first edition), while certainly recognizing Mises's role in suggesting the *monetary* aspect of the Austrian Cycle Theory, saw his own work on the "real" aspects of the cycle as stemming more generally from Austrian capital theory.[20]

There seems little doubt, however, that the core of the "Austrian" (or even the "Hayekian") Theory of the Trade Cycle ultimately derives, virtually entirely, from the pioneering work contained in those few pages in Mises's 1912 treatise on monetary theory. Certainly, the theory outlined in those pages owed much to the earlier ideas acknowledged by Mises; and it is unquestionably the case that it was Hayek's careful and original elaboration in the 1930s of the Misesian outline which became best known to the economics profession. Despite all this, however, no account of Mises's contributions can fail to recognize the pivotal role played by Mises's own theory of the trade cycle. Writing in 1951, Ludwig Lachmann put it this way: "Almost forty years ago Professor Mises, through a brilliant interpretation of an idea of Wicksell, became the first exponent of what has come to be known as 'The Austrian Theory of the Trade Cycle.'"[21]

THE MISESIAN THEORY OF THE TRADE CYCLE

Mises apparently did not, in 1912, *set out* to provide a theory of the trade cycle. His theory emerged as an almost incidental by-product of his exploration of the theory of banking (especially the influence of the banking system which results from its ability to issue "fiduciary media"). The term "fiduciary media" was apparently introduced by H. E. Batson, the 1934 translator of the second edition of Mises's book into English (TMC, appendix B, 482), but Mises himself adopted this term for his own use

---

20. See Hayek's preface to the 2nd edition of *Prices and Production*, xiii.

21. Ludwig M. Lachmann, "The Science of Human Action," *Economica* 18 (November 1951); 412–27; reprinted in Ludwig M. Lachmann, *Capital, Expectations, and the Market Process*, ed. W. E. Grinder (Kansas City: Sheed, Andrews and McMeel, 1977), 105.

in his later work. Mises defined "fiduciary media" as that amount of "money-substitutes"[22] against which the debtors do *not* in fact keep a 100 percent reserve of "money proper" (HA, 433).

In the course of this exploration, Mises examined the influence on the rate of interest exercised by an expansion in the issue of fiduciary media. Following Wicksell, Mises concluded that such expansion would reduce the "money rate of interest" ("the rate of interest that is demanded and paid for loans in money or money-substitutes") below the "natural rate of interest" (the rate "that would be determined by supply and demand if actual capital goods were lent without the mediation of money") (TMC, 355). He then examined the consequences of the resulting "Wicksellian" divergence of the money rate of interest below the natural rate. Using Böhm-Bawerkian capital-and-interest theory (TMC, 339n), he demonstrated that the consequence would be a tendency for producers to enter into more "roundabout" processes of production than are in fact warranted by the true availability of consumer goods that will be needed "to support the labourers and entrepreneurs during the longer period" (TMC, 361). Mises then traced the series of market reactions through which the "equilibrium of the loan market is reestablished after it has been disturbed by the intervention of the banks" (TMC, 362). Because the "period of production" has been lengthened more than is consistent with the underlying facts, an inevitable consequence must be the "reduction of the quantity of goods available for consumption. The market prices of consumption goods rise and those of production goods fall. . . . That is, the rate of interest on loans rises again, it again approaches the natural rate" (TMC, 362–63). (Mises is *extremely* brief in this last statement. He relies on the reader's understanding of the Böhm-Bawerkian insight that the money rate of interest simply corresponds, in a smoothly running economy at a given level of production, to the excess value of consumer goods at a given date, over the value—the spot prices—of the inputs invested at an earlier date in their production.)

This understanding of how the money rate of interest, initially depressed by bank fiduciary media expansion, is forced back up by reasser-

22. "Money-substitutes" are "[c]laims to a definite amount of money, payable and redeemable on demand, against a debtor about whose solvency and willingness to pay there does not prevail the slightest doubt." (Mises, HA, 432.)

tion in the market of the underlying realities (i.e., the refusal by consumers to postpone their demand for immediate consumption goods), leads directly to a theory of crises. Mises sees the economic crisis as expressing "the loss of some of the capital invested in the excessively lengthened roundabout processes of production. It is not practicable to transfer all of the production goods from those uses that have proved unprofitable [because the market has pushed interest rates higher than the levels that had previously made those longer processes appear to be profitable] into other avenues of employment . . . there is a loss of value. . . . Economic goods which could have satisfied more important wants have been employed for the satisfaction of less important" (TMC, 364). Insofar as many of these capital inputs are specific and not easily transferable, entrepreneurs suffer losses, and are forced to cancel projects. As Mises asserts: "Our theory of banking . . . leads ultimately to a theory of business cycles" (TMC, 365).

Mises maintained this theory of the business cycle, apart from minor revisions, both in his 1928 monograph and in his 1949 treatise. And although Hayek developed the "real" elements of the business cycle theory far more carefully and extensively in his 1931 *Prices and Production,* it does seem fair to bracket Mises and Hayek as having adhered basically to the same, shared, theory.[23] In his classic League of Nations volume surveying and classifying theories of the business cycle, Gottfried Haberler lists, in alphabetical order, Hayek, Machlup, Mises, Robbins, Röpke, and Strigl as exponents of what he called the neo-Wicksellian version of the "monetary over-investment theory" of the business cycle.[24] Clearly, Mises was the source for almost of all these writers, most of whom—as well as Haberler himself—were Mises's disciples in one sense or another. Haberler recognizes that while Wicksell "has provided the theoretical basis for this theory," Wicksell himself followed a different theory of the business cycle.

23. For a recent discussion of differences between the Misesian and the Hayekian versions of the theory see Jean-Gabriel Bliek, "Hayek's Anti-Cycle Theory as the Rule of Necessity," in *Journal des Economistes et des Etudes Humaines,* 9, no. 4 (December 1999): 589–607.

24. Gottfried Haberler, *Prosperity and Depression: A Theoretical Analysis of Cyclical Movements,* 3rd edition (Lake Success, N.Y.: United Nations, 1946), 32f.

Certain characteristic features of the Misesian theory should be emphasized:

(a) The theory finds the source of the cycle problem to lie in the expansion of the money supply. (Mises's theory of banking demonstrates the ability of the banking system to achieve such expansion.) In this, Mises saw himself as a follower of those British economists of the mid-nineteenth century who offered the Currency School's explanation, in terms of monetary expansion, for the crises of its time.

(b) Mises's theory then follows Wicksell in focusing attention upon the way in which such monetary expansion generates a money rate of interest that is systematically (and misleadingly) below that natural rate of interest which expresses the true willingness of market participants to postpone immediate consumption enjoyments for the sake of greater future gains.

(c) The theory then traces the consequences of this aberration for the production plans undertaken by entrepreneurs. They are led to make irreversible, but "erroneous," plans based on the *apparent* profitability of such plans (as reflecting the falsely low rates of money interest). These errors will inevitably be revealed; their revelation manifests itself in the form of abandoned projects and sudden drastic reductions in the market values of those projects.

(d) The erroneous quality of these production plans consists in their requiring consumers (because of the longer "waiting period" entailed by greater "roundaboutness") to be denied a greater volume of immediate consumer goods than these consumers are in fact prepared to agree to. It is here that the Austrian focus on the time-dimension of production finds its expression. It is the rate of interest which has the function of balancing the desire of consumers for consumption goods *now* with their desire for a compensatingly larger volume of such consumption goods *later*. The misleadingly low money rate of interest encourages producers to ignore the true needs of consumers for immediate consumer satisfactions. But these ignored underlying truths will inevitably emerge—in the form of shortages of consumer goods which push up their prices to the point where the rate of interest has been forced by the market toward its "true," natural level. This latter correction, revealing the errors of production processes begun under false assumptions, takes the form, as we have seen, of the crisis phase of the business cycle. In *Human Action,* Mises put it this way: "The whole entrepreneurial class is, as it were [during the boom phase of the cycle], in the position of a master-builder whose task it is to erect a building out of a limited supply of building materials. If this man overestimates the quantity of the available supply, he drafts a plan for the execution of which the means at his disposal are not sufficient. He oversizes the groundwork and the foundations and only discovers later in the progress of the construction that he lacks the material needed for the completion of the structure" (TMC, 560). The loss of value, the abandonment of projects in midstream, which occur during the crisis and downturn phases of the cycle, are clearly analogous to the unfinished, abandoned buildings.

(e) The entire thrust of the theory is that it serves as a textbook example of the *non*-neutrality of money. Monetary expansion certainly has affected—in disastrous fashion—the structure of the real production economy.

In his 1912 outline of the theory, Mises does not appear to have explicitly attributed to the government any crucial role in the monetary expansion responsible for the boom phase of the cycle (and thus, in Mises's theory, for the eventual crisis phase and subsequent depression). But in his 1928 and 1949 treatments, Mises is most emphatic in laying at the door of governmentally installed central banks the ultimate responsibility for the distortions (and eventually the depressions) which arise out of the expansion of fiduciary media. He refers, in particular, to the practice of considering it the duty of central banks of issue "to shield the banks which expanded circulation credit from the consequences of their conduct," in order to soften the economic hardships experienced during the crisis.[25] Mises was caustic in his condemnation of such public policy attitudes. The "practice of intervening for the benefit of banks, rendered insolvent by the crisis, and of the customers of these banks, has resulted in suspending the market forces which could serve to prevent a return of the expansion. If the banks emerge from the crisis unscathed . . . what remains to restrain them from embarking once more on an attempt to reduce artificially the interest rate on loans and expand circulation credit. . . ?"[26]

25. Mises, "Monetary Stabilization and Cyclical Policy" (1928), in *On the Manipulation of Money and Credit*, 141.

26. Ibid., 142.

In *Human Action*, Mises developed the thesis that, in the absence of central bank control over the banking system, competition between private banks in the market would tend to limit credit expansion (and thus remove the source of the business cycle aberrations). "Government interference" in the banking sector is therefore held ultimately responsible for credit expansion. This policy of encouraging credit expansion has its source in "the erroneous assumption that credit expansion is a proper means of lowering the rate of interest permanently and without harm to anybody but the callous capitalists" (HA, 443f). Quoting from Mises's 1928 discussion, Haberler cites Mises as maintaining that the root cause of the cyclical character (of the boom and its aftermath) is the ideology which considers the reduction of the rate of interest to be desirable and the "inflationary expansion of credit to be the best way of achieving that objective."[27]

But this ideology in favor of lower interest rates is based, Mises believed, in economic ignorance. Market-generated rates of interest have an important economic function to perform and arise out of an essential aspect of human nature. And it is Mises's radically "Austrian" theory of capital and interest to which we now turn.[28]

c. *The Theory of Capital and Interest*

As we have seen, the "Austrian" Theory of the Trade Cycle combined a key Wicksellian insight (on the divergence between the "money" rate of interest and the "natural" rate of interest) with ideas concerning the time-dimension of production, which had their source in Böhm-Bawerk's famous theories concerning capital and interest. Mises accepted key elements from Böhm-Bawerk's theories; but he also gradually grew dissatisfied with other elements in those theories. The first edition of his 1912 *Theorie des Geldes und der Umlaufsmittel* used Böhm-Bawerk's approach to the theory of capital-using production and interest without reservations. His 1924 second edition of that work, however, contained a rather lengthy

27. Haberler, *Prosperity and Depression*, 65.

28. For a somewhat more detailed account of Mises's views on these topics, see Israel M. Kirzner, *Essays on Capital and Interest: An Austrian Perspective* (Cheltenham, UK and Brookfield: Elgar, 1996), essay 3.

footnote both praising Böhm-Bawerk for a "great achievement" and indicating some serious disagreement with his approach (TMC, 339n). Mises also used that footnote to refer to an anticipated "special study" of his own on the problem of interest, which he hoped would "appear in the not-too-distant future." That special study never did appear, and apart from a number of brief observations on the area of capital and interest which appeared in various writings of Mises over the years, it was not until his 1940 treatise, *Nationalökonomie,* that Mises presented his complete theory of interest (along with a series of carefully formulated statements concerning the use of the term "capital" in theoretical discussion, with special critical emphasis upon its use in discussions of interest theory). This theory of interest he developed was so radical and so striking that when Frank Knight wrote his 1941 review article, he chose to concentrate virtually his entire discussion—in an article highly critical of Mises—on that topic, entitling it "Professor Mises and the Theory of Capital."[29]

There are certain fascinating highlights in the history of theories of capital and interest that are reflected in Knight's trenchant article. Knight was himself, it should be noted, the author of an approach to capital and interest theory which was advanced as a vigorously argued alternative to the Böhm-Bawerkian (i.e., the "Austrian") theory. (In fact Knight was endorsing and expanding on positions taken much earlier by the U.S. economist John Bates Clark, who had engaged in a celebrated controversy with Böhm-Bawerk around the turn of the century.) Knight had objected to key "Austrian" features of Böhm-Bawerk's theories; his criticisms of Mises's 1940 treatment of these issues arose out of the circumstance that Mises was even more "Austrian" than his mentor (Böhm-Bawerk) had been. What aroused Knight's analytical ire in Mises was, in particular, those areas in which Mises believed that his mentor had not proceeded consistently enough, or far enough, in the strictly "Austrian" (i.e., subjective) direction.

This is not the place for a detailed account of the agreements and disagreements between Böhm-Bawerk, Mises, and Knight.[30] But it is important to indicate some of the doctrinal background against which we must try to understand Mises's own positions on, and his contributions to, the

---

29. *Economica* 8 (November 1941).
30. On this see the present writer's essay cited above, n. 28.

theory of capital and interest. These positions reflect profound philo-sophical insights that Mises translated into the logic of their economic implications. Yet much in Mises's position has left many of his readers—even those not nearly as critical of Mises as Knight was—puzzled. In the following we attempt to outline Mises's position as clearly as possible, while recognizing some of the difficulties that many of his readers have encountered.

CAPITAL, INTEREST, AND TIME

Mises built solidly on the Böhm-Bawerkian insights concerning time; where he differed with Böhm-Bawerk was in his insistence on a more radically subjective perspective on the role of time than he found in his mentor's work. Mises emphasized his debt to "the imperishable merits of Böhm-Bawerk's contributions," in regard to the role of time (HA, 489); but he was not satisfied with his teacher's treatment. Böhm-Bawerk had emphasized the fact that production is a time-consuming ("roundabout") process; he had used this time-dimension of production as the source of explanation for the phenomenon of interest in a producing economy. For Böhm-Bawerk, interest emerged because entrepreneur-producers must, in order to engage today in time-consuming processes of production, persuade owners of resources to advance the services of their resources in processes, the fruits of which can be expected only at a later date. Resource owners will not, Böhm-Bawerk believed, be prepared to do so (i.e., to forgo more immediate extraction of consumer satisfaction from these owned resources) unless the fruits of these time-consuming pro-duction processes exceed in value alternative rewards available to these resource owners through immediate exchanges in today's spot markets. They will not be prepared to do so because of what came to be called "positive time preference"—a term loosely referring to preference for immediate, rather than postponed, reward. Mises took issue with the reli-ance which Böhm-Bawerk placed on the *psychological* basis for positive time preference (we shall refer briefly to this issue later on). In addition, he believed that Böhm-Bawerk had, surprisingly, become a victim of a fallacy which Böhm-Bawerk had himself prominently refuted: the belief that interest emerges as a result of the productivity of capital.

Earlier theorists had believed that since time-consuming processes of production require capital, it is the *productivity* of capital, manifested in the enhanced value of the fruits of time-consuming production processes, which is the source of interest. Interest was seen as the fruit of a tree called "capital." Mises read Böhm-Bawerk's theory of interest as somehow still recognizing a role, in the generation of interest, played by the higher productivity of longer, more "roundabout" processes. Mises (following, in this regard, earlier work of the U.S. economist F. A. Fetter) found this to be inexplicable. Böhm-Bawerk had himself demonstrated the fallacy of the productivity theory of interest. If a tree is expected today to produce a steady annual stream of fruit in future years, this productivity will be entirely reflected in the tree's current market value. If a capital good can, through its investment today in a time-consuming process of production, generate a high-valued stream of output in the future, the value of that output will tend to be fully anticipated in today's market value of that capital good. This value will, in the absence of other causes for an interest phenomenon, rise to the point where the *physical* productivity of the capital good will be utterly unable to provide any flow of *value* return like the kind that we find in the real-world phenomenon of interest. Mises found it simply unintelligible that Böhm-Bawerk, who had so thoroughly and trenchantly deployed this kind of reasoning to refute the earlier productivity theorists, should have himself reverted to a theory which included productivity elements.

Mises found Böhm-Bawerk's treatment to be also faulty in the latter's discussions of time as if it somehow comes to be "congealed" in the durable things produced during time-consuming production processes. For Mises, time enters our understanding of the phenomena of interest strictly in its ex ante sense. In making decisions in a multi-period world, producers, consumers, and resource owners treat time in a *forward-looking* manner. An economics that focuses analytically (as Austrian economics does) upon *decisions* rather than upon *things,* cannot, therefore, treat time in its elapsed sense. It is this fact which led Mises to reject an important element in the Böhm-Bawerkian system: the elapsed, "average period of production." For Mises, the role that time "plays in action consists entirely in the *choices* acting man makes between periods of production of different length. The length of time expended in the past for the production of capital goods available today does not count at all. . . . The 'average period of production' is an empty concept" (HA, 488–89; emphasis supplied). Mises had apparently carefully studied the ideas of philosophers regarding the nature of time, drawing particularly on Henri

Bergson. Mises identified the idea of time as "a praxeological category." "Action is always directed toward the future." "The present offers to acting opportunities and tasks for which it was hitherto too early, and for which it will be hereafter too late" (HA, 100–101). From this perspective, it is clear that Mises could not endorse the Böhm-Bawerk-Hayek notion that the capital stock of a society, at a given point in time, possesses a "time-structure." (Hayek's use of this concept constitutes one significant difference between his own elaboration of the Austrian Theory of the Trade Cycle and that of Mises.)

Indeed, Mises objected altogether to the use of the term "capital" to refer to the "totality of the produced factors of production." Such a totality is "a description of a part of the universe" that is "of no use in acting." Moreover, the use of a notion like aggregate "real capital" had been responsible for the "blunder" of explaining interest "as an income derived from the productivity of capital" (HA, 263). Instead, Mises endorsed Menger's use of the term "capital" as an accounting concept. "Capital is the sum of the money equivalent of all assets minus the sum of the money equivalent of all liabilities as dedicated at a definite date to the conduct of the operations of a definite business unit" (HA, 262). Capital is a correlate of the accounting notion of income. "The calculating mind of the actor draws a boundary line between the consumer's goods which he plans to employ for the immediate satisfaction of his wants and goods of all orders . . . which he plans to employ for providing by further acting, for the satisfaction of future wants. . . . That amount which can be consumed within a definite period without lowering the capital is called income." This use of the term "capital" is sharply distinguished, in Mises's terminology, from the term "capital goods." The presence of capital goods (produced factors of production) attests to the adoption by producers of time-consuming production processes. But there is no need whatsoever to refer to the totality of such capital goods. And "[t]here is no question of an alleged productivity of capital goods" (HA, 493); if it is profitable to engage in a time-consuming process of production this is attributable entirely to the selection by the producer of the appropriate time-profile for the production process.

For Mises, then, the phenomenon of interest is in no sense a correlate of anything that might be called capital or capital goods. Although interest typically emerges in a world that uses capital goods, and in which capital accounting plays a crucially important role, interest is not the productivity return on any abstract totality that might be called "capital," nor is it the expression of the "productivity" of capital goods.

Instead, interest represents the economic manifestation of what Mises believed to be a universal (a "categorial") element in human action, the element of positive time preference. This element generates a characteristic pattern in the structure of inter-period prices, which expresses itself, in the loan market, as what we know as the phenomenon of interest. The element of time preference and the existence of the phenomenon of interest do not in any way *depend* on the role of production in economic life. "Productivity" is *not* the source of interest. Interest would occur even in a world in which no production takes place. But in our world, in which production *does* take place, the phenomenon of interest generates profoundly important implications. Because production takes time, the market decisions of producers, resource owners, and consumers, must very definitely take account of the interest phenomenon. The choice by producers of a process of production must pay careful attention to the length of time involved, for the duration of which interest will have to be paid. The choices made will of course determine (and be expressed in) the kind and durability of the tools (the "capital goods") that will be developed and deployed, the technology that will be utilized, and the kind and durability of the produced consumer goods. The inter-temporal market, the market in which producing entrepreneurs necessarily function, tends to ensure that prices (including the rates of interest) guide decision makers to take appropriate account of both the time preferences of market participants (resource owners and consumers) and the production possibilities associated with alternative production processes (involving different technologies and different time profiles).

It is this perspective upon the nature and market function of interest which undergirded Mises's lifelong concern with the dangers represented by ideologies and political programs that considered it possible and desirable to eliminate interest, or at least to engineer reduction in its rate. As we have seen in this chapter, it was this kind of ideological misunderstanding concerning interest that Mises blamed for the pain and suffering implicit in the trade cycle. Artificially low interest rates resulting from the expansion of the money supply (through "fiduciary media" creation) tends to distort production decisions, misleading producers to undertake processes of production unwarranted (in the length of their time profiles) by the inter-period structure of consumer preferences. As we saw earlier, a portion of the stock of capital goods assembled by producers will sooner or later suffer a severe loss of market value, as projects come necessarily to be abandoned as the true time preferences of market participants reassert themselves.

THE NATURE AND THE SOURCE OF POSITIVE TIME PREFERENCES

Virtually everything presented in the preceding section as Mises's views (on interest and capital-using production) could rest on an understanding of positive time preference as a widely observed empirical phenomenon rooted in commonly encountered psychological regularities. But Mises was emphatic in insisting on the "categorial" character of the time preference phenomenon. One of the sources of Mises's dissatisfaction with Böhm-Bawerk's views on interest arises precisely out of this position. Böhm-Bawerk's "demonstration of the universal validity of time preference is inadequate," Mises maintained, "because it is based on psychological considerations" (HA, 488). For Mises, on the other hand, time preference emerges as a "praxeological theorem," flowing out of the essential quality of human action. "Time preference is a categorial requisite of human action. No mode of action can be thought of in which satisfaction within a nearer period of the future is not—other things being equal—preferred to that of a later period. The very act of gratifying a desire implies that gratification at the present instant is preferred to that at a later instant" (HA, 484).

Readers of Mises have had difficulty in appreciating this characteristic example of Misesian a priorism. Mises himself grappled with a number of the problems found with (and the counter-examples offered against) this view of time preference as embedded categorially in the very notion of action (HA, 489). However, relatively few followers of Mises have found it necessary to accept his views on this matter. It is perhaps worthwhile to point out, nonetheless, that quite apart from the question of whether positive time preference is simply an empirical regularity, or something which emerges inescapably from the very logic of human action, Mises's notion of time preference is not quite the same as that to be found in mainstream neoclassical treatments of interest. These neoclassical treatments follow the path marked out by the prominent early-twentieth-century American economist Irving Fisher (especially in his 1930 *The Theory of Interest*).

Fisher developed a neoclassical theory of interest which, following Böhm-Bawerk's "Austrian" approach to a considerable extent, saw interest as resulting from the interplay between subjective elements (based on time preference, or, in Fisher's terminology, "impatience") and objective elements (the physical productivity of more time-consuming production processes). In Fisher's theory (and in modern more technically sophisticated versions of that theory) time preference expresses itself as a preference between *dates*—receipts available at date t_1 are preferred to receipts available at date t_2 (since t_2 is later than t_1).

Now it seems easy to imagine scenarios in which an individual *might* prefer the receipt of an item at the later (t_2) date rather than at the earlier (t_1) date. Someone in winter might prefer to receive a load of ice in six months' time (during the summer) rather than now. A prospective student might, in the year 2001, prefer to receive the academic calendar for the 2002–2003 academic year a year later (rather than immediately). These possibilities need not worry a neoclassical economist who builds his ideas of positive time preference on observed empirical regularities; these cases will be considered as relatively unusual cases that do not disturb the validity of the general assumption of positive time preference. But for Mises, who argues for the logical *inevitability* of positive time preference, such exceptions have sometimes been thought to pose problems.

However, we should recognize that these kinds of "exceptions" do not qualify as cases of negative time preference *at all*. (This itself has nothing to do with the question of whether or not positive time preference is *logically* entailed by the very concept of human action.) For Mises, wherever the specific *date* (at which an item is to be received) alters its valuation in the eyes of an agent, *regardless of that date's closeness (to the moment at which preferences are registered)*, this means that it is the date itself (rather than its *distance in time* from the moment of evaluation) that is governing the evaluation. For Mises, time preference refers not to dates, but to *future distance* from the moment of evaluation. Of course the date *at* which ice is available, the date *at* which an academic calendar is available, may affect its subjective evaluation. But for Mises, *that* kind of influence upon valuation is not what he understood by the notion of time preference. Time preference, for Mises, refers to the *sense of futurity*. A given receipt anticipated further in the future is valued (now), with positive time preference, at a relatively lower level than that same receipt anticipated sooner in the future. The notion of "a given receipt" may certainly itself be affected by circumstances, such as summer heat, which are associated with *date*. In Mises's terminology, however, time preference is unaffected by such considerations; Misesian time preference is relevant to *futurity*, not to dates. One may not be prepared to follow Mises in seeing the logical inevitability of positive time preference. Nonetheless one should recognize that such "exceptions" as ice-next-summer versus ice-in-today's-winter do not, for Mises, challenge any such claimed inevitability.

MONEY, CYCLES, AND INTEREST: CONCLUDING OBSERVATIONS

Many if not most of the policy debates between economists, and between the exponents of clashing political positions on economic affairs during the twentieth century, have concerned the topics dealt with in this chapter. For the central decades of this century the dominant orthodoxy in the economics profession endorsed, in regard to these debates, the theoretical perspectives and policies associated with the work of John Maynard Keynes.[31] The Keynesian perspective focused attention on the interaction between key *aggregate* economic variables; it generated, in this way, an entirely new branch of economics, macroeconomics. This macroeconomic perspective focused attention, in particular, upon the adequacy of *aggregate demand* to sustain the volume of production needed to maintain "full employment" of resources (and, in particular, of labor). This perspective generated an attitude toward governmental economic policy that emphasized the government's alleged ability to manipulate monetary and fiscal policy variables so as to ensure full employment. Ludwig von Mises adopted a vigorously dissenting stance toward this Keynesian economics. Although he rarely offered frontal rebuttal to Keynesian theory, his contributions to the topics dealt with in this chapter constituted a well-developed (if implicit) basis for his rejection of Keynesianism.[32]

---

31. Keynes's influential work was *The General Theory of Employment, Interest and Money* (London: Macmillan, 1936).

32. See however the two essays (originally published in 1948 and 1950, respectively) republished as chapter 4 ("Stones into Bread: The Keynesian Miracle") and chapter 5 ("Lord Keynes and Say's Law") in Ludwig von Mises, *Planning for Freedom and Other Essays and Addresses,* 2nd edition (South Holland, Ill.: Libertarian Press, 1962).

This basis differed, at least in part, from the neoclassical orthodoxy which preceded Keynes (and which Keynes chose to call "classical"); it also differed from the late-twentieth-century neoclassical approaches that have, to a large extent, replaced the Keynesian orthodoxy of earlier decades.

Although we cannot offer here a nuanced account of the differences between Mises's positions and those of his Keynesian and non-Keynesian fellow economists, a few general remarks on these issues may usefully conclude the present chapter. Certainly, Mises rejected (as other economists in the Austrian tradition have rejected) a "macroeconomic" emphasis upon interacting aggregates. Moreover, given his understanding of the dynamic ("disequilibrium") character of the market process (the entrepreneurially competitive process discussed in chapter 4), Mises was unconcerned with the possibility of a chronic ("equilibrium") inadequacy of aggregate demand that might be responsible for systematic, large-scale unemployment. As noted in this chapter, Mises found the causes of business crises (and thus of the bouts of unemployment which typically accompany them) not in inadequate demand, but in the unsustainable projects initiated during booms as a result of artificially low rates of interest caused by monetary expansion. For Mises, what tends to ensure fullest feasible levels of production (and thus of resource employment) is the dynamism of the entrepreneurial market process. It turns out, then, that the Keynesian and similar programs calling for such policies as budgetary deficits (insofar as these must entail monetary expansion), expanded size of the governmental sector of the economy, and manipulation of prices of all kinds (especially including minimum wage laws and manipulation of the interest rate as a policy tool) were seen by Mises as policies likely to exacerbate, rather than to alleviate, cyclical volatility in capitalist systems.

For the concluding three or four decades of his life, which coincided with the heyday of Keynesian influence, Mises was often considered simply old-fashioned and obstinately orthodox in his resolute resistance to the brave new economic policies advanced in the post–World War II years. In fact he was consistently adhering to a set of theories the subtleties of which were simply not appreciated in the avalanche of the new Keynesian orthodoxy. As we now enter the twenty-first century, we encounter a more sensitive openness in the economics profession to the advantages of entrepreneurial competition within an institutional framework of secure individual rights. It is to be hoped and anticipated that the ideas of Ludwig von Mises on money, cycles, and interest may now evoke fresh consideration, and perhaps fuller and more sympathetic understanding, than they received during his own lifetime—and especially during his declining years.

6. MISES: FREE-MARKET
ECONOMIST OF THE CENTURY

This concluding chapter offers an outline of an aspect of Mises's economics that is, in one sense, the most important aspect of all. Indeed, it is this aspect which probably identifies, for many observers, the position occupied by Mises in twentieth-century economics: for better or for worse, Mises is best known not so much as an outstanding economic theorist, not so much for his central role in the development of twentieth-century Austrian economics, but as the most outspoken, most trenchant, and most passionate defender of free-market capitalism—of laissez-faire— of the twentieth century. This chapter will present certain elements in Mises's economics that have not been covered in any of the preceding chapters. But it will also pull together certain implications of a number of topics that were dealt with in earlier chapters in order to help us understand the basis for the strong positions which Mises took regarding central governmental planning (socialism) and governmental intervention into an otherwise free-market economy.

It is important, for the purposes of this book, to bring these implications together for two distinct reasons. First, in the last analysis, these implications have, more than other aspects of his work, decisively shaped Mises's lifework and its public influence. Second, these implications throw significant light on some otherwise overlooked aspects of the substance of his scientific economics. To best appreciate what we mean in this latter regard, it may be useful to confront directly an apparent puzzle in Mises's strong statements in favor of laissez-faire economic policy.

MISES, *WERTFREIHEIT*, AND THE SCIENTIFIC
CASE FOR THE FREE MARKET

We saw at the end of chapter 3 that Mises was emphatic in endorsing Max Weber's doctrine of *wertfreiheit*. Weber had shown the dangers for social scientists of failing to maintain a careful separation between their objective, impartial statements in their role as scientists, on the one hand, and their personal ("nonscientific") beliefs, values, and preferences, on the other. Mises (unlike a number of economists who were otherwise highly sympathetic to his economics) thoroughly agreed. Economics, he insisted, "is perfectly neutral with regard to all judgments of value. . . ."

Although economics is, he stated, "the foundation of politics and of every kind of political action," it itself is "apolitical" (HA, 884f). Whether one is made happy or unhappy by the conclusions of economics does not affect the validity of these conclusions. And these scientific conclusions should not be presented in a manner that might suggest that they *did* make the economist happy (or otherwise).

Now economists have struggled, at least for a century, to spell out the philosophical guidelines that can enable us to translate strictly positive statements of scientific economics into normative guides for policy makers in a way that can invest such normative advice with the authority of science. Value-free medical science research can lead to sound, life-saving, medical advice. Value-free economic science should be able similarly to generate sound economic policy advice. But the history of economics shows how elusive is the goal of justifying the scientific character of such policy advice.

Out of the attempts to provide such justification has emerged a vast literature dealing with the foundation of what is called *welfare economics*. The classical economists had believed that appropriate economic policy could be identified as that which could increase the "*wealth*" of a nation. When neoclassical economists, toward the close of the nineteenth century, revealed the subtleties and pitfalls which surrounded attempts to pinpoint the meaning of the term, "an increase in the wealth of a nation," they were compelled to seek a substitute criterion. A good deal of neoclassical welfare economics assessed the "goodness" of policy in terms of its ability to increase the "economic *welfare*" of a nation. A dominant strand of twentieth-century welfare economics has believed it possible to judge policy in terms of its impact on the *efficiency* with which a society allocates its scarce resources. But for Austrian economics, none of these attempts can be judged as adequate. The subjectivism of Austrian economics reveals how unsatisfactory it is to work with any notion of aggregate, objective wealth as a policy maximand. (In this, Austrians were thoroughly in tune with their colleagues in other neoclassical schools of economic thought.) Similarly, however, the methodological individualism of Austrian economics renders any notion of aggregate social well-being (of the sort the British neoclassicals—Marshall and Pigou—had developed) to be thoroughly suspect. For similar reasons (as well as for other very important "knowledge" considerations raised by Hayek) Austrians have rejected the idea of social efficiency as a meaningful, relevant yardstick with which to assess the economic goodness of public policy. But all this offers Austrians a most serious challenge. If we lack a scientific standard by which to recognize economic success or economic failure, what *can* we, as scientists rather than political advocates, say about socialism, for example, or about interventionism, without violating the professional standard of *wertfreiheit*, that Mises had so thoroughly accepted as his own? How could Mises, in his role as objective scientist (as distinct from his political position as a classical liberal), denounce governmental price-fixing? How could he denounce central bank inflation of the money supply? How could he denounce government antitrust policy? or protectionism?

MISES, SCIENCE, AND ECONOMIC GOODNESS

Mises never did explore in any detail the difficulties surrounding the translation of positive economic science into policy advice. He appeared to believe that the economic goodness or badness of a policy could, if the relevant economic theory is thoroughly understood, easily be recognized. Several strands of reasoning in this regard seem to have been taken for granted by Mises. Once we understand the existence and operation of economic "law," and the possibly counter-intuitive outcomes explained by such "law," Mises believed, we can immediately recognize that policy makers (who have instituted economic policies *without* understanding such economic "law") are likely unwittingly to set in motion, through their policies, chains of economic causation which generate outcomes entirely different from (even opposite) *those aimed at by the policy makers themselves.* (It was this likelihood, Mises believed, that explains the tendency for politicians to *deny* the teachings of economics. No one welcomes a science which purports to tell one that one is acting foolishly. It is much easier to endorse intellectual efforts to discredit economic science.) At any rate, Mises believed, we have here clear identification of one kind of "bad" economic policy. A policy is "bad" not because it produces results which the *economists,* as citizens, do not like, but because it leads to results at variance with the objectives *aimed at for that policy by the policy makers themselves.*

A second criterion for judging the economic goodness or badness of a policy is the possibility or impossibility of the successful completion of the plans which that policy encourages. As we saw in the preceding chapter, Mises believed that the central bank inflation that feeds the boom phase of the business cycle does so by encouraging producers to undertake projects that it will be impossible to complete (because these projects, based on "falsely" low money rates of interest, call for sacrifices of consumer goods that the public is in fact not prepared to make). The inflationary policy is thus "bad" economic policy because it encourages plans that are doomed to failure. As we shall see, Mises's criticism of the economic performance of a socialist economy involves his demonstration of the *impossibility* of central planning (in a sense that will be made clear below). Socialism is *not* a "good" economic system; it is predicated on the feasibility of an undertaking (central planning) that is in fact impossible to implement. A policy is "bad" not because economists, as citizens, do not like it, but because it generates plans by individual entrepreneur-producers that they will find impossible to complete.

There appears to be yet a third important basis upon which Mises may have implicitly judged the goodness or badness of economic policy. This has to do with the idea of "consumer sovereignty." As we noticed in chapter 4, Mises believed, *as a proposition of positive economics,* that, with certain exceptions, market outcomes are determined by consumer preferences. Decisions by producers and by resource owners are, in a free-market society, motivated by the desire to anticipate the spending decisions of consumers. (To say that free markets are subject to consumer sovereignty is not to say that free markets "maximize social efficiency," or "maximize aggregate social utility." It is merely to say that all changes in production decisions, all changes in the pattern of resource allocation, are changes calculated—by those decision makers with the most to gain by correct decision making—to take account of consumer preferences, as expressed in their spending decisions.) There are grounds for believing that, in his criticism of what he judged to be unsound economic policies, Mises was simply assuming that his readers held consumer sovereignty to be a desirable feature in an economic system. To show that government intervention frustrates consumer sovereignty is thus to convince these readers that such intervention is, in *their* view, to be deplored. An economic policy is "bad," not because economists, in their capacity as citizens, do not like it, but because it tends to encourage decisions by prospective producers which do not pay all possible regard to the changing patterns of consumer preference.

We can now understand how Mises came to believe that economic science leads us ineluctably to the conclusion that a policy favoring unfettered free markets, a policy of laissez-faire, of capitalism without any government intervention, is scientifically demonstrated to be the best policy. A free market works in a systematic way to encourage coordination among the decisions of market participants, with the motivating force being the needs and preferences of consumers. "The coordination of the autonomous actions of all individuals is accomplished by the operation of the market" (HA, 725). A free market will tend to generate decisions that *can* be successfully implemented and which respect and *do* express consumer sovereignty. If policy makers understand the economics of the free market, their pursuit of laissez-faire will produce results consistent with their expectations, results that will represent successfully completed decisions by market participants, and results that will represent the sovereignty of the consumers. On the other hand, Mises was convinced, intervention by the state can only frustrate the achievement of such results. The most extreme form of state intervention is, of course, the form of economic organization called socialism. And, as we saw in earlier chapters, Mises threw down the gauntlet, with regard to the economics of socialism, as early as 1920. Throughout his life Mises was to consider his work in regard to the possibility or impossibility of central economic planning under socialism to be among the most important of his entire career.

THE ECONOMICS OF SOCIALISM

Mises's theoretical challenge to the possibility of central socialist planning was presented (in a social science journal, *Archiv für Sozialwissenschaft und Sozialpolitik*) under the title "Die Wirtschaftsrechnung im Sozialistischen Gemeinwesen" in 1920—a time when socialism was, to put it mildly, being very seriously advocated in post–World War I Austria. The article was included, with some revisions, in his important 1922 book-length study of the economic and sociological aspects of socialism, and was translated into English in 1935, when it was included in a book, edited by Hayek, entitled *Collectivist Economic Planning: Critical Studies of the Possibilities of Socialism*. Mises's article and book initiated a celebrated debate among economists, one that is still continuing, in fact, to this very day. Mises's critique of the possibility of central socialist planning was grounded in his emphasis upon the most fundamental of economic insights, the role of *economic calculation*.

The foundation of economic efficiency, Mises pointed out, is the rational calculation of benefits and costs, the rational weighing of alternatives. Such calculation is straightforward for the simple conditions under which a Robinson Crusoe must operate. But it becomes much more complicated under less simple conditions. To "choose whether we shall use a waterfall to produce electricity or extend coal-mining and better utilize the energy contained in coal, is quite another matter. Here the processes of production are so many and so long, the conditions necessary to the success of the undertaking so multitudinous, that we can never be content with vague ideas. To decide whether an undertaking is sound we must calculate carefully" (s, 114).

Such calculation cannot, of course, be conducted in terms of heterogeneous physical units (of alternative inputs and/or outputs); such calculation must be conducted in terms of common units of *value*. Under market conditions such units of value are furnished by the money prices that prevail. Calculation using such market prices as the basis for comparison is certainly not perfect, Mises recognized; but its imperfections are sufficiently tolerable for entrepreneur-producers under capitalism to engage in calculative, rational decision making. Mises did not, in asserting the possibility of calculative decision making under capitalism, claim that such decision making conduces to a social optimum. He merely pointed out the possibility of rational individual decision making. Capitalism is based on individual plans (and on their market interaction); such plans are constrained, within the limits of market conditions, to be rational. In contrast, Mises argued, the rational basis for central planning under socialism (that central planning which is, under socialism, intended to replace the independent decisions of individual capitalist producers) is simply absent. There are no indicators of value that might serve as the basis for economic calculation by would-be central planners. "The theory of economic calculation," Mises concluded, "shows that in the socialistic community economic calculation would be impossible" (s, 131).

Mises's contention rests on the circumstance that, by definition, *the socialistic community does not include a market for resource services.* Money prices for *consumer goods* might be imagined for the socialist economy. "But since the prices of the various factors of production (including labor) could not be expressed in money, money could play no part in economic calculations" (s, 121). Production decisions can be *calculated* decisions only if the decision makers can assign *values* to units of resources (based on their potential usefulness in alternative available processes of production). But would-be socialist planners have no market-generated money factor prices available to them. Their decision-making must be made, in effect, in physical terms, something utterly inconsistent with rational economic planning with regard to resource allocation.[1] Rational central planning, under socialism, is simply impossible.

It should be emphasized that, in declaring socialist central planning to be an impossibility, Mises was not declaring it impossible for a socialist economy to exist—even for a period of decades. He was not at all disturbed by the circumstance that the Soviet Union's existence was a protracted one. He was merely declaring it impossible for the decisions made in such an economy to be "rational," i.e., to be consistent with the priorities that the planners themselves wish to maintain. A socialist economy can continue to "exist" even when the goods produced are not the ones which the planners prefer (over alternatives that might have been produced). A socialist economy can continue to "exist" even when resources are used in wasteful fashion (i.e., in ways that result in fewer of the desired bundles of consumer goods than might have been achieved by a more rational allocation pattern). But clearly a socialist economy, without the possibility of rational economic calculation, is doomed to inefficiency and thus, at least relatively, to poverty and stunted growth. The poverty in which the masses lived in the Soviet Union was something that Mises's theory explained superbly well. Mises dealt a devastating blow to the illusion that the extraordinary record of economic growth in capitalist economies during the preceding century, the dramatic rises in standards of living in Western market-based societies, could be duplicated without a market for resource services. Mises showed socialism, insofar as it had been proposed as an *economic* system of organization, to be an utter failure.

No account of the remarkable (and quite fierce!) debate among economists that was initiated by Mises's critique can be provided here.[2] I do,

---

1. For the relation between Mises's statement of the problems confronting economic calculation under socialism and Hayek's articulation of this problem in terms of dispersed knowledge (under socialism) of relevant scarcities, see Israel M. Kirzner, *The Driving Force of the Market,* chapter 8. There is no question that in the eyes of the public, Hayek was Mises's most articulate and influential supporter in regard to his critique of the economics of socialism.

2. For an account of the inter-war debate, see T. J. Hoff, *Economic Calculation in the Socialist Society* [translation of the 1938 Norwegian original] (London: William Hodge, 1949). For a superb account bringing the story up to the 1980s, see Don Lavoie, *Rivalry and Central Planning: The Socialist Calculation Debate Reconsidered* (Cambridge: Cambridge University Press, 1985).

however, wish to emphasize that Mises's argument was based solidly on his "Austrian" understanding of the market. This understanding (as we saw in chapter 4) sees the market not as a system somehow yielding instantaneous equilibrium patterns of resource allocation, but as a continuous process in which dynamic price and quality competition between producer-entrepreneurs is (on the basis of the perceived pure profit opportunities inherent at each moment in the continually changing arrays of market prices) continually modifying patterns of resource allocation so as better to anticipate consumer preferences. The resource market prices which are lacking under socialism cannot, in this understanding, be replaced by centrally promulgated (nonmarket) "prices" on the basis of which "calculation" can be conducted. (Misunderstanding on this score was responsible for significant confusion in the debate which followed Mises's 1920 paper.[3] To understand Mises's criticism of the socialist economy one must first understand his appreciation of the dynamic, entrepreneurially competitive character of the market economy.) But Mises's reasoning on behalf of the capitalist market economy was not confined to his powerful critique of its socialist alternative. Mises was convinced that economic prosperity requires not simply a market economy. He believed that prosperity calls for a market economy that is in no way "hampered" by the kinds of government intervention which have in fact characterized Western capitalist countries during the twentieth century.

THE MIXED ECONOMY: THE IMPOSSIBILITY OF A STABLE "THIRD WAY"

Mises was well aware of the political attractiveness of interventionism as economic policy. If socialism was the most serious threat in the immediate post–World War I years, interventionism was the enduring twentieth-century danger for capitalism. Especially after its disastrous experience of the depression during the thirties, public opinion in Western capitalist economies clamored for regulation, controls, and other forms of direct or indirect government intervention in markets—in order, as the public saw it, to protect against the hazards and/or excesses of laissez-faire. Politicians catering to this widespread demand for proactive governmental

3. On this see Don Lavoie, ibid.

economic policy (especially in the years of the so-called Keynesian revolution) offered economic programs seeking to offer the best of both worlds: the advantages of free-market capitalism with the perceived protections of centrally planned fiscal, monetary, and market regulation. Textbooks on economic principles taught millions of students that the mixed economy was the virtually unanimous choice of enlightened modern economists. Mises would have none of this.

Mises believed that the idea of a mixed economy as a viable "third way" was simply a myth. And, he emphasized, he believed this idea to be an entirely dangerous myth. Mises's intellectual onslaught against interventionism goes back at least to the twenties.[4] But it was especially during the last decades of his life that Mises devoted himself to developing his critique of interventionism. Among the targets of Mises's scathing criticism were virtually all the manifestations of the interventionist program: antitrust policy, price controls of all kinds (with perhaps especial emphasis on minimum wage laws and rent controls), inflationary monetary policy, budgetary deficits, farm subsidies, tariff protection, nationalization of foreign-owned companies, income and wealth transfers, and on and on. All the programs that make up what is euphemistically termed the "modern welfare state" came under his withering attack.

All of these interventionist policies, Mises pointed out, are either doomed to failure—because they fly in the face of consumer preferences and will thus fail to achieve their objectives—or will generate unwelcome results not at all intended by the policy makers themselves. Minimum wage legislation (and "pro-union" legislation interfering with the competitive process of the labor market) will yield unemployment (EFI, 29, 67, 71). Legislation aimed at the large size of major business firms (or their high concentration within industries) will raise costs to the consuming public (EFI, 208). Inflationary monetary policy generates slumps (EFI, 107), and hurts the public, particularly the poor, who own savings and other assets (EFI, 34f, 103f, 188ff); eventually such policy can lead to hyperinflation (EFI, 83). Keynesian full employment policy invariably turns out to be inflationary, with all its unfortunate results (EFI, 76–81). U.S. farm policy has led to the farmer's complete loss of economic independence

---

4. In fact he had, already in 1929, published a work with the title *Kritik des Interventionismus* (Jena: Gustav Fischer, 1929).

(EFI, 208f). Inheritance taxes encourage precisely the kind of concentration in business that interventionists profess to oppose (EFI, 210).

But the worst result of interventionist policies is that they lead inevitably to further and further government control of the economy. Interventionism is a slippery slope leading to socialism. Again and again Mises dismissed the idea of a viable, stable economic system that is neither one of socialist planning nor one of capitalist free enterprise. There is, Mises argued, a built-in dynamic in a regime of government intervention that inevitably sets in motion a systematic series of changes leading in the direction of complete socialism.[5] By "government intervention" Mises was referring to "interference with the market" (EP, 40), to governmental activities or decrees which force "the entrepreneurs and capitalists to employ some of the factors of production in a way different from what they would have resorted to if they were only obeying the dictates of the market" (HA, 718). The form of socialism to which the interventionist system is tending is what Mises called the "Hindenburg pattern of socialism" (HA, 723), one in which *nominal* features of a market economy (such as private property ownership, prices, wages, and interest rates) are retained but in which in fact market participants "are bound to obey unconditionally the orders issued by the government's supreme office of production management" (HA, 717).

The reason why this dynamic renders a system of interventionism unstable is that acts of intervention tend to produce results "which—from the point of view of their own advocates and the governments resorting to them—are more unsatisfactory than the previous state of affairs which they were designed to alter" (EFI, 55). A philosophy that sustains interventionism as a way of dealing with apparently undesirable features of the economy will then tend to generate new acts of intervention in order to deal with the unfortunate results of the earlier acts of intervention. Thus, governments who find certain commodity market prices to be "too high," are tempted to impose price ceilings. Such price ceilings, simple economics predicts, tend to produce commodity shortages. To cope with these shortages (and the arbitrariness of resulting patterns of consumption)

---

5. For a full-length study of this kind of dynamic, see Sanford Ikeda, *Dynamics of the Mixed Economy, Toward a Theory of Interventionism* (London and New York: Routledge, 1997).

the government is likely to impose rationing, and/or to extend price controls to the resource markets, etc.[6]

It should be noted that in criticizing the interventionist program (and in declaring illusionary the idea that the interventionist system could be a stable alternative to both socialism and laissez-faire capitalism), Mises emphasized that he did not at all deny the need for, and a proper role for, government. Unlike some of his followers,[7] Mises did not at all question the need for government, and this was with full awareness of all its coercive apparatus "for violent prevention and suppression of antisocial action on the part of refractory individuals and groups of individuals" (HA, 719).[8] Mises was no anarchist; he did not even see the government as a "necessary evil" to be minimized (EFI, 57). He saw government, with its function of protecting private property rights, as an essential prerequisite for the free-market society. Government, he emphasized, is a *beneficial* institution in that it makes possible the cooperative achievements of the market. The political problem presented for all eras, however, is that this valuable institution is vulnerable to the danger of becoming tyrannical and totalitarian. In our time, in addition, such danger has extended to more subtle and more powerful forms, in that it is obscured and disguised by the illusion that interference with the market sovereignty of consumers is somehow in the economic interest of the public. This is the source of the willingness of the public to endorse expansions in the role of government, beyond its valuable and necessary function of ensuring the inviolability of property rights, to outright interference in the way such property rights are deployed in free markets. Such interference, Mises was convinced,

6. Ludwig von Mises, "Middle-of-the-Road Policy Leads to Socialism," in *Planning for Freedom and Other Essays and Addresses*, 22f.

7. The late Murray N. Rothbard was notable as the prominent follower and exponent of Mises who articulated a particularly strong form of unqualified libertarian philosophy. See especially his *For a New Liberty: The Libertarian Manifesto* (revised edition) (New York and London: Collier Macmillan, 1978). It should be noted that Rothbard did not subscribe to Mises's insistence on the need for (and possibility of) a sharp separation between the *wertfrei* propositions of economic science and the value-laden statements of political-philosophical discourse.

8. See also Mises, HA, 149: "The state is essentially an institution for the preservation of peaceful interhuman relations. However, for the preservation of peace it must be prepared to crush the onslaughts of peace-breakers."

necessarily tends to undermine those powerful but sensitive webs of interpersonal cause-and-effect that we call the market process. A policy of interventionism is, in effect, a policy to replace the market by the state.

Mises did not hesitate to express his views on interventionism even where they seemed to put him at odds with his most admired and influential intellectual allies. Friedrich Hayek, whom we saw to be one of Mises's strongest supporters in his critique of socialism, published his celebrated *Constitution of Liberty* in 1960. Mises reviewed this work and termed it a "great book," providing "a brilliant exposition of the meaning of liberty and the creative powers of a free civilization" (EFI, 151f). Yet Mises pulled no punches in expressing his disappointment with Hayek's treatment, in that book, of a number of features of the welfare state. "In fact," Mises wrote, "the Welfare State is merely a method for transforming the market economy step by step into socialism" (EFI, 151). Indeed, Mises continued, Hayek's own "searching analysis of the policies and concerns of the Welfare State" cannot fail to convey how these policies must fail to achieve their designed objectives, inducing "further acts of intervention . . . until all economic freedom has been virtually abolished. What emerges is the system of all-round planning, i.e., socialism of the type which the German Hindenburg plan was aiming at in the first World War and which was later put into effect by Hitler after his seizure of power and by the British Coalition Cabinet in the Second World War" (EFI, 152).

MISES, ECONOMICS, AND CLASSICAL LIBERALISM

Mises's convictions concerning the *economic* goodness of laissez-faire capitalism were separate from, but closely linked to, his own advocacy of classical liberalism as a *political* program. Throughout his career as an economist Mises insisted on the objective, nonpolitical, impartial character of his science, and yet he also passionately believed in and advocated (as a nonscientific, value-laden ideal) the political program of classical liberalism.[9] At times, Mises may have *seemed* to ignore the

---

9. We use here the term "classical liberalism" to distinguish it, of course, from what has, since before the middle of the twentieth century, been termed liberalism in the U.S. Mises generally used the term "liberalism" in what Leland Yeager refers to as "the European and etymologically correct sense of the word." See Yeager's introduction to *Nation, State, and Economy: Contributions to the Politics and History of Our Time* [1919], by Ludwig von Mises (New York: New York University Press, 1983), xi.

distinction between his science and his political convictions; the truth is that the distinction is indeed a subtle one, yet one which Mises articulated with great precision. "Liberalism . . . is a political doctrine. It is not a theory, but an application of the theories developed . . . especially by economics to definite problems of human action within society." Economic science is value-neutral, but "as a political doctrine liberalism is not neutral with regard to values and the ultimate ends sought by action. It assumes that all men or at least the majority of people are intent upon attaining certain goals. . . . While . . . economics . . . uses the terms happiness and removal of uneasiness in a purely formal sense, liberalism attaches to them a concrete meaning" (HA, 153f).

The distinction between classical liberalism and economics is an especially subtle one for Mises because he saw the former as a direct application of the scientific conclusions of the latter. Economics, for Mises, teaches that free markets permit and enable participating individuals to achieve their own goals through mutual cooperation and exchange. These teachings, Mises maintained, were first developed as "scientific theory without any thought of its political significance" (LCT, 195). The ideology of liberalism that was *derived* from this positive theory applied the theory to develop a political program through which man in society may act to achieve his goals, insofar as man is presumed to "prefer life to death, health to sickness, nourishment to starvation, abundance to poverty" (HA, 154).

The closeness between Mises's liberalism and his economics expresses Mises's *utilitarian* perspective. Liberalism deploys the teachings of economics to articulate its political program. But for Mises the teachings of economics seem inevitably to lead (on utilitarian grounds) to that very political program. "One cannot understand liberalism without a knowledge of economics. For liberalism is applied economics; it is social and political policy based on a scientific foundation" (LCT, 195). As William Baumgarth explained, Mises sought to offer a theory of society that is as value-free as conceivably possible. For Mises, classical liberalism does not *need* to depend, for its moral force, upon the asserted ethical imperatives of such categories as freedom or justice; its moral force flows out of economic understanding as it relates to the actual motives of men in society, whatever they may be. Mises's "attempt to offer such a theory was a bold one and went as far in the direction of utilitarianism as perhaps it is possible to go."[10] Baumgarth himself had serious doubts as to the moral *persuasiveness* of a political program which avoids ethically imperative reference to categories such as "justice" and "honor." Yet it is quite certain that for Mises, the ideal he constructed virtually purely from his economic science provided an ideology sufficiently heady to invest his entire career with a passion and sense of dedication rarely to be found in scientific work. Indeed, there is no doubt that the passion Mises poured into his scientific work derived in large measure from his awareness of its relevance to the political program he believed flowed from it.

Although we do not have any published writings expressing Mises's classical liberal outlook before his 1919 *Nation, State and Economy*, we can surmise that he imbibed this outlook much earlier, during his years of immersion in the pre–World War I Austrian School.[11] In his monograph *The Historical Setting of the Austrian School of Economics*, published when he was eighty-eight years of age, Mises revealed a good deal of the political context of the *methodenstreit* which raged around the turn of the century and earlier between the Austrian School and the German Historical School. One can sense in Mises's language and references the moral contempt with which he (and presumably the early Austrians) viewed the professors of the German School, and his conviction that the political loyalties of these professors and their followers led directly from their roles as the "intellectual bodyguard of the House of Hohenzollern"[12] to their becoming supporters of the Nazis after World War I (HSAS, 32). It was in Bismarck's Germany that the government inaugurated "its *Sozialpolitik*, the system of interventionist measures such as labor legislation, social security, pro-union attitudes, progressive taxation, protective tariffs, cartels and dumping" (HSAS, 30). The German Historical School provided the intellectual

10. William Baumgarth, "Ludwig von Mises and the Justification of the Liberal Order," in *The Economics of Ludwig von Mises: Toward a Critical Reappraisal*, ed. L. Moss (Kansas City: Sheed and Ward, 1976), 97.

11. See Mises, NR, 19f, for some hints of how, as a university student, Mises, who at first considered liberalism to be "an obsolete world view," came gradually to appreciate it.

12. This was the noble house, the Prussian electors and kings, from which sprang the German Kaisers.

ammunition for these policies. Its political influence "consisted in the fact that it rendered Germany safe for the ideas, the acceptance of which made popular with the German people all those disastrous policies that resulted in the great catastrophes. The aggressive imperialism that twice ended in war and defeat, the limitless inflation of the early Twenties, the *Zwangswirtschaft* and all the horrors of the Nazi regime were achievements of politicians who acted as they had been taught by the champions of the Historical School" (HSAS, 31). Mises clearly identified himself with what he called "the liberalism of the Austrian economists" who rejected the German Historical School (HSAS, 34).

In the American environment of the 1940s in which Mises found himself upon his arrival in his new country, and in the immediate postwar years, Mises was, as was noted in chapter 1, often considered a "conservative." He was a staunch opponent of the social measures which had been introduced by Franklin D. Roosevelt in the wake of the depression of the 1930s; he was unflagging in his opposition to the Keynesian fiscal and monetary policies that acquired enormous popularity during those years. With both major U.S. political parties supporting these interventionist measures (with greater or lesser degrees of enthusiasm, or with greater or lesser degrees of comprehensiveness), Mises found himself not merely out of step with prevailing fashions in economic policy; he found himself treated as an extremely (perhaps absurdly) conservative figure, one vainly attempting to restore a laissez-faire regime that had been decisively rejected, both intellectually and politically, decades earlier. And it is true that Mises found support among men and organizations associated with the "rock-ribbed" conservative wing of the Republican Party. Yet Mises never did see himself as a conservative; he was outspoken in his explicit identification of (classical) liberalism as his own political ideology. It is ironic but significant that in the semantic confusions of his time, those who in the U.S. termed themselves "liberals" (appropriating the term from the classical liberals in order to describe their own interventionist program—the very opposite of the position held by the classical liberals) were seen by Mises as following precisely those statist, conservative-authoritarian policies and philosophies against which the champions of his own classical liberalism had, in an earlier age, been radical rebels.[13] Leland Yeager has accurately described Mises's position: "Mises was emphatically not a conservative. His book [the 1919 *Nation, State and Economy*] rails repeatedly against political and economic privilege. He championed political democracy as well as a free-market economy. He admired democratic revolutions against hereditary and authoritarian regimes. . . ."[14]

ECONOMICS, AUSTRIAN ECONOMICS, AND THE CASE FOR THE FREE MARKET

Both fervent proponents and fierce critics of free-market capitalism have often pointed out the obvious relevance of neoclassical economics (the economics which has, for a good part of the twentieth century, been understood as the economic orthodoxy) for the defense of capitalism. Marxists and other critics of free-market capitalism have never ceased to denounce neoclassical economics, with the standard theory of market price as its core, precisely because that economics appears to provide powerful ammunition for asserting the economic efficiency of the capitalist system. George Stigler, associated with a far more benign appreciation of capitalism, has pointed out that, as compared with other fields of social science, economics tends to instil in its practitioners a generally less skeptical (and often in fact a more favorable) attitude toward the achievements of the market.[15] It is neoclassical economics which seems to demonstrate the benign power of Adam Smith's "invisible hand" to generate prices and allocate resources in systematic, and apparently desirable, fashion. In order to argue any economic failures in capitalism it is clearly necessary to undermine the core teachings of neoclassical economics, or, at any rate, to challenge the relevance of its well-behaved theoretical models to the complex realities of the world in which we must live.

13. In this, Mises's position was very similar to that of F. A. Hayek, whose 1944 *Road to Serfdom* pointed out the parallels between the "liberal" interventionist programs of the Western democracies and the roots of Nazi Germany. See also Hayek's essay, "Why I Am Not a Conservative," published as a postscript to F. A. Hayek, *The Constitution of Liberty* (Chicago: University of Chicago Press, 1960), 397–411.

14. Yeager, introduction to *Nation, State, and Economy*, xi.

15. George J. Stigler, "The Politics of Political Economists," *Quarterly Journal of Economics* (November 1959): 522–32.

It must seem surprising, then, to discover that during much of the twentieth century, it was orthodox economics itself that was made to serve as the intellectual basis for the widespread interventionism that has characterized the century (and especially the decades coinciding with and immediately following Mises's arrival in the U.S.). What explains this apparent paradox is that economists did indeed challenge the relevance of the neoclassical models to the real world.

The real world, many economists argued, unlike the neoclassical theoretical world, is a world of imperfect competition, a world pervaded by externalities, a world rendered unstable by the volatility and possible inadequacy of aggregate demand. This stance allowed economists to pay some lip-service to the elegance of the orthodox models, while at the same time insisting on the need for government interventions to deal with the problems, rampant in the real world, for which the orthodox models had no explanation and no solution. The growth of interventionism as a political ideology was thus parallel to the trend within the economics profession to use the "unrealism" of its models to demonstrate the *shortcomings* of free-market capitalism. To Ludwig von Mises these developments made no sense at all. A convincing case can be made that what enabled Mises to resist the fashionability of the interventionist economics of his time was the uniquely *Austrian* character of his own economics.

The truth is that the Austrian tradition that Mises had received and that he extended and deepened never did accept as central those rarefied models of perfectly competitive equilibrium that the midcentury critics of laissez-faire capitalism deployed to demonstrate that system's real-world shortcomings. As we saw in chapter 4, Mises worked with a theoretical construct that focused upon dynamic entrepreneurial competition in a world of disequilibrium. It was in the context of this dynamically competitive process—rather than in the unrealistic perfectly competitive equilibrium models of midcentury neoclassical microeconomics—that Mises saw the benign market process at work. It was this process, a process at work no less in the area of the monetary sector of the market than in the real sector, which Mises believed to constrain resource prices and resource allocation patterns, interest rates, and the value of money, to take account of hitherto overlooked (or unanticipated) changes in consumer preferences.

There is no contradiction between this disequilibrium framework of Mises's Austrian economics and the facts of the real world. The lessons

Mises learned regarding the achievements of the free market emphatically *did* apply to the world for which public policy must be formulated. For Mises, in order to understand the relevance of the theory of the market process to the defense of free-market capitalism, it was not necessary to extend the technical sophistication of market models; it was simply necessary to appreciate the subtleties of the market process itself. The logic of economic reasoning in the 1950s and the 1960s was no different from, and had lost none of its real-world relevance in comparison to, the economic reasoning of the 1920s. For Mises, the economists of the postwar years had disastrously lost their way. In fact, it seemed to him that it was the very advances in the technical sophistication of midcentury economics that were to blame for this tragic misuse of the science. It was this which drove Mises, during the last decades of his career, to attempt again and again to clarify what he believed to be the true epistemological and methodological foundations of economics.

MISES: THE FREE-MARKET ECONOMIST OF THE CENTURY

Few will argue with the judgment that, in terms of the vigor and passion with which he attacked socialist and interventionist alternatives to laissez-faire capitalism, Ludwig von Mises was the foremost economist of the twentieth century.[16] What we have seen is that in thus defying the conventional policy wisdom of his century, Mises was simply articulating the straightforward implications of his own strictly scientific contributions to the positive, objective discipline of pure economics. Both in his positive economics and in his policy positions, Mises was virtually

16. The statement in the text certainly recognizes the role played, during the past four decades, by the (post-Knightian) Chicago School in nudging public opinion in the U.S. toward a more favorable attitude toward free markets. In particular, Professor Milton Friedman (see especially his *Capitalism and Freedom* [Chicago: University of Chicago Press, 1962]) has exercised an influence far wider than that of Mises. Nonetheless, in terms of vigor, passion, and sheer consistency, the statement in the text should command general agreement. It should of course be noted that the economics underlying the Chicago School's pro-market positions is quite different from that of Mises. For Chicago, it is the assumption of rapid attainment by markets of results approximating those inherent in the model of perfectly competitive equilibrium that provides the analytical basis. As we have seen both in chapter 4 and in the present chapter, this was certainly *not* the basis for Mises's own positions.

alone. He watched with sadness twentieth-century developments both in economics and in the public policy fashions sweeping the nominally capitalist societies of the West. "The public discussion of economic problems ignores almost entirely all that has been said by economists in the last two hundred years. Prices, wage rates, interest rates and profits are treated as if their determination were not subject to any law. Governments try to decree and to enforce maximum commodity prices and minimum wage rates. Statesmen exhort businessmen to cut down profits, to lower prices, and to raise wages as if these matters were dependent on the laudable intentions of individuals. In the treatment of international economic relations people blithely resort to the most naïve fallacies of Mercantilism. Few are aware of the shortcomings of all these popular doctrines, or realize why the policies based upon them invariably spread disaster" (HA, 879f).

Mises could suggest only one way to combat these "sad facts": "by never relaxing in the search for truth" (HA, 880). Mises's entire career as an economist—from his Vienna days as a brilliant young scholar and as one deeply involved in the hectic world of post–World War I public policy, to his years in Geneva as a renowned senior scholar, to his three decades of lonely, unfashionable teaching and writing in the U.S. during his old age—represented Mises's extraordinary, courageous, sustained fulfillment of this ideal. He never faltered in his belief that the "body of economic knowledge is an essential element in the structure of human civilization; it is the foundation upon which modern industrialism and all the moral, intellectual, technological, and therapeutical achievements of the last centuries have been built" (HA, 885). Mises persisted "in the search for truth" in the face of the disdainful dismissal of his work by the professional economics establishment of his time because he saw his work as essential for the preservation of human civilization.

At the dawn of the twenty-first century, there is reason to believe that the work of the foremost free-market economist of the twentieth century will not be forgotten.

The central purpose of this work has been to set forth, in outline, the economic thought of Ludwig von Mises. The story of Mises's economics ends, in one sense, with the conclusion of Mises's life. And the story we have told in this book is therefore, in this sense, ended. But there is of course another sense in which the story of Mises's economics has continued to unfold *after* his death. Although our own purpose has not been to tell the story of the impact which Mises's work has had upon late-twentieth-century economic thought, we must certainly, in doing justice to Mises's contributions, take brief note of the remarkable resurgence of Austrian Economics that has occurred since 1973. That resurgence has consisted primarily in the rediscovery of the vitality and cogency of Mises's ideas.

During a period in which the mainstream of economic theorizing has pursued the path of formal, technical sophistication, many younger economists, disenchanted with the aridity and artificiality of the model-building approach, have found intellectual stimulation and satisfaction in Mises's relatively simple, but powerful and fundamental, insights. After decades during which the need for and value of government intervention in the market economy were the unquestioned bases of public policy, after decades during which socialism was admired as a viable and morally attractive alternative to "unbridled" capitalism, Misesian views concerning the economic incoherence of socialism—and the case for complete, or virtually complete, laissez-faire—have somehow become part and parcel of respectable public policy discourse. (Certainly these latter developments can, in great part, be attributed also to other intellectual currents, as well as historical and political changes which extend far beyond the direct scope of Mises's economics.)[1]

Karen Vaughn has recently described this revival. As she points out, there would have been little doubt among economists in 1974 (the year after Mises's death) "that the Austrian school was a closed chapter in the history of economics." But it is today obvious that such predictions were sorely mistaken. "Austrian concerns such as imperfect information, time and market coordination are now part and parcel of modern economics. . . . Even more surprising, articles devoted to research from an overtly

1. See above, chapter 6, n. 16.

Austrian perspective now routinely find their way into respectable, if not elite, academic journals. Mainstream publishers . . . are all publishing books about the Austrian school. . . . There are institutes and programmes named after both Mises and Hayek on both sides of the Atlantic. . . ."[2]

Mises may not have agreed with a good deal of the "new" Austrian economics. Many of the new Austrian economists came to question specific parts of the Misesian system. But there can be no doubt that the prime moving element responsible for the resurgence of the Austrian tradition was the impact of the work of Mises himself. Sometimes Mises's disciples have disagreed among themselves regarding Mises's views on specific issues, or regarding the interpretation to be placed on some of his more cryptic statements. Some followers of Mises have, with more than a hint of aggressiveness, believed themselves to be more "pure" Misesians than others. Some followers of Mises have learned to appreciate the complementarities between Mises's own work and that of his most famous fellow-Austrian, Friedrich Hayek; others have held that Hayek's work differs radically from that of his mentor. Out of the debates—sometimes inspiring and intellectually fertile, sometimes disappointing and intellectually dispiriting—on these issues, a broad group of scholars has emerged who are all working within the Austrian tradition, and who recognize the work of Mises as being the most powerful and radical expression of that tradition in the twentieth century.

It is notoriously hazardous to predict the future course of intellectual history. Yet this writer believes that the resurgence of interest in the Austrian tradition and in the Misesian approach will endure. This does not mean that Misesian positions on method, on markets, on monetary and trade cycle theory, and on capital theory will necessarily command the agreement of future economists. It does not even mean that a live, identifiable Austrian tradition in economics will be a reality in, say, fifty years. It means, rather, that the broad sweep of Mises's view of the workings of the market economy—his focus on human action, on the purposefulness of action, on the entrepreneurial element in the market process, on the subjectivism with which economic understanding must be pursued—will continue to find a place within the menu of intellectual options available

2. Karen I. Vaughn, "The Rebirth of Austrian Economics: 1974–99," *Economic Affairs: Journal of the Institute of Economic Affairs*, 20, no. 1 (March 2000): 40–43.

in twenty-first-century economics. These themes are too compelling, too persuasive, and too obviously fertile to be lost in the technicalities of any future economics. For the future historian of twenty-first-century economic thought, it will inevitably be necessary to recognize the impact of a remarkable twentieth-century Austrian economist, Ludwig von Mises.

ARTICLES OF NOTE ON

MISES AND HIS WORK

MISES AND THE RENAISSANCE
OF AUSTRIAN ECONOMICS

Mises was a towering figure: he represented uncompromising intellectual integrity, the courageous pursuit of ideas regardless of the crop of unpopularity which he well knew he would reap. His scholarship was extraordinary; his wisdom legendary; the profundity of his insights into social processes has probably never been surpassed. Much has been written about his passionate championship of individual liberty; it is only natural that exponents of the several different streams of social philosophy to whom individual liberty is of importance are each eager to recognize Mises as a source for their respective positions on the ideological spectrum. I, too, wish to draw attention to Mises the proponent of individual liberty, but I wish to do so in a context for which matters of ideological emphasis are, nonetheless, wholly irrelevant. Let me explain.

A number of writers have, on occasion, claimed to have perceived a contradiction in Mises. On the one hand Mises was an outspoken exponent of the Weberian view that economic science can and must be *wertfrei* (value-free). Economic science can and must be pursued in a manner that carefully distinguishes between the personal opinions and value-judgements of the economist, and the objective, interpersonally valid conclusions of science. On the other hand Mises was the impassioned defender of the free-market, full of scorn for the pretensions of central planners and interventionists to replace or supplement the spontaneous market with contrived arrangements by the state. It has seemed difficult, for a number of writers, to reconcile these different aspects of Mises. Yet, to anyone who heard Mises lecture on these topics, there can be no doubts concerning his position; there is certainly no contradiction in that position.

For Mises economic science is very definitely *wertfrei*. The demonstrations that wage controls tend to produce specific consequences, that rent controls tend to produce specific consequences, or that foreign exchange controls tend to produce specific consequences—these are not matters

From *Homage to Mises: The First Hundred Years,* ed. John K. Andrews Jr. (Hillsdale, Mich.: Hillsdale College Press, 1981), 14–18. Reprinted by permission of Hillsdale College Press.

of opinion, they are the conclusions of science. Whether one approves or disapproves of these consequences, whether the fulfillment of these lessons of science be welcomed or feared, affects not in the slightest the truth of the proportions which assert these tendencies. Yet for Mises economics does not operate in an ivy-clad vacuum; it is impossible to ignore the fact that these consequences do not in general coincide with the goals which the proponents of controls purport to cherish. From the perspective of *these* goals, then, these policies are simply wrong and muddleheaded policies. No doubt, in articulating these judgements it was difficult for Mises altogether to conceal his own passionate sense of human tragedy entailed by the pursuit of such bad policies—but what made these policies bad policies in the view of Misesian applied economic science was not Mises's own opinions, but the opinions of those who wrongheadedly sought to promote their announced goals by policies that tend to produce consequences precisely the opposite of these goals.

Now, there can be no doubt that for Mises, the *value* of the value-free pursuit of economic truth, was extremely high. For Mises the systematic search for economic truths is an activity that is eminently worthy of human endeavor. This sense of worth had its source in Mises's passionate belief in human liberty and the dignity of the individual. For Mises the preservation of a society in which these values can find expression depends, in the last resort, upon the recognition of economic truths. But, paradoxically enough, Mises was convinced that these deeply held values can be promoted, through the advancement of social science, only if scientific activity is itself conducted as an austerely dispassionate undertaking. If economic science is to attain a credibility beyond that achieved by crass propaganda, it must earn that credibility by impartial concern for truth. The values to be achieved by economics require value-freedom in economic investigation.

How tragic, then, it must have been for Mises in the latter half of his life to observe the direction taken by economics. So far from economic science demonstrating those truths upon which, for Mises, the very future of civilized society depends, we had an atmosphere of professional opinion in which the prestige of science was deployed to deride the very possibility of spontaneous market solutions to social problems. In virtually every area in economics, it seemed to turn out, chaos and misery were shown to be bound to ensue unless market forces are curbed, redirected or superseded by the firm, benevolent hand of an all-wise government. For Mises these sadly mistaken conclusions meant a two-fold tragedy. First, they represented serious error in the understanding of economic phenomena; second, they constituted a tragic perversion of science for ends diametrically opposed to those which, for Mises, confer worth and beneficent purpose upon the distinterested study of economics. The possibility that today, as we mark the one-hundredth birthday of our teacher, the climate of professional opinion may to some extent be changing, offers us an opportunity to appraise the place of Mises within the broader perspective of the history of economic understanding. Let us briefly recount part of the story of Austrian economics.

When Carl Menger published his *Grundsätze* in 1871, the subjectivist revolution that he initiated against classical economic theory was audacious and sweeping. This revolution was, as is well-known, paralleled by comparable intellectual currents in England and Lausanne. Jevons and Walras are, along with Menger, generally credited with focusing attention on the critical role played by subjectivist, marginal-utility-inspired forces underlying the demand side of the market. By the eve of World War I these new developments had become the established orthodoxy: Alfred Marshall in England and John Bates Clark in the United States provided the core of what is still today the standard body of microeconomics. Despite some recognized differences of emphasis separating the various major schools of theoretical economics, it was generally held that what they shared in common (especially as contrasted both with the classical theorists and with the anti-theorists of the younger Historical School) far outweighed what distinguished them from one another. It seems fair to say that Mises, as well as other Austrian economists of the first half of this century, shared in this sense of fellow-feeling with their colleagues of other schools. For Mises the approving label "modern economics" applied to *all* the post-1870 currents of theoretical economics. It was this which appears responsible for the opinion, accepted at least in part by Mises, Hayek and other Austrian economists of the time, that what was valuable in the earlier Austrian tradition had become benignly absorbed into the mainstream of twentieth century economics by about 1931, sixty years after the appearance of Menger's *Grundsätze,* and at the midpoint of the century which we are today celebrating.

Yet I believe it must be argued that this view (still maintained in standard histories of economic thought) has, since 1931, been revealed to have been profoundly mistaken. The course of mainstream economics during the past fifty years surely establishes beyond question (a) that what separated the early Austrians from their fellow economists elsewhere was far more significant than had been appreciated—even by Austrians themselves; (b) that it was the complete failure of these uniquely "Austrian" elements to have been meaningfully accepted into mainstream economics that has been responsible for those massive developments in standard economics since the Thirties that cast so depressing a shadow over Mises's later years.

The historic contribution of Mises, I submit, was represented not so much, perhaps, by the magisterial works that he produced in 1912, or 1922, in 1933, or 1940—as by his courageous, lonely vigil during the arid decades of the Forties, Fifties and Sixties, a vigil marked by a stream of unpopular books and papers, and by patient, unperturbed teaching and lecturing to whomever he was able to influence. It was this painful, unappreciated work which kept Austrian ideas alive during the years of eclipse. It is surely only as a result of this work that most of us who are here in Hillsdale today, are indeed here. And it is as a result of this work, I have reason to hope, that we can look to a resurgence of awareness on the part of economists generally, of the fundamental Austrian insights, and of their crucial importance for economic understanding.

Let us recall that oft-quoted sentence of Hayek's in which he suggested that "it is probably no exaggeration to say that every important advance in economic theory during the last hundred years was a further step in the consistent application of subjectivism." (*The Counter-Revolution of Science,* Free Press, 1955, p. 31). The legacy of Carl Menger was one to which subjectivism was the very essence; the direction in which the Austrian tradition pointed, was one leading almost inescapably to more and more consistent application of the subjectivist insights. And it was, to cite Hayek once again, Mises who, moving ahead of his colleagues, carried out this development most consistently (*ibid.,* p. 210).

What I wish to suggest here is that in the first half century of Austrian economics the members of the school were themselves not fully aware of how deeply their subjectivism set them apart from their non-Austrian fellow-economists. One is not always aware of the air one breathes. It was perhaps not until Mises (in his *Grund-probleme* of 1933) and Hayek (in *Individualism and Economic Order* and in the *Counter-Revolution of Sciences*) had articulated some of the more radical implications of the subjectivist approach, that it was possible to realize the extent of the gulf that separated the Austrian theory of the market process from the neo-Walrasian theory of market equilibrium. Austrian economics may have shared much in common with the economics of Alfred Marshall and of Leon Walras. But surely one crucial difference stands out. The latter schools, we are now in a position to see, pointed to a natural line of development that led to a positivist, instrumentalist view of economic theory, a view for which human purposefulness, error, surprise and the subjectivism of expectations are matters of embarrassment. It was the Austrian tradition, on the other hand that pointed in the direction of the consistent application of subjectivism.

The realization that economic science, praxeologically conceived, fits not at all into the standard paradigms of the philosophers of the natural sciences, is a lesson still not fully learned. Paradoxically enough, it was the *eclipse* of Austrian economics during the mid-twentieth century that has helped us glimpse the far-reaching truths contained in this lesson. During an era in which methodological individualism was forgotten in mainstream economics, in which scope for error or for entrepreneurial discovery was at least implicitly denied, in which clarity of theoretical insight was carelessly bartered for a pottage of econometric techniques—it was during such an era that Austrian economists came to appreciate the character of a praxeologically conceived science of human action.

So that we have before us a most interesting episode in the history of ideas. A body of work, a unique approach to its field of study, decisively loses scientific popularity. From the perspective of the newly regnant orthodoxy this now fashionable approach is in fact perceived as a crude, introspective, discredited, almost pre-scientific line of work that has come to be replaced by sophisticated mathematical techniques, and hard-headed empirical and econometric realism. And yet that body of work not only refuses to die. On the contrary, its very unfashionability generates a hitherto-absent degree of self-awareness—and plants the seeds for its renewed growth and revitalization. Thus it was that, during the Forties, Fifties and Sixties Austrian economics declined to permit itself to be relegated to the dustbin of intellectual history. Instead Austrian economics identified itself with unprecedented clarity not as a primitive approach displaced by intellectual advance, but rather as a unique set of ideas the subtlety of which had hitherto escaped attention. Sooner or later the richness of these ideas, and the depth of understanding they convey, would come to be appreciated. If there is hope today for a resurgence in

Austrian economics, then the unsung contributions of Mises during the decades of eclipse indeed assume historic proportions.

There is, in fact, considerable room for hope. At the very time when mainstream orthodoxy has never been more technically sophisticated, more sensitive to the complexities of social interaction—there is deep unrest in the economics profession. Faculty members and graduate students perceive a yawning gulf between the smoothly-oiled models on their blackboards and the seething reality in the streets around them. Self-criticism and bleak methodological introspection among economists— even among the high priests of contemporary orthodoxy—are becoming almost standard features in the academic environment. In this climate Misesian ideas are finding, once again, attentive ears in the economics profession. It is exciting work to nurture those hopeful signs of Austrian resurgence. I am, for example, most pleased to report that this month my own New York University will conduct a scholarly conference in honor of the Mises centenary. During this conference some twenty economists from all over the U.S. and Europe will gather in New York to discuss new work now being written in the light of Mises's own contributions.

It is impossible, of course, to predict precisely where this kind of intellectual development will take us. But it is surely clear that the rekindled interest in the ideas of subjectivism, the replacement of a positivistic economic science by one sensitive to the methodological uniqueness that derives from attention to human purposefulness and to human error, are developments which the economics profession can no longer in good conscience refuse to come to grips with. Out of this intellectual ferment appears to be emerging a sympathetic reappraisal of the ideas of earlier Austrian economics (whether in the area of capital theory, of competition theory, or of monetary theory) that were ignominiously discarded from the mainstream in years past.

Here, surely, Mises's historic role comes into focus in a bright new light. Mises was not merely the intellectual leader of the Austrian School during the central decades of the twentieth century. He was, surely more importantly, responsible for rescuing subjectivism from an otherwise certain death in the chokingly hostile environment of post–World War II positivism. Looking to the future, I would submit, it is our obligation to see to it that indeed Mises will be remembered in the long sweep of the history of economic thought as the pivotal figure responsible for a late twentieth century rediscovery of the fruitfulness and the subtlety of subjectivist economics. In this rediscovery process, the Misesian commitment to strict ideological neutrality, to an almost puritanical *wertfreiheit,* must never be relaxed. And yet, one senses, it is precisely the truths that such a *wertfrei* pursuit of praxeology can reveal, that would be likely to gladden the heart of Mises the devoted adherent of the ideals of Western civilization, the passionate lover of human liberty.

MISES AND THE AUSTRIAN TRADITION

We are witnessing what appears to be at least a modest revival of interest in the Austrian tradition on the part of the economics profession. There can be no doubt that this revival is to be attributed to the tenacity with which Mises continued to pursue his writing and teaching when it appeared that the profession had decisively turned its collective back on that tradition.[1] Much, perhaps most, of Mises's substantive contributions to economics had been completed before Mises arrived in the United States early in World War II. But the decades that followed witnessed an explosion of work in economics along lines that Mises considered profoundly mistaken. Instead of developing theory informed by subjectivist insights, the profession was turning toward a mindless and spuriously quantitative empiricism; instead of pursuing the subtle social processes set in motion by interacting, purposeful human individuals, the profession was entranced by the "hydraulics" of dubious models constructed from crude aggregative components. The Austrian-trained economists who had sought the intellectual leadership of Mises in Vienna during the twenties and thirties became, as a result of the imminent conflagration in Europe, geographically scattered and disorganized. During the lonely decades that followed, undeterred by thinly disguised disparagement on the part of his professional colleagues, and without the suitable academic base to which his stature and contributions entitled him, Mises continued to publish prolifically and to teach and lecture to whoever would listen.

In the 1960s and 1970s it appeared that economists were retreating, to a degree, from some of the aggregative excesses that had marked the immediate postwar era. There has been a return, in the professional mainstream, to a theoretical perspective aware of the importance of the microfoundations of the discipline. There has been a return to the neoclassical theory developed during the half-century following the marginalist revolution of the 1870s—a milieu in which the Austrian tradition in economics originated and flourished.

Yet the mainstream neoclassical revival of the past two decades has by no means constituted a return to the perspectives of the Austrian tradition. This may, at first glance, appear paradoxical. For many historians of thought, after all, the Austrian school is considered simply one of the intellectual tributaries from which the neoclassical mainstream took its source. Yet the truth is that the body of thought that developed in Vienna from Menger to Mises embodied insights that never were absorbed into the neoclassical tradition that drew from the confluence of Marshallian and Walrasian doctrine. A persuasive case can be made that the cracks and strains developing recently within the structure of contemporary economic theory, can be attributed precisely to the absence, in the dominant neoclassical tradition, of those Austrian insights.[2] It is no accident, therefore, that at this time of dilemma within economics, the ideas of the Austrians, and of Mises in particular, are being rediscovered. The perspective that Mises steadfastly pursued during the inhospitable forties and fifties has come to be seen as offering for the eighties a remarkably sensitive understanding of the operation of modern economic systems.

MISES AND THE MODERN AUSTRIAN REVIVAL

The chapters in this book reflect, in many ways and in different degrees, this recognition. There have been occasions in the past when admirers of the economic contributions of Ludwig von Mises have been accused, not entirely without grounds, of according his views the unswerving acceptance ordinarily reserved for incontrovertible truth. There are, no doubt, altogether understandable sociological forces inducing such uncritical attitudes toward a great but neglected thinker on the part of admirers dismayed by contemptuous treatment of him. Fortunately, the rediscovery in recent years of the brilliance, power, and depth of Mises's work has substantially eliminated the forces that might induce such unswering acceptance. Mises's ideas are being treated with the respect they so richly deserve: they are discussed extensively, seriously, and critically. The reader of this book will, therefore, encounter lively and uninhibited discussion of a number of fundamental Misesian ideas as well as innovative attempts to reappraise such ideas in the light of recent work by leading contributors to other traditions within the modern literature. But whether these chapters represent departures from Misesian orthodoxy, or revised assessment of the role of Mises in the history of economic thought, or measured reaffirmation of Misesian insights, they share an awareness of the subtle and profound aspects of the Misesian economic system that set it apart from the contemporary mainstream and that account for the thoroughly Misesian character and outlook of the modern Austrian revival. The various issues in Misesian economics raised in this book may be grouped under four headings: (1) the choice of economic method; (2) the nature of human action; (3) the character of the market process; and (4) the Misesian system as a framework for applied economic theory. It may be useful to show how thoroughly interrelated these groups of issues are within the Misesian system.

THE MISESIAN SYSTEM

For Mises the *market* constitutes a social process made up of the systematic sequences of decisions of interacting purposeful individual human beings continually discovering what they believe to be better ways of improving their respective situations. From this overall vision of the market process flow a number of the characteristically Misesian insights. We note immediately, of course, that the emphasis on social processes of discovery at once demotes the concept of market equilibrium from any position of centrality (as it enjoys, for example, in neoclassical orthodoxy). On the other hand the perceived systematic character of the social-discovery process renders it far away indeed from any conception of the market as sheer, unorganized chaos. (As Roger Garrison points out in chapter 11, the Austrians occupy, on more than one theoretical issue, a comfortable middle ground!) Several chapters grapple with the problems faced in demonstrating the systematic character of the market process.

The Misesian view of the market is peopled by purposeful individuals—human beings continually making discoveries. This feature of the Misesian view entails an unorthodox view of the analytical unit in economic theory—the individual decision, as expressed in human action. At the same time, because this view of the analytical basis for economic theory places so much emphasis on an unobservable—the purposefulness held to actuate human behavior—it follows that the epistemological character of the discipline, and hence the method appropriate to it, differs sharply from those relating to the physical sciences. In this, too, Mises found himself in disagreement with his fellow economists. In these regards (as well as in regard to Mises's well-known dismissal of the use of mathematics in economics) several chapters subject the Misesian position to searching and critical analysis.

The Misesian notion of purposeful human action bears resemblance in many respects, of course, to the concept of the individual decision in standard neoclassical microeconomic theory. But it is by now fairly well recognized that for Mises human action embraced far more than the simple economizing decision of neoclassical theory. The difference between the two concepts draws attention, in turn, to different levels of subjectivism identified in chapters of this book. Methodological individualism, although insisting on tracing market phenomena back to their roots in individual action, is consistent, in principle, with a variety of levels at which the subjectivity of action may be recognized. At the lowest level, perhaps, the individual is viewed as merely reacting in programmed, maximizing fashion to the environment that confronts him. Subjectivism is here confined to recognizing the given configuration of tastes and expectations with which the individual is somehow viewed as being endowed. At higher levels, on the other hand, the individual decision may be recognized as incorporating in an essential way the *discovery* of what that environment is or is likely to be. Or again, it may be held as *creating* that environment in devising feasible courses of action that were hitherto nonexistent. In discussions of these higher levels of subjectivism, Mises's vision of the entrepreneurial character of individual action has been compared or contrasted with the view of the decision extensively developed by George Shackle. In view of the radical indeterminacy emphasized by Shackle in his discussions of human decisions, these comparisons raise issues that extend, in turn, once again to the very possibility of systematic market processes. If the human decision is as spontaneous, creative, and dynamically subjective as both Mises and Shackle appear to maintain, is it still possible to speak meaningfully of systematic processes of discovery? From such themes it is but a short distance to explicit consideration of the role of uncertainty in the Misesian system. To what extent is the concept of human action inseparable from that of continuous, kaleidic change in the environment? The exploration of these delicate themes, along lines both more and less sympathetic to Mises's views, occupies much of several chapters in this book.

Mises was not merely an abstract theorist. He viewed his theories as providing the analytical framework within which to assess real-world problems and policies. Thus his view of the market as a process called for a sharp departure from the orthodox neoclassical perception of both the meaning and virtues of competition. Moreover, Mises's view of the market as a process of discovery entails rather definite implications for the analysis and assessment of monopoly resource ownership and of government intervention in markets—without, it must be emphasized, departing, he believed, one iota from the valuefree stance of the detached scientist. His views on these and related matters are critically examined in this book.

MISES AND THE FUTURE OF AUSTRIAN ECONOMICS

The chapters in this book, as well as the conference discussions that they generated, reveal modern Austrians to be far from unanimity on numerous fundamental issues. At times it may even appear legitimate to question the very existence of a clearly defined, generally accepted body of Austrian doctrine. Yet I believe that, on reflection, it can be maintained fairly that: (1) despite their disagreements Austrian economists do by and large share an overall perspective on the nature and tasks of economic science that permits their designation as a distinct school of thought; (2) this shared overall perspective, when understood against the sweep of the developments in twentieth-century thought, is unquestionably the heir of the earlier Austrian tradition; and (3) the strains and stresses evident at the frontiers of the present Austrian revival are the healthy products of attempts to reconcile Austrian insight with intellectual developments elsewhere in social science.

To the development of this shared overall Austrian perspective, and to the ferment and sense of excitement now evident in the resurgence of interest in this Austrian perspective, Mises's contributions have been crucial and decisive. The true memorial to Ludwig von Mises will be the future work within the Austrian tradition that these contributions continue to generate.

NOTES

1. Because of the focus on the Misesian contributions to current ferment at the frontiers of economics, no attempt has been made here to provide an appraisal of Mises in broader terms. We are fortunate in that a significant literature exists that provides excellent material on Mises, including a wealth of biographical and bibliographical detail. Readers may obtain a perspective on Mises's greatness as man and as social scientist

from the following works: M. Sennholz, ed., *On Freedom and Free Enterprise* (Princeton, N.J.: D. Van Nostrand, 1956), a *Festschrift* (festival writing) on the fiftieth anniversary of Mises's doctorate from the University of Vienna; Mont Pelerin Society, *Tribute to Mises, 1881–1973* (Chislehurst, Kent: Quadrangle Publications, n.d.); Margit von Mises, *My Years with Ludwig von Mises* (New Rochelle, N.Y.: Arlington House, 1976); L. S. Moss, ed., *The Economics of Ludwig von Mises, toward a Critical Reappraisal* (Kansas City: Sheed and Ward, 1976); Ludwig von Mises, *Notes and Recollections* (South Holland, Ill.: Libertarian Press, 1978), including postscript by Hans F. Sennholz; Percy L. Greaves, Jr., introduction to Ludwig von Mises, *On the Manipulation of Money and Credit* (Dobbs Ferry, N.Y.: Free Market Books, 1978); J. K. Andrews, ed., *Homage to Mises, the First Hundred Years* (Hillsdale, Mich.: Hillsdale College Press, 1981). For a comprehensive bibliography of Mises's writings the reader is referred to Bettina Bien [Greaves], *The Works of Ludwig von Mises* (Irvington-on-Hudson, N.Y.: Foundation for Economic Education, 1969).

2. See, for example, D. Bell and I. Kristol, eds., *The Crisis in Economic Theory* (New York: Basic Books, 1981).

To attempt to discuss Mises's views on entrepreneurship calls for far more than just the exposition of one specific economic function in the Misesian system—it is to seek to lay bare the very essence of that system. A fairly strong case can be made to support the claim that for Mises the core of economic understanding consists in appreciation of the entrepreneurial character of the market process. "The driving force of the market, the element tending toward unceasing innovation and improvement, is provided by the restlessness of the promoter and his eagerness to make profits as large as possible."[1] To understand adequately the function fulfilled by the Misesian entrepreneur is to understand what sets the economics of Ludwig von Mises apart from the economic orthodoxy of his time. At the time when we honor the one hundredth anniversary of Mises's birth, and in an intellectual epoch in which we are witnessing the remarkable and encouraging resurgence of interest in Mises's ideas and writings, it is wholly appropriate to devote special attention to the place occupied by the entrepreneur in the Misesian "Science of Human Action." Let us study a paragraph from Mises's magnum opus.

> The entrepreneur is the agency that prevents the persistence of a state of production unsuitable to fill the most urgent wants of the consumers in the cheapest way. All people are anxious for the best possible satisfaction of their wants and are in this sense striving after the highest profit they can reap. The mentality of the promoters, speculators, and entrepreneurs is not different from that of their fellow men. They are merely superior to the masses in mental power and energy. They are the leaders on the way toward material progress. They are the first to understand that there is a discrepancy between what is done and what could be done. They guess what the consumers would like to have and are intent upon providing them with these things. In the pursuit of such plans they bid higher prices for some factors of production and lower the prices of other factors of production by restricting their demand for them. In supplying the market

From *Wirtschaftspolitische Blätter* 28, no. 4 (Vienna: 1981): 51–57.
1. L. v. Mises, *Human Action: A Treatise on Economics,* New Haven, 1949, p. 256.

with those consumers' goods in the sale of which the highest profits can be earned, they create a tendency toward a fall in their prices. In restricting the output of those consumers' goods the production of which does not offer chances for reaping profit, they bring about a tendency toward a rise in their prices. All these transformations go on ceaselessly and could stop only if the unrealizable conditions of the evenly rotating economy and of static equilibrium were to be attained.[2]

The foregoing paragraph points, I believe, to three interrelated themes unique to the Misesian entrepreneurial function. In what follows we shall develop these three aspects of Misesian entrepreneurship so as to draw attention to this uniqueness. The three central ideas we shall examine are: (a) the recognition of the entrepreneurial element in each individual market participant; (b) the insight into entrepreneurship as the driving force behind the equilibrating tendencies within the price system; (c) appreciation for the entrepreneurial basis for the social efficiency achieved by the market economy.

HUMAN ACTION AND MARKET ENTREPRENEURSHIP

"The mentality of the promoters, speculators and entrepreneurs is not different from that of their fellow men." Elsewhere Mises is even more explicit in recognizing the entrepreneurial element in the human action engaged in by each individual. "In any real and living economy every actor is always an entrepreneur."[3] What Mises means is that the market process is kept in motion by the purposeful actions of human beings eager to enhance their positions. These purposeful actions call for continuous assessment of the possibilities relevant to an uncertain future. This speculative activity is inseparable from the human condition, whether one is a high-flying business promoter or whether one is safely ensconced in a bureaucratic sinecure. To be human is to be compelled to speculate.

On the other hand Mises recognizes that some human beings are more gifted speculators than others. In the market economy there is a tendency for those who are "superior to the masses in mental power and energy" to become specialized in the function of market entrepreneurship. So that

---

2. Op. cit., p. 333.
3. Op. cit., p. 253.

the notion of entrepreneurship for Mises may refer on the one hand to a broadly conceived speculative element suffusing all human action, or it may refer more narrowly to the specialized economic function exercised by those who display business leadership.[4]

In more orthodox versions of modern microeconomics, it is worthy of remark, both levels of entrepreneurship fail to receive recognition. It is by now fairly well known that in contemporary neo-Walrasian microeconomic theory there is virtually no scope for market entrepreneurial activity. In equilibrium there are no profits for the entrepreneur to win, and no losses for him to avoid; he has simply nothing to do. And similarly in the microeconomic world peopled by market participants whose sole decision-making responsibility is that of correctly computing the solutions to constrained maximization problems, there is no scope for any speculative dimension to choice. (It is this, of course, which has led Shackle to interpret modern microeconomics as having in fact extruded genuine choice from its purview.)[5]

For the Misesian system, on the other hand, this entrepreneurial element is something that can simply not be lost sight of at any level. The analysis of individual choice can never forget that in making his decisions man is choosing between uncertain future alternatives that he must himself identify. Choice cannot be considered apart from the eagerness with which the chooser seeks correctly to envisage the future and its possibilities. For analytical purposes, it is true, it is convenient to imagine a separate entrepreneurial function exercised in the market. And, as noted, the superior speculative abilities of some in fact permit the flesh-and-blood identification of entrepreneurial businessmen. But the basic insight remains that the unit of analysis for the methodologically individualistic economics of Mises is explicitly endowed with an important entrepreneurial dimension.

ENTREPRENEURSHIP AND THE EQUILIBRATING FORCES OF THE MARKET

For Mises the activities of the entrepreneur are responsible for the agitation of the market that would "stop only if the unrealizable conditions of the evenly rotating economy and of static equilibrium were to be

---

4. Op. cit., pp. 255f.

5. See, for example, the profound and extended critique of neoclassical theory contained in G. L. S. Shackle, *Epistemics and Economics,* Cambridge, 1972.

attained." As Mises expressed it elsewhere, the "activities of the entrepreneurs are the element that would bring about the unrealizable state of the evenly rotating economy if no further changes were to occur."[6] In recognizing this outcome of entrepreneurship Mises's position is to be sharply distinguished from the (separate) views of the two other major theorists of the entrepreneurial role, Schumpeter and Knight. For neither of these two writers is entrepreneurship perceived as the equilibrating factor in the market process.

For Schumpeter, in fact, the essence of entrepreneurship is that it consists in disrupting existing equilibrium states. For Schumpeter "the perennial gale of creative destruction"[7] that is the central feature of capitalism, is a series of entrepreneurial rebellions against existing settled patterns of production. These rebellions constitute the "spontaneous and discontinuous changes in the channel of the circular flow"[8] that make up what Schumpeter in his 1911 book called "economic development"— a phenomenon which he described as entirely "foreign to what may be observed . . . in the tendency towards equilibrium."[9]

For Knight (and his followers) the entrepreneur tries his best to cope with the uncertainty of business conditions; he has chosen to bear the brunt of this uncertainty by accepting contractual responsibility for the prices paid for the resources used in production. Profit emerges as "the residuum of product remaining after payment is made at rates established in competition with all comers for all services of men or things for which competition exists."[10] It results from the unpredictable changes which inevitably render these competitive rates "incorrect," as perceived from the perspective of subsequent events. There is nothing in Knightian entrepreneurship to link it with the equilibrating process in the course of which competitively equilibrium prices are determined.

In emphasizing the equilibrating function of the entrepreneur Mises is not only directing our attention to an important insight into the entrepreneurial role; he is, perhaps even more importantly, expounding a

---

6. Mises, op. cit., p. 335.

7. J. A. Schumpeter, *Capitalism, Socialism and Democracy*, New York, 3rd Edition, 1950, p. 87.

8. J. A. Schumpeter, *The Theory of Economic Development*, Cambridge, 1934, p. 65.

9. Op. cit., p. 64.

10. F. H. Knight, *Risk, Uncertainty and Profit*, Boston, 1921, p. 308.

particularly penetrating view on the character of the market process itself. If there is any system in markets, if market prices are anything other than randomly wandering terms of exchange—this is to be attributed to entrepreneurial activity. Entrepreneurial activity is thus responsible for far more than the bids and offers that competitively hammer out market prices; it is this activity that ensures, in addition, that these prices display a tendency to converge towards the pattern consistent with the evenly rotating economy. Of course Mises hastens to describe the evenly rotating economy as an "unrealizable" state. But for Mises what is unrealizable is the end-state itself; such a state is not realizable because of the incessant, kaleidic change that envelops human life. The equilibrating process, however (which would, in the altogether imaginary absence of change, continue until the evenly rotating economy would be attained), is not at all a matter only of the imagination. It is the overriding theme that at all times governs the course of real-world market prices. What Mises has taught us is that this powerful equilibrating tendency is set in motion and maintained by the eager competition of profit-seeking entrepreneurs endeavoring to serve consumers more efficiently.

The part played in the Misesian equilibration process by the free interplay of competitive entrepreneurial activity has not always been adequately understood. It was totally overlooked by many of those who responded to Mises's 1920 challenge to the possibility of economic calculation under socialism. A number of economists developed theoretical schemes for centrally planned systems that were to work with "prices" promulgated on a trial and error basis by the central authorities. These schemes assumed that the socially-coordinative results achieved through market prices can, in principle, be similarly attained through the use of non-market price systems. What these writers failed to recognize, in this attempt to meet Mises's arguments, was that for Mises the results achieved through market prices are inseparable from the profit-motivated endeavors of competing entrepreneurs that drive the market. To talk of non-market prices—prices without entrepreneurs—as able to simulate the market, is thus profoundly to misunderstand the market process itself.[11]

---

11. For a full analysis of this misunderstanding see the unpublished doctoral dissertation of D. Lavoie, Rivalry and Central Planning: A Re-examination of the Debate over Economic Calculation Under Socialism, New York University, 1981.

ENTREPRENEURSHIP AND THE SOCIAL
EFFICIENCY OF THE MARKET

The last-mentioned issue relating to the possibility of economic calcula-tion under socialism, links directly with the last of the three themes we identified in the paragraph cited from Mises, early in this paper. Entre-preneurship in the market economy is responsible for whatever social-economic efficiency the market is able to deliver. "The entrepreneur is the agency that prevents the persistence of a state of production unsuit-able to fill the most urgent wants of the consumers in the cheapest way." This theme is in fact closely associated with the preceding theme, that of the equilibrating tendency with which entrepreneurial activity endows market prices.

From the Misesian perspective, the absence of the conditions required for the evenly rotating economy constitutes and expresses an inadequate adjustment to the realities embedded in the juxtaposed patterns of con-sumer attitudes on the one hand, and of production possibilities tech-nologically feasible with available resources, on the other. This lack of adjustment to the realities is referred to in the cited paragraph from Mises as the "discrepancy between what is done and what could be done." And, as Mises explains, it is the leadership displayed by profit-motivated entre-preneurs that uncovers discrepancies of this kind. Wherever what is done falls short of what could be done, there is scope for pure entrepreneur-ial gain. Wherever entrepreneurs are at liberty to pursue possibilities for such pure gain, they will tend to unearth the discrepancies that underlie these profit possibilities. The very same market process which tends, as seen in positive analysis, towards the equilibrium configuration of prices, constitutes at the same time (what must, from the normative perspective, be seen as) a process of the elimination of social waste and inefficiency.

For Mises the social efficiency of the market is not to be looked for in the optimality conditions that may be satisfied in market general equilibrium. This is so not merely because the general equilibrium state is "unrealizable." More importantly this is the case because from the Misesian perspective the really exciting and significant normative properties of the market consist in the ability of the market process to identify and eliminate social inefficien-cies that have arisen out of sheer error and misinformation. From this per-spective, the market is seen as a means of communication in a very special sense. It is not merely that, with equilibrium prices prevailing, each mar-ket participant is aware of all that he needs to know in order to participate cooperatively in a smoothly working social system of decentralized decision-making controlled by no one at all. Rather the market is the vehicle whereby existing socially-wasteful processes of production come to the attention of entrepreneurs who tend to notice where and how the resources can be reallocated to more socially valuable uses. The opportunities for profits and the situations threatening losses noticed by entrepreneurs act as the spurs to a continual process of progressive replacement of less efficient by more efficient patterns of resource deployment. It is in this way that entrepreneurs, besides being responsible for the equilibrating forces in the market, are also the "leaders on the way toward material progress."

In this Misesian process of leadership toward material progress we must understand the role of entrepreneurial discovery as broadly as can be. Not only do entrepreneurs discover discrepancies between what is being done and what could now be done with today's technology. Entrepreneurs are, in addition, the agents for the discovery of altogether new ways of doing things, of altogether new things worth doing, that also, in the widest sense of the phrase, represent discrepancies between what is being done and what could be done. A pattern of resource allocation that would be optimal from the perspective of the technological knowledge actually possessed today, will surely, from the perspective of tomorrow's technology, be seen to have been "inefficient." Entrepreneurial responsiveness to the lure of pure profits available (so to speak) "around the corner," is the social device that points society towards the discovery of that new, as yet undreamed of, technology. It is here, of course, that the innovative role assigned by Schumpeter to his entrepreneur, finds its place naturally within the broader Misesian theory. The capitalist process of creative destruction which is for Schumpeter an essentially disruptive process, becomes visible, in the Misesian system, as a *response* to what will, in hindsight, be viewed as the fundamentally incomplete adjustment (to the "true" realities) that was present in what (viewed from the contemporaneous perspective) *appeared* as the fully equilibrated state.

THE MISESIAN SYSTEM: BETWEEN SCYLLA AND CHARYBDIS

We are now in a position to appreciate the relationship which the Misesian theory of the entrepreneurial market process bears to alternative perspectives. At the risk of oversimplifying complex and subtle issues (and, indeed, of possibly engaging in mild caricature), we offer the following sketch of the available theoretical alternatives.

The Neoclassical Orthodoxy

In this view the analysis of the market proceeds, in principle, as if the future holds no surprises. While acknowledging the importance of the acquisition of information, and of the need to address the stochastic character of economic phenomena, the orthodox approach tends to view the market as at all times peopled by successfully maximizing individuals each of whom knows exactly how much ignorance he possesses and how worthwhile it would be to reduce that ignorance by specified doses. The markets peopled by these maximizing individuals are, in this orthodoxy, usually envisioned as clearing immediately, with prices leaping instantaneously to sustain the market-clearing equilibrium. In this approach there has been virtually no analysis of entrepreneurship because there is really no need for entrepreneurial activity. There is no need for alertness to possible future changes, because the future is, in effect, presumed already known (or, at any rate, market participants effectively know as much about the future as they would be prepared to pay for). Markets reach equilibrium effortlessly; no tortuous entrepreneurial process of equilibration is called for.

The Radical Uncertainty Challengers

Although it has long been (and still continues to be) dominant in economics, the neoclassical orthodoxy has, in recent decades, become the target of relentless criticism by those who have rebelled against the refusal of orthodox theory to recognize the radical uncertainty within which human choices are made. In particular the critics' ire has been directed against the very heart of theoretical orthodoxy: the notion of general equilibrium seen as the stable center of gravity for the entire market system. For critics such as a Joan Robinson, a G. L. S. Shackle, or an L. M. Lachmann, the rot at the heart of orthodox microeconomics consists in its refusal to recognize the impact of the sheer unknowability of the future in a world of kaleidic change. The various critics differ drastically in their own positive positions, but they share a common conviction that the vision of the market as an equilibrating system is, to put it mildly, deeply flawed. And it is uncertainty that is responsible for this rejection of the market as an equilibrating system.

The Misesian Vision: The Entrepreneurial Process

Against the background of this challenge to neoclassical orthodoxy—a challenge that, while it has not yet quite shaken the pillars of the economics profession, is yet far from having been without significant impact—it is possible to appreciate the richness and subtlety of the Misesian view. On the one hand Mises is fully sensitive to the uncertainty that envelops individual human action, and that surrounds the entire body of market transactions. In fact Mises insists on placing uncertainty at the center of his system. On the other hand Mises does not perceive any incompatibility between his recognition of uncertainty and his emphasis on the powerful equilibrating forces of the market. Quite the contrary, the equilibrating forces of the market are driven by the activities of that very agent whose sole analytical function is that of imagining the future in the face of the all-pervading fog of uncertainty.

Of course Mises never falls into the error of treating the market as if it has attained the unrealizable state of equilibrium. But neither does he fail to stress the systematic manner in which entrepreneurial profit-motivated endeavor works to discover and eliminate the maladjustments which constitute the state of disequilibrium. Perhaps the most encouraging intellectual development in economics in the last few years has been a growing appreciation—even if still all too limited—of the profound insights embodied in the Misesian understanding of the entrepreneurial character of the market process.[12]

12. For further analysis of the entrepreneurial role, the reader is referred to I. M. Kirzner, *Competition and Entrepreneurship*, University of Chicago Press, 1973, and *Perception, Opportunity and Profit*, University of Chicago Press, 1979.

UNCERTAINTY, DISCOVERY, AND HUMAN ACTION: A STUDY OF THE ENTREPRENEURIAL PROFILE IN THE MISESIAN SYSTEM

A central element in the economics of Ludwig von Mises is the role played by the entrepreneur and the function fulfilled by entrepreneurship in the market process. The character of that process for Mises is decisively shaped by the leadership, the initiative, and the driving activity displayed and exercised by the entrepreneur. Moreover, in an intellectual edifice built systematically on the notion of individual *human action*— on the manner in which reasoning human beings interact while seeking to achieve their individual purposes—it is highly significant that Mises found it of relevance to emphasize that each human actor is always, in significant respects, an entrepreneur.[1] The present paper seeks to explore the character of Misesian entrepreneurship, with special reference to the influence exercised by the inescapable uncertainty that pervades economic life. Both at the level of isolated individual human action and at the level of entrepreneurial activity in market context, we shall be concerned to determine the extent to which the Misesian entrepreneur owes his very existence and his function to the unpredictability of his environment and to the ceaseless tides of change that undergird that unpredictability.

On the face of it, this question may not seem worthy of new research. Mises, it may be pointed out, expressed himself quite clearly on numerous occasions to the effect that the entrepreneurial function is inseparable from speculation with respect to an uncertain future. For example he wrote that "the entrepreneur is always a speculator."[2] Or, again, he wrote that "entrepreneur means acting man in regard to the changes occurring in the data of the market."[3] Moreover when Mises points out that every individual acting man is an entrepreneur, this is because "every action is embedded in the flux of time and thus involves a speculation."[4] In other words the entrepreneurial element cannot be abstracted from the notion of individual human action, because the "uncertainty of the future is already implied in the very notion of action. That man acts and that the future is uncertain are by no means two independent matters, they are only two different modes of establishing one thing."[5]

Thus it might seem that the essentiality of uncertainty for the Misesian entrepreneur hardly needs to be established anew. Certainly any thought of questioning that essentiality must, it might appear, be quickly dismissed.

What I shall argue in this chapter is not that the role of uncertainty in the function of the Misesian entrepreneur may be any less definitive than these clear-cut statements imply but that this role is a more subtle one than may on the surface appear to be the case. It is this subtlety in the role played by uncertainty in the Misesian system, I believe, that sets that system apart in significant respects from the views of other economists (such as Knight or Shackle) who have emphasized the phenomenon of uncertainty in the context of the market.

THE BACKGROUND OF THE PRESENT EXPLORATION

In earlier forays into the field of the Misesian entrepreneur, I developed an interpretation of the entrepreneurial function in which the role of uncertainty, while recognized and certainly not denied, was not emphasized. This failure to emphasize uncertainty was quite deliberate and was indeed explicitly acknowledged.[6] Instead of emphasizing the uncertainty in which entrepreneurial activity is embedded, these earlier treatments stressed the element of *alertness to hitherto unperceived opportunities* that is, I argued, crucial for the Misesian concept of entrepreneurship.[7] Since my position explicitly recognized the element of change and uncertainty, while it claimed to be able to explicate the elusive quality of entrepreneurship without need to emphasize the uncertainty element, it is perhaps not surprising that my treatment has drawn fire from two different perspectives. A number of critics have felt rather strongly that failure to emphasize the role of uncertainty renders my understanding of entrepreneurship fundamentally defective. At least one critic, on the other hand, has been persuaded by my exposition of entrepreneurship to the point that even my frugal references to uncertainty as an inescapable characteristic of the entrepreneurial scene appear altogether unnecessary and are seen as productive of confusion. Since all these critics are basically in agreement with me, I believe, on the broad accuracy of the general entrepreneurial character of the market process that I ascribe to Mises, it has for some time been my hope to delve into these questions more thoroughly. Some further brief recapitulation of these earlier discussions seems in order as an introduction to our present exploration.

My emphasis on alertness to hitherto unperceived opportunities as the decisive element in the entrepreneurial function stemmed from my pursuit of a didactic purpose. This purpose was to distinguish the analysis of the market *process* (a process in which the entrepreneur plays the crucial role) as sharply as possible from the analysis of equilibrium states (in which all scope for entrepreneurial activity has been assumed away). In equilibrium, it turns out, all market decisions have somehow come already into complete mutual coordination. Market participants have been assumed to be making their respective decisions with perfectly correct information concerning the decisions that all other participants are making at the same time.[8] So long as the underlying present consumer attitudes and production possibilities prevail, it is clear that we can rely on the very same set of decisions being made in each of an indefinite number of future periods. On the other hand, in the absence of such complete equilibrium coordination of decisions, a market process is set in motion in which market participants are motivated to learn more accurately to anticipate the decisions of others; in this process the entrepreneurial, profit-motivated discovery of the gaps in mutual coordination of decisions is a crucial element. Entrepreneurial activity drives this market process of mutual discovery by a continually displayed alertness to profit opportunities (into which the market automatically translates the existing gaps in coordination). Whereas entrepreneurial activity is indeed speculative, the pursuit of profit opportunities is a purposeful and deliberate one, the "emphasis on the element of alertness in action [was] intended to point out that, far from being numbed by the inescapable uncertainty of our world, men *act upon their judgments of* what opportunities have been left unexploited by others."[9]

In developing this aspect of entrepreneurship I was led to emphasize the capture of pure entrepreneurial profit as reducible essentially to the exploitation of arbitrage opportunities. Imperfect mutual awareness on the part of other market participants had generated the emergence of more than one price for the same bundle of economic goods; the entrepreneur's alertness to the profit opportunity presented by this price discrepancy permits him to win these profits (and, in so doing, tends to nudge the prices into closer adjustment with each other). In so emphasizing the arbitrage character of pure profit, emphasis was deliberately withdrawn from the speculative character of entrepreneurial activity that wins pure profit by correctly anticipating *future* price movements.[10]

A number of (otherwise friendly) critics expressed serious reservations concerning my deliberate lack of stress on the speculative character of entrepreneurial activity. Henry Hazlitt pointed out that my repeated references to the entrepreneur's perceiving of opportunities fail to make clear that at best the entrepreneur *thinks* that he perceives opportunities; that what an entrepreneur "acts on may not be a perception but a *guess.*"[11] Murray Rothbard has endorsed a discussion by Robert Hébert in which my definition of the entrepreneur is sharply distinguished from that of Mises: "Mises conceives of the entrepreneur as the uncertainty bearer. . . . To Kirzner, on the other hand, entrepreneurship becomes reduced to the quality of *alertness;* and uncertainty seems to have little to do with the matter."[12] Although conceding that my treatment of the entrepreneur has "a certain amount of textual justification in Mises," Rothbard sees this not as providing genuine support for my reading of the Misesian entrepreneur but as being the result of a "certain uncharacteristic lack of clarity in Mises's discussion of entrepreneurship."[13]

In a most thoughtful paper by Lawrence H. White several years ago, he too deplored my deliberate failure to emphasize uncertainty in the analysis of entrepreneurship. This treatment, White argues, fosters neglect of important features of entrepreneurial activity that arise precisely from the passage of time and from the uncertainty generated by the prospect of unanticipated changes bound to occur during the journey to the future. To compress entrepreneurial activity into an arbitrage box is, in particular, to fail to recognize the highly important part played by entrepreneurial *imagination.*[14]

On the other hand my treatment of entrepreneurship has been criticized by J. High from a diametrically opposite point of view. High accepts the definition of entrepreneurship in terms of alertness to opportunities for pure profit. He proceeds to point out that "[n]othing in this definition requires uncertainty. The definition requires ignorance, because the opportunity has not been discovered earlier; it requires error, because the opportunity could have been discovered earlier, but the definition does not require uncertainty."[15] High is therefore critical of passages in which uncertainty is linked specifically with entrepreneurship.[16]

Clearly the role of uncertainty in the entrepreneurial environment, and in particular its relationship to the entrepreneur's alertness to error, demands further explication. What follows may not satisfy my critics (from both wings). I trust, however, that my discussion of some of the perhaps less obvious links between uncertainty and alertness will, if it does not quite absolve me of the charge of intransigence, at least bear witness to my grateful acknowledgment of the very deep importance of the problems raised by my critics.

Our inquiry will be facilitated by a careful examination of the sense in which each individual engaging in human action is, as already cited from Mises, exercising entrepreneurship.[17] Or, to put the issue somewhat differently, it will be helpful to explore more precisely what it is that distinguishes human action from purely calculative, allocative, economizing activity.

I have argued in earlier work that the concept of human action emphasized by Mises includes an ineradicable entrepreneurial element that is absent from the notion of economizing, of the allocation of scarce resources among competing ends, that was articulated by Lord Robbins.[18] On the face of it there appear to be two distinct aspects of Misesian human action that might be considered to set it apart from Robbinsian economizing activity. We shall have to ask whether these are indeed two distinct aspects of human action and how they relate to the entrepreneurial element that human action contains (but which Robbinsian allocative activity does not). These two aspects of human action (not present in economizing activity) may be identified as (1) the element in action that is beyond the scope of "rationality" as an explanatory tool, and (2) the element in action that constitutes discovery of error. Let us consider these in turn.

THE LIMITS OF RATIONALITY

Perhaps the central feature of purely economizing activity is that it enables us to explain behavior by reference to the postulate of rationality. With a given framework of ranked goals sought, and of scarce resources available to be deployed, rationality (in the narrow sense of consistency of behavior with the relevant given ranking of ends) assures a unique pattern of resource allocation; decision making can be fully understood in the light of the given ends-means framework. There is no part of the decision that cannot be accounted for; given the framework, the decision taken is fully determined (and therefore completely explained); any other decision would have been simply unthinkable.

On the other hand the notion of Misesian human action embraces the very adoption of the ends-means framework to be considered relevant. The adoption of any particular ends-means framework is a step which is logically (although not necessarily chronologically) prior to that of allocating means consistently with the given ranking of ends. If the human decision is to be perceived as including the selection of the ends-means framework, then we have an element in that decision that cannot, of course, be explained by reference to rationality. Consistency in action is not sufficient to account for that ranking of ends in terms of which consistency itself is to be defined. So that the totality of human action cannot, even in principle, be explained on the basis of rationality. A science of human action cannot fail to acknowledge—even after full recognition of the formidable explanatory power of the postulate of rationality—that human history, depending as it does on unexplained adoption of goals and awareness of means, contains a strong element of the unexplained and even the spontaneous. These are themes that have, of course, been extensively developed by G. L. S. Shackle. "Choice and reason are things different in nature and function, reason *serves* the chosen purposes, not performs the selection of them."[19] "A man can be supposed to act always in rational response to his 'circumstances': but those 'circumstances' can, *and must,* be in part the creation of his own mind. . . . In this loose-textured history, men's choices of action being choices among thoughts which spring indeterminately in their minds, we can deem them to *initiate* trains of events in some real sense."[20]

In an earlier era, much criticism of the role of the rationality postulate in economic theory focused on the place of apparently nonrational behavior, behavior arising out of impetuous impulse or out of unthinking habit.[21] It is simply unrealistic, these criticisms ran, to assume that economic activity represents the exclusive result of deliberation. Man acts all too often without careful deliberation; he does not weigh the costs and benefits of his actions. This is not the place to evaluate these criticisms or deal with the debates that they engendered three-quarters of a century ago and more. But it is perhaps important to point out that limits of rationality discussed in this section have little to do with the arguments based on impulsiveness and on habit bondage. It is not at all being argued here that human action involves the *thoughtless* selection of goals. Human decision making may of course involve the most agonizingly careful appraisal of alternative courses of action to choose that which seems likely to offer the most estimable of outcomes. In emphasizing that the rationality postulate is unable to explain the selection of the relevant ends-means framework, we are not suggesting that that selection occurs without deliberation, but merely that the results of that deliberation cannot be predicted on the basis of the postulate of consistency; that deliberation is essentially creative. One may predict the answer that a competent mathematician will arrive at when he tackles a given problem in computation (in the same way that one may know in advance the answer to that problem that will be yielded by an electronic computer); but one cannot, in the same way, predict which computational problem the mathematician will deliberately choose to tackle (as one may not be able to predict which problems will be selected to be fed into the electronic computer).

The matter may be presented in an alternative version. One may always distinguish, within each human decision an element into which thought enters in self-aware fashion from an element into which thought enters without self-awareness. A man desires a specific goal with great eagerness; but deliberation persuades him, let us imagine, that it is in his interest not to reveal that eagerness to others (say, because others might then spitefully wish to deny that goal to him). The studied nonchalance with which he masks his pursuit of the goal exhibits scope for both elements: (1) his apparent nonchalance is indeed deliberate and studied, he knows precisely the reason why it is important that he pretend disinterest; but (2) he may not be at all self-aware as to how he arrived at this judgment to act on the assumption that others may spitefully seek to frustrate his achievement. He simply decides so to act. His decision is to refrain from naively pursuing with evident eagerness that which he eagerly desires; but his decision is yet naive in the sense that he has not, for example, sought (as reasons having to do with long-term strategy might well suggest) to ostentatiously pretend unawareness of the spitefulness of the others. No matter how calculative a man's behavior may be, it seems impossible to avoid having accepted, without calculation, some framework within which to self-consciously engage in cost-benefit comparisons. A man decides to display behavior *a*. We may call the mental activity of making that decision, activity *b*. Now the man *may* have decided (in the course of decision-making activity *c*) to engage in decision-making activity *b* (or he may have simply and impulsively engaged in decision-making activity *b*). But even if engaging in decision-making activity *b* (as a result of which behavior *a* was chosen) was itself the outcome of "higher" decisions, at some level our decision maker's highest decision was made quite unselfconsciously.

This extra-Robbinsian aspect of human action, the aspect which involves the creative, unpredictable selection of the ends-means framework, can also be usefully stated in terms of *knowledge*. Given his knowledge of the relevant ends-means framework, man's decision can be predicted without doubt; it is simply a matter of computation. To the extent, however, that man must "decide" what it is, so to speak, that he knows, and that this determination is not, in general, based ineluctably on other knowledge unambiguously possessed, man's behavior is not at all predictable. What a man believes himself to know is not itself the result of a calculative decision.[22] This expression of the notion of the existence of limits to rationality will facilitate our insight into the important linkage that exists between these limits and the phenomenon of uncertainty.

In the absence of uncertainty it would be difficult to avoid the assumption that each individual does in fact already know the circumstances surrounding his decision. Without uncertainty, therefore, decision making would no longer call for any imaginative, creative determination of what the circumstances really are. Decision making would call merely for competent calculation. Its results could, in general, be predicted without doubt. Human judgment would have no scope. "With uncertainty absent, man's energies are devoted altogether to doing things; . . . in a world so built . . . it seems likely that . . . all organisms [would be] automata. . . ."[23] "If man knew the future, he would not have to choose and would not act. He would be like an automaton, reacting to stimuli without any will of its own."[24] Thus the extra-Robbinsian aspect of human action, the aspect responsible for rendering human action unpredictable and incompletely explainable in terms of rationality, arises from the inherent uncertainty of human predicament. If, then, one chooses to identify entrepreneurship with the function of making decisions in the face of an uncertain present or future environment, it certainly appears that Misesian human action does (while Robbinsian economizing does not) include an entrepreneurial element.

But before making up our minds on this point, we must consider that second element, mentioned at the end of the preceding section, that distinguishes Misesian human action from Robbinsian allocative decision making.

THE DISCOVERY OF ERROR

To draw attention to this element in human action I shall draw on an earlier paper in which I attempted to identify that which might represent "entrepreneurial profit" in successful individual action in a Crusoe context.[25] Entrepreneurial profit in the Crusoe context, it turned out, can be identified only where Crusoe discovers that he has up until now attached an erroneously low valuation to resources over which he has command. Until today Crusoe has been spending his time catching fish with his bare hands. Today he has realized that he can use his time far more valuably by building a boat or making a net. "He has discovered that he had placed an incorrectly low value on his time. His reallocation of his labor time from fishing to boat-building is an entrepreneurial decision and, assuming his decision to be a correct one, yields pure profit in the form of additional value discovered to be forthcoming from the labor time applied."[26] This (Crusonian) pure profit arises from the circumstance that at the instant of entrepreneurial discovery Menger's law is violated. Menger's law teaches that men value goods according to the value of the satisfactions that depend on possession of those goods. This law arises from man's propensity to attach the value of ends to the means needed for their achievement. At the moment of entrepreneurial discovery Crusoe realizes that the ends achievable with his labor time have higher value than the ends he had previously sought to achieve:

> The value Crusoe has until now attached to his time is *less* than the value of the ends he now seeks. This discrepancy is, at the level of the individual, pure profit. . . . Once the old ends-means framework has been completely and unquestionably replaced by the new one, of course, it is the value of the new ends that Crusoe comes to attach to his means. . . . But, during the instant of an entrepreneurial leap of faith . . . there is scope for the discovery that, indeed, the ends achieved are more valuable than had hitherto been suspected. *This,* is the discovery of pure (Crusonian) entrepreneurial profit.[27]

Scope for entrepreneurship thus appears to be grounded in the possibility of discovering error. In the market context, the state of general equilibrium, providing as it does absolutely no scope for the discovery of profitable discrepancies between prices and costs, affords no opportunity for entrepreneurial discovery and turns out to be populated entirely by Robbinsian maximizers. In the same way, it now appears, the situation in which Crusoe is errorlessly allocating his resources—with the value of ends being fully and faultlessly attached to the relevant means in strict accordance with Menger's law—affords no scope for the entrepreneurial element in human action. Human action, without scope for the discovery of error, collapses into Robbinsian allocative activity.

Clearly this way of identifying the entrepreneurial element that is present in Misesian human action but absent in Robbinsian economizing activity fits in well with the approach that defines entrepreneurship as alertness to hitherto unperceived opportunities.[28] In the market context entrepreneurship is evoked by the presence of as yet unexploited opportunities for pure profit. These opportunities are evidence of the failure of market participants, up until now, to correctly assess the realities of the market situation. At the level of the individual too, it is then attractive to argue, an entrepreneurial element in action is evoked by the existence of as-yet-unexploited private opportunities. To act entrepreneurially is to identify situations overlooked until now because of error.

UNCERTAINTY AND/OR DISCOVERY

Our discussion has led us to identify two apparently distinct elements in human action, each of which possesses plausible claims as constituting that entrepreneurial element in action that sets it apart from purely calculative economizing activity: (1) On the one hand we saw that it appears plausible to associate entrepreneurship with the department within human action in which the very framework for calculative economizing activity is, in an open-ended, uncertain world, selected as being relevant. It is here that we would find scope for the unpredictable, the creative, the imaginative expressions of the human mind—expressions that cannot themselves be explained in terms of the postulate of consistency. Thus entrepreneurship, at the Crusoe level, arises uniquely and peculiarly from the circumstance that, as a result of the inescapable uncertainty of the human predicament, acting man cannot be assumed to be sure of the framework relevant for calculative activity. He must, using whatever entrepreneurial gifts he can display, *choose* a framework. (2) On the other hand, as we have seen, it appears perhaps equally plausible to associate entrepreneurship with that aspect of human action in which the alert individual realizes the existence of opportunities that he has up until now somehow failed to notice. Scope for entrepreneurship, at the Crusoe level, arises then not from the present uncertainty that must now be grappled with in decision making but from earlier error from which entrepreneurial discovery must now provide protection.

We must emphasize that these alternative identifications of the entrepreneurial element in action do appear, at least on a first scrutiny, to be genuinely different from one another. It is of course true that past error (from which, on the one view, we look to entrepreneurial discovery to provide a rescue) may be attributed to the pervasive uncertainty that characterizes our world (and to the inevitably kaleidic changes responsible for that uncertainty). But to discover hitherto unnoticed opportunities (unnoticed because of past failure to pierce correctly the fog of uncertainty) does not at all seem to be the same task as that of selecting between alternative present scenarios for the future within which calculative activity is to be undertaken. Moreover, whatever the possible reasons for past error, error itself implies merely ignorance, not necessarily uncertainty.[29] To escape ignorance is one thing; to deal with uncertainty is another.

This tension that we have discovered at the level of human action in the Crusoe context, between present uncertainty and earlier error as sources of entrepreneurship, is clearly to be linked immediately with our more general exploration in this chapter. This chapter is concerned with determining the extent to which the Misesian entrepreneur is to be perceived as the creature of uncertainty. The tension we have now discovered between present uncertainty and earlier error corresponds exactly to the disagreement that we encountered between those who see the Misesian entrepreneur as essentially the bearer of market uncertainty and those who see him as the discoverer of earlier market errors. It is my contention that our awareness of this apparent tension can in fact shed light on certain subtleties in the concept of entrepreneurship likely otherwise to be overlooked. Our procedure to develop this claim will be as follows: We will seek to show that, on a deeper understanding of the meaning of uncertainty and of the discovery of error at the level of individual action, the tension between them dissolves in a way that will reveal the full significance of entrepreneurial alertness at the level of the individual. Thereafter we will pursue the analogy between the scope of entrepreneurship at the individual level and that of the entrepreneurship at the level of the market, drawing on this analogy to identify precisely the relative roles, in market entrepreneurship, of uncertainty and of alertness.

ACTION AND ALERTNESS

Man acts, in the light of the future as he envisages it, to enhance his position in that future. The realized consequences of man's actions, however, flow from the impact of those actions on the actual (as contrasted with the envisaged) course of future events. The extent to which man's plans for the enhancement of his future prospects are fulfilled depends on the extent to which the future as he has envisaged it corresponds to the future as it in fact occurs. There is no natural set of forces or constraints assuring correspondence between the envisaged future and the realized future. The two may, it seems at first glance, diverge from one another with complete freedom. The future course of events is in general certainly not constrained by past forecasts; nor, unfortunately, are forecasts constrained by the actual future events these forecasts seek to foretell. On the face of it, then, with nothing to guarantee correspondence between the actual future and the future as it is envisaged, it might seem as if successful action were entirely a matter of good fortune. Indeed, if man is aware of this apparent lack of ability to envisage the future correctly except as a matter of sheer good fortune, it is not clear why (apart from the joys of gambling itself) man bothers to act at all. But of course the overwhelming fact of human history is that man does act, and his choices are made in terms of an envisaged future that, although by no means a photographic image of the future as it will actually unfold, is yet not entirely without moorings in regard to that realized future. "To be genuine, choice must be neither random nor predetermined. There must be some grounds for choosing, but they must be inadequate; there must be some possibility of predicting the consequences of choice, but none of perfect prediction."[30] "The essence of the situation is action according to *opinion*, . . . neither entire ignorance nor complete and perfect information, but partial knowledge."[31] The genuine choices that do, we are convinced, make up human history express man's conviction that the future as he envisages it does hold correspondence, in some degree, to the future as it will in fact unfold. The uncertainty of the future reflects man's awareness that this correspondence is far from complete; the fact that he acts and chooses at all reflects his conviction that this correspondence is far from negligible. Whence does this correspondence, incomplete though it may be, arise? If there are no constraints assuring correspondence, how is successful action anything but the sheerest good fortune?

The answer to this dilemma surely lies in the circumstance that man is *motivated* to formulate the future as he envisages it, as accurately as possible. It is not a matter of two unfolding tapestries, one the realized future, the second a fantasized series of pictures of what the first might look like. Rather, acting man really does try to construct his picture of the future to correspond to the truth as it will be realized. He really does try to glimpse the future, to peer through the fog. He is thus motivated *to bring about* correspondence between the envisaged and the realized futures. Man's purposeful efforts to better his condition are responsible not only for his choices as constructed against a given envisaged future; that purposefulness is, perhaps even more importantly, responsible for the remarkable circumstance that that envisaged future does overlap significantly with the future as it actually unfolds. (Of course, these forecasts need not be made, explicitly, prior to action; they are embedded, possibly without self-awareness, in action itself.) We call this motivated propensity of man to formulate an image of the future man's *alertness*. Were man totally lacking in alertness, he could not act at all: his blindness to the future would rob him of any framework for action. (In fact, were man totally lacking in potential for alertness, it would be difficult to identify a notion of error altogether: were unalert man to act, it would not be on the basis of an erroneously forecast future. It would be on the basis of no relevant forecast at all. Not recognizing that he might—had he been more alert—have avoided the incorrect picture of the future, he could not in any meaningful sense blame himself for having erred.)

It will surely be acknowledged that this alertness—which provides the only pressure to constrain man's envisaged future toward some correspondence with the future to be realized—is what we are searching for under the phrase "the entrepreneurial element in human action." Robbinsian allocation activity contains no such element, because within the assigned scope of such defined activity no possible divergence between a future as envisaged and a future to be realized is considered. What is incomplete in the notion of purely allocative activity is surely to be found precisely in this abstraction from the desperately important element of entrepreneurship in human action.

It should be observed that the entrepreneurial alertness we have identified does not consist merely in "seeing" the unfolding of the tapestry
of the future in the sense of seeing a preordained flow of events. Alertness must, importantly, embrace the awareness of the ways in which the
human agent can, by imaginative, bold leaps of faith, and determination,
in fact *create* the future for which his present acts are designed. As we
shall argue in a subsequent section, this latter expression of entrepreneurial alertness does not affect its essential formal character—which
remains that of assuring a tendency for the future context envisaged as
following present action to bear some realistic resemblance to the future
as it will be realized.

We must notice, in understanding this entrepreneurial element in
human action, two aspects of it: (1) We note what provides the scope for
entrepreneurship. This scope is provided by the complete freedom with
which the future as envisaged might, without entrepreneurial alertness,
diverge from the future as it will in fact be. Entrepreneurial alertness has a
function to perform. (2) We note what provides the incentive that switches
on entrepreneurial alertness. This incentive is provided by the lure of pure
entrepreneurial profit to be grasped in stepping from a less accurately
envisaged future to a more accurately envisaged one. Each step taken in
moving toward a vision of the future that overlaps more significantly with
the truth is not merely a step toward truth (that is, a positive entrepreneurial success); it is also a profitable step (that is, a step that enhances the
value of the resources with which action is available to be taken).

Viewed from this perspective, the tension between the uncertainty-
environment in which action occurs, on the one hand, and the
discovery-of-error aspect of action, on the other, can be seen to dis-
solve at a glance. These two aspects of action can be seen immediately
as merely two sides of the same entrepreneurial coin. If uncertainty
were merely an unpleasant condition of life to which man must pas-
sively adjust, then it would be reasonable to distinguish between the
quite separate activities of bearing uncertainty on the one hand and
of discovering error on the other. Escaping from current errors is one
thing; grappling with the uncertainty of the future is another. But,
as we have noticed, to choose means to *endeavor,* under the incentive
to grasp pure profit, to identify a more truthful picture of the future.
Dealing with uncertainty is motivated by the profit to be won by avoiding error. In this way of viewing the matter the distinction between

escaping current error and avoiding potential future error is unimportant. The discovery of error is an interesting feature of action because it offers incentive. It is this incentive that inspires the effort to pierce the fog of uncertainty that shrouds the future. To deal with uncertainty means to seek to overcome it by more accurate prescience; to discover error is merely that aspect of this endeavor that endows it with incentive attraction. The imagination and creativity with which man limns his envisaged future are inspired by the pure gains to be won in ensuring that that envisaged future is in fact no less bright than that which can be made the truth.

We shall find in the next section that these insights surrounding entrepreneurship at the level of individual action have their exact counterparts in entrepreneurship in the market context. It will be useful to summarize briefly the key points we have learned about individual entrepreneurship:

1. Entrepreneurship in individual action consists in the endeavor to secure greater correspondence between the individual's future as he envisages it and his future as it will in fact unfold. This endeavor consists in the individual's alertness to whatever can provide clues to the future. This alertness, broadly conceived, embraces those aspects of imagination and creativity through which the individual may himself *ensure* that his envisaged future will be realized.

2. Scope for entrepreneurship is provided by the uncertainty of the future. For our purposes uncertainty means that, in the absence of entrepreneurial alertness, an individual's view of the future may diverge with total freedom from the realized future. In the absence of entrepreneurial alertness it is only sheer chance that can be responsible for successful action.

3. Incentive for the "switching on" of entrepreneurial alertness is provided by the pure gain (or avoidance of loss) to be derived from replacing action based on less accurate prescience by action based on the more realistically envisaged future. The avoidance of entrepreneurial error is not merely a matter of being more truthful, it happens also to be profitable.

ENTREPRENEURSHIP IN THE MARKET

Our examination of the entrepreneurial element in individual action permits us to see the role of entrepreneurship in the market in a fresh light. We shall discover, in the market context, elements that correspond precisely to their analogues in the individual context. Let us consider what happens in markets.

In a market exchanges occur between market participants.[32] In the absence of perfect mutual knowledge, many of the exchanges are inconsistent with one another. Some sales are made at low prices when some buyers are buying at high prices. Some market participants are not buying at all because they are unaware of the possibility of buying at prices low enough to be attractive; some are refraining from selling because they are unaware of the possibility of selling at prices high enough to be attractive. Clearly the actions of these buyers and sellers are, from the perspective of omniscience, uncoordinated and inconsistent. We notice that, although the assumption of perfect knowledge that is necessary for market equilibrium would constrain different transactions in the market to complete mutual consistency, the actuality of imperfect knowledge permits these different transactions in different parts of the market to diverge with apparently complete freedom. What alone tends to introduce a modicum of consistency and coordination into this picture, preventing a situation in which even the slightest degree of coordination could exist only as a matter of sheerest chance, is market entrepreneurship, inspired by the lure of pure market profit. We are now in a position to identify, in the market context, elements that correspond to key features already identified in the context of individual entrepreneurship.

Corresponding to uncertainty as it impinges on individual action, we have market discoordination. The freedom with which an individual's envisaged future may diverge from the future to be realized, corresponds precisely to the freedom with which transactions made in one part of the market may diverge from transactions made elsewhere. In the absence of entrepreneurship it is only out of the purest chance that market transactions by different pairs of buyers and sellers are made on anything but the most wildly inconsistent terms. There is nothing that constrains the mutually satisfactory price bargain reached between one pair of traders to bear any specific relation to corresponding bargains reached between other pairs of traders.

Corresponding to error at the level of the individual, we have price divergence at the level of the market. Perfect knowledge (such as in Robbinsian individual allocative activity) precludes error. Market equilibrium (implied by universal perfect knowledge) precludes price divergences.

The individual entrepreneurial element permits the individual to escape from the distressing freedom with which divergences between envisaged futures and realized futures may occur; the entrepreneur fulfills the same function for the market. The function of the entrepreneur is to bring different parts of the market into coordination with each other. The market entrepreneur bridges the gaps in mutual knowledge, gaps that would otherwise permit prices to diverge with complete freedom.

Corresponding to the incentive for individual entrepreneurship provided by more realistic views of the future, we have, at the market level, the incentive provided by opportunities for pure entrepreneurial profit. Market profit consists in the gap between prices generated by error and market inconsistency—just as the source for private gain is to be discovered in a present divergence between the imagined and the actual future.

The following are propositions, in the context of the market, that concern entrepreneurship; they correspond precisely to those stated at the conclusion of the preceding section:[33]

1.° Entrepreneurship in the market consists in the function of securing greater consistency between different parts of the market. It expresses itself in entrepreneurial alertness to what transactions are in fact available in different parts of the market. It is only such alertness that is responsible for any tendency toward keeping these transactions in some kind of mutual consistency.

2.° Scope for market entrepreneurship is provided by the imperfect knowledge that permits market transactions to diverge from what would be a mutually inconsistent pattern.

3.° Incentive for market entrepreneurial activity is provided by the pure gain to be won by noticing existing divergences between the prices at which market transactions are available in different parts of the market. It is the lure of market profits that inspires entrepreneurial alertness.

TIME, UNCERTAINTY, AND ENTREPRENEURSHIP

Our analogy between entrepreneurship at the level of the individual and entrepreneurship in the market emphasized only the most salient respects of the analogy. Certain additional features of the entrepreneurial function in the market need to be dealt with more extensively. In the individual context the divergence (which it is the function of entrepreneurship to limit) was a divergence between anticipated and realized future.

Its source in uncertainty was immediately apparent. In the market context the divergence (which it is the function of entrepreneurship to limit) was a divergence between the transactions in different parts of the market. Its source was stated in terms of imperfect mutual knowledge among market participants. Its relationship to uncertainty was not asserted. This requires both amplification and modification.

Our statements concerning market entrepreneurship were couched in terms of the market for a single commodity within a single period. It should be clear that nothing essential is lost when our picture of the market is expanded to include many commodities and, in particular, the passage of time. This should of course not be understood to mean that the introduction of the passage of time does not open up scope for additional insights. We merely argue that the insights we have gained in the single-period context for entrepreneurship are not to be lost sight of in the far more complex multiperiod case.

When we introduce the passage of time, the dimensions along which mutual ignorance may develop are multiplied. Market participants in one part of today's market not only may be imperfectly aware of the transactions available in another part of that market; they also may be imperfectly aware of the transactions that will be available in next year's market. Absence of consistency between different parts of today's market is seen as a special case of a more general notion of inconsistency that includes also inconsistency between today's transactions and those to be transacted next year. A low price today may be in this sense inconsistent with the high prices that will prevail next year. Scope for market entrepreneurship, in the context of the passage of time, arises then from the need to coordinate markets also across time. Incentive for market entrepreneurship along the intertemporal dimension is provided not by arbitrage profits generated by imperfectly coordinated present markets but, more generally, by the speculative profits generated by the as yet imperfectly coordinated market situations in the sequence of time. And, of course, the introduction of entrepreneurial activity to coordinate markets through time introduces, for individual entrepreneurs engaged in market entrepreneurship, precisely the considerations concerning the uncertain future that we have, until now, considered only in the context of the isolated individual.

It is because of this last circumstance that we must acknowledge that the introduction of the passage of time, although leaving the overall formal function of market entrepreneurship unchanged, will of course introduce substantial modification into the way we must imagine entrepreneurship to be exercised concretely. It is still the case, as noted, that the entrepreneurial function is that of bringing about a tendency for transactions in different parts of the market (conceived broadly now as including transactions entered into at different times) to be made in greater mutual consistency. But whereas in the case of entrepreneurship in the single-period market (that is, the case of the entrepreneur as arbitrageur) entrepreneurial alertness meant alertness to present facts, in the case of multiperiod entrepreneurship alertness must mean alertness to the future. It follows that market entrepreneurship in the multiperiod case introduces uncertainty as facing the entrepreneur not only as in the analogy offered in the preceding section—where the market analogue for uncertainty turned out to be the freedom with which transactions in different parts of today's market may unconstrainedly diverge from being mutually consistent—but also as in the simple sense of the entrepreneur's awareness of the freedom with which his own envisaged future (concerning future market transactions) may diverge from the realized future. In particular the futurity that entrepreneurship must confront introduces the possibility that the entrepreneur may, by his own creative actions, in fact *construct* the future as *he* wishes it to be. In the single-period case alertness can at best discover hitherto overlooked current facts. In the multiperiod case entrepreneurial alertness must include the entrepreneur's perception of the way in which creative and imaginative action may vitally shape the kind of transactions that will be entered into in future market periods.

Thus the exercise of entrepreneurial alertness in the multiperiod market context will indeed call for personal and psychological qualifications that were unneeded in the single-period case. To be a successful entrepreneur one must now possess those qualities of vision, boldness, determination, and creativity that we associated earlier with the entrepreneurial element in isolated individual action with respect to an uncertain future. There can be no doubt that in the concrete fulfillment of the entrepreneurial function these psychological and personal qualities are of paramount importance. It is in this sense that so many writers are undoubtedly correct in linking entrepreneurship with the courage and vision necessary to *create* the future in an uncertain world (rather than with merely seeing that which stares one in the face).

However, the function of market entrepreneurship in the multi-period context is nonetheless still that spelled out in the preceding section. What market entrepreneurship accomplishes is a tendency for transactions in different parts of the market (including the market at different dates) to become coordinated. The incentive that inspires this entrepreneurial coordination is the lure of pure profit—the difference in market values resulting from hitherto less complete coordination. These insights remain true for the multiperiod case no less than for the arbitrage case. For some purposes it is no doubt important to draw attention to the concrete psychological requirements on which successful entrepreneurial decision making depends. But for other purposes such emphasis is not required; in fact such emphasis may divert attention from what is, from the perspective of the overall functioning of the market system, surely the essential feature of entrepreneurship: its market-coordinative properties.

Let us recall that at the level of the individual, entrepreneurship involved not merely the bearing of uncertainty but also the overcoming of uncertainty. Uncertainty is responsible for what would, in the absence of entrepreneurship, be a failure to perceive the future in a manner sufficiently realistic to permit action. Entrepreneurship, so to speak, pushes aside to some extent the swirling fogs of uncertainty, permitting meaningful action. It is this function of entrepreneurship that must be kept in view when we study the market process. The uncertainty that characterizes the environment within which market entrepreneurship plays its coordinative role must be fully recognized; without it there would be no need and no scope for entrepreneurship. But an understanding of what entrepreneurship accomplishes requires us to recognize not so much the extent to which uncertainty is the ineradicable feature of human existence but rather the extent to which both individual action and social coordination through the market can occur significantly despite the uncertainty of the future (and in spite also of the uncertainty-analogue that would, in the absence of the arbitrageur, fog up even the single-period market).

FURTHER REFLECTIONS ON UNCERTAINTY AND ALERTNESS

Thus we can see how those writers who have denied that the pure entrepreneurial role involves the bearing of uncertainty were both correct and yet at least partly irrelevant. Both J. A. Schumpeter[34] and J. B. Clark insisted that only the capitalist bears the hazards of business; the pure entrepreneur has, by definition, nothing to lose.[35] No doubt all this is true, as far as it goes, But what is important about linking the entrepreneur with the phenomenon of uncertainty is not that it is the entrepreneur who accepts the disutilities associated with the assumption of the hazards of business in an uncertain world. What is important is that the entrepreneur, motivated by the lure of pure profits, attempts to pierce through these uncertainties and endeavors to see the truth that will permit profitable action on his part.

A number of economists may be altogether unwilling to accept the notion of alertness with respect to uncertain future. In fact many may wish to reject the very formulation we have employed to schematize the uncertainty of the future. For us uncertainty meant the essential freedom with which the envisaged future may diverge from the realized future. Entrepreneurial alertness means the ability to impose constraints on that freedom, so that the entrepreneur's vision of the future may indeed overlap, to some significant extent, with that future that he is attempting to see. But many will be unwilling to treat the future as something to be seen at all. "The present is uniquely determined. It can be seen by the eye-witness.... What is the future but the void? To call it the future is to concede the presumption that it is already 'existent' and merely waiting to appear. If that is so, if the world is determinist, then it seems idle to speak of choice."[36] Similarly many are unwilling to see the entrepreneur as "alert to opportunities" if this terminology implies that future opportunities already "exist" and are merely waiting to be grasped, "Entrepreneurial projects are not waiting to be sought out so much as to be thought up."[37]

What perhaps needs to be emphasized once again is that in using phrases such as "grasping future opportunities," "seeing the future correctly or incorrectly," or the "divergence between the envisaged future and the realized future," we do not wish to imply any determinacy regarding the future. No doubt, to say that one sees the future (with greater or lesser accuracy) is to employ a metaphor. No doubt the future that one "sees" is a future that may in fact be constructed significantly by one's action, which is supposed to be informed by that very vision. But surely these metaphors are useful and instructive. To dream realistically in a way that inspires successful, creative action is to "see correctly" as compared to the fantasies that inspire absurd ventures or the cold water poured by the unduly timid pessimist that stunts all efforts at improvement. "The future," we have learned, "is unknowable, though not unimaginable."[38] To acknowledge the unknowability of the future is to acknowledge the essential indeterminacy and uncertainty surrounding human existence. But surely in doing so we need not consign human existence to wholly uncoordinated chaos. To speak of entrepreneurial vision is to draw attention, by use of metaphor, to the formidable and benign coordinative powers of the human imagination. Austrian economists have, in principled fashion, refused to see the world as wholly knowable, as suited to interpretation by models of equilibrium from which uncertainty has been exhausted. It would be most unfortunate if, in pursuing this refusal, economists were to fall into a no-less-serious kind of error. This error would be the failure to understand how entrepreneurial individual action, and the systematic market forces set in motion by freedom for entrepreneurial discovery and innovation, harness the human imagination to achieve no less a result than the liberation of mankind from the chaos of complete mutual ignorance. Mises's concept of human action and his analysis of the role of entrepreneurial market processes surely remain, in this regard, unique and as yet insufficiently appreciated contributions to the profound understanding of human society.

NOTES

1. L. von Mises, *Human Action* (New Haven: Yale University Press, 1949), p. 253.

2. Ibid., p. 288.

3. Ibid., p. 255.

4. Ibid., p. 254.

5. Ibid., p. 105.

6. I. M. Kirzner, *Competition and Entrepreneurship* (Chicago: University of Chicago Press, 1973), pp. 86–87.

7. Ibid., chap. 2. See also I. M. Kirzner, *Perception, Opportunity, and Profit* (Chicago: University of Chicago Press, 1979), chap. 10.

8. F. A. Hayek, *Individualism and Economic Order* (London: Routledege and Kegan Paul, 1949), p. 42.

9. Kirzner, *Competition and Entrepreneurship*, pp. 86–87. (Italics in original.)

10. Such activity was subsumed under arbitrage by pointing out the formal similarity between (1) buying and selling in different markets today and (2) buying and selling in different markets at different dates. (See Kirzner, *Competition and Entrepreneurship*, pp. 85–86.)

11. Henry Hazlitt, review of *Competition and Entrepreneurship*, in *Freeman* (December 1974): 759. Similar concerns seem to be expressed in a review of *Competition and Entrepreneurship* by Percy L. Greaves, Jr. in *Wertfrei* (Spring 1974): especially pp. 18–19.

12. See unpublished paper by Murray N. Rothbard, "Professor Hébert on Entrepreneurship," pp. 1–2. Reprinted with permission.

13. Ibid., p. 7.

14. L. H. White, "Entrepreneurship, Imagination, and the Question of Equilibrium," unpublished paper (1976). See also L. H. White, "Entrepreneurial Price Adjustment" (Paper presented at Southern Economic Association meetings Washington, D.C., November, 1978), p. 36, n. 3.

15. J. High, review article on *Perception, Opportunity and Profit* in *Austrian Economics Newsletter* (Spring 1980): 14.

16. High's criticisms of my references to uncertainty as a characteristic of the entrepreneurial environment focus most specifically on what he believes to be my use of uncertainty to "serve as the distinguishing characteristic between entrepreneurship and luck" (ibid.). Here there seems to be a definite misunderstanding of my position. So far from the presence of the uncertainty surrounding entrepreneurship being what separates entrepreneurial profit from the lucky windfall, almost the exact reverse is the case. What marks entrepreneurial profit as different from the lucky windfall is that the former was, despite the (inevitable) uncertainty that might have discouraged the entrepreneur, in fact deliberately pursued. Where luck confers gain may well reflect the circumstance that the uncertainty of this gain deterred the actor from even dreaming of winning it. High's reading apparently resulted from his understanding a passage that he cites (from Kirzner, *Perception, Opportunity and Profit*, pp. 159–160) to represent the case of a purely lucky gain. In fact the passage cited does not refer to luck at all. If one knows that one's labor can convert low-valued leisure into high-valued apples, the apples one so gains through one's hard work do not constitute a lucky windfall. The point of the cited passages is that Menger's law shows how there is no value gain at all derived from that labor, since one would already have attached the higher value of the ends to the available means. Our discussion in this chapter, however, proceeds on the assumption that High's unhappiness at my treatment of uncertainty in entrepreneurship does not rest solely on the validity of the way in which I distinguish entrepreneurial profits from windfall gains.

17. Mises, *Human Action*, p. 253.

18. See Kirzner, *Competition and Entrepreneurship*, pp. 32–35. See also Kirzner, *Perception, Opportunity and Profit*, pp. 166–168.

19. G. L. S. Shackle, *Epistemics and Economics* (Cambridge: Cambridge University Press, 1972), p. 136. (Italics in original.)

20. Ibid., p. 351.

21. See also Kirzner, *The Economic Point of View* (Princeton: Van Nostrand, 1960), p. 167.

22. See also Kirzner, *Perception, Opportunity and Profit*, chap. 9.

23. F. H. Knight, *Risk, Uncertainty and Profit* (New York: Houghton Mifflin, 1921), p. 268.

24. Mises, *Human Action*, p. 105.

25. See Kirzner, *Perception, Opportunity and Profit*, chap. 10, especially pp. 158–164.

26. Ibid., p. 162.

27. Ibid., p. 163.

28. See, for example, Kirzner, *Competition and Entrepreneurship*, p. 39.

29. See note 15 of this chapter.

30. B. J. Loasby, *Choice, Complexity and Ignorance* (Cambridge: Cambridge University Press, 1976), p. 5.

31. Knight, *Risk, Uncertainty and Profit*, p. 199.

32. Our discussion proceeds in terms of the market for a single commodity. It could be couched, without altering the essentials in any respect, in more general terms. See also the subsequent section of this chapter.

33. The three pairs of statements may be viewed as additions to the two lists of twelve statements developing the analogy between the individual and the market, provided in Kirzner, *Perception, Opportunity and Profit*, chap. 10, pp. 170–172, 173–175.

34. J. A. Schumpeter, *The Theory of Economic Development* (Cambridge, Mass.: Harvard University Press, 1934), p. 137; J. A. Schumpeter, *History of Economic Analysis* (Oxford: Oxford University Press, 1954), p. 556. See also S. M. Kanbur, "A Note on Risk Taking, Entrepreneurship and Schumpeter," *History of Political Economy* 12 (Winter 1980): 489–498.

35. J. B. Clark, "Insurance and Business Profit," *Quarterly Journal of Economics* 7 (October 1892): 46 (cited in Knight, *Risk, Uncertainty and Profit*, p. 38).

36. Shackle, *Epistemics and Economics*, p. 122.

37. White, "Entrepreneurship, Imagination," p. 7.

38. L. M. Lachmann, "From Mises to Shackle: An Essay," *Journal of Economic Literature* 14 (March 1976): 59.

MISES AND HIS UNDERSTANDING
OF THE CAPITALIST SYSTEM

To someone not familiar with Mises's understanding of the market, there would, on the surface of Mises's exposition, appear to be a puzzling tension in that exposition—a tension having to do with some very basic elements of Mises's position. We shall find that the resolution of this tension is, once it has been explained, fairly obvious, but we shall also find that a careful consideration of this resolution can help us more fully appreciate the uniqueness (and the intellectual integrity) of Mises's understanding of the capitalist system.

A TENSION WITHIN MISES'S ECONOMICS?

The apparent tension in Mises to which we refer relates to the nature and significance of the market prices for inputs and outputs which emerge at each moment in the real world. These actual market prices are described by Mises as reflecting an "equilibrium of demand and supply"; they actually equalize "the size of the demand" with "the size of supply"; in the "unhampered market," any "deviation of a market price from the height at which supply and demand are equal is"—apparently instantaneously—"self-liquidating" (Mises, 1966, p. 762). It is on this basis that Mises pronounces any government interference with market prices of commodities, of resource services (including wage rates), (i.e. any requirement that a price at a given date be different from the value which the unhampered market would have generated for that date) as disturbing the "equilibrium of demand and supply" (ibid.), and therefore, in general, as producing results which are (from the perspective of the government itself) worse, not better, than the conditions which the government wished to improve.

Professor Salerno has interpreted this Misesian position to mean that all market prices are "market-clearing prices" (Salerno, 1993, p. 121); he has interpreted this position as asserting that "the constellation of resource prices that emerges on a market unhampered

From Israel M. Kirzner, *The Driving Force of the Market: Essays in Austrian Economics* (New York and London: Routledge, 2000), 165–79; the original source is *Cato Journal* 19, 2 (1999). Reprinted by permission.

by legal restrictions *always* reflects the circumstance that existing resources are devoted to their most valuable uses as determined by entrepreneurial appraisements of future output prices" (ibid.). The impression conveyed here is that actual market prices are, in the relevant sense, the "correct" prices, the prices that ensure that resources are channelled to their most valuable uses. Interference with these prices necessarily obstructs the efficiency with which the market allocates resources.

And yet, on the other hand, Mises is clearly entirely aware that the market prices at any given date are almost certainly not the "correct" prices. In Salerno's words, market prices are, as a consequence of the unavoidable errors of entrepreneurial judgment under uncertainty, "also disequilibrium prices" (ibid.). In Mises's own words, the market prices at any given date are, in contrast to the imaginary prices that would characterize the imaginary "final state of rest" (Mises, 1966, p. 245), seen as "*false* prices" (ibid., p. 338; emphasis in original). It is the market *process* during which the competition of profit-seeking entrepreneurs modifies these false prices, tending to ensure that they be replaced by prices more closely and "truthfully" reflecting the underlying preferences of the consumers. What stimulates this process is the realization by entrepreneurs that the existing market-generated pattern of resource allocation is *not* the ideal one. There is, in fact, "a discrepancy between what is done and what could be done" (ibid., p. 336).

One can surely sympathize with the beginner-reader of Mises who finds himself puzzled by these statements which seem, when taken together, to claim that actual market prices are the correct, equilibrium, prices, but that they are also false, disequilibrium, prices; that the pattern of resource allocation actually achieved at any given date is optimal, but is, at the same time, not at all as efficient as it might be.

TENSION RESOLVED

A more mature student of the Misesian system is able to reassure such a puzzled beginner. There is no internal tension in Mises's exposition. What needs to be understood is the distinction between what Mises calls "the plain state of rest" (or simply "the state of rest") (Mises, 1966, pp. 244ff.) on the one hand, and what he calls the "final state of rest" (a state not identical with, but closely related to Mises's concept of the "evenly rotating economy"—the Misesian concept which is the closest to standard

Walrasian general equilibrium[1]), on the other. It is not our purpose here to elaborate on Mises's "final state of rest" or on his "evenly rotating economy." What we wish to do is to clarify key aspects of Mises's "plain state of rest." For students coming to Mises from a background in standard microeconomic theory, it is easy to misunderstand Mises's "plain state of rest." It is easy to misunderstand it, in particular, as corresponding to the mainstream short-run equilibrium state. This might lead the student to misunderstand Mises's statements concerning the "equilibrium of demand and supply," in a particular market, as corresponding to the conditions prevailing at the intersection of the Marshallian demand and supply curves. But this would be quite mistaken. The Marshallian intersection refers to a state of affairs in which all participants (and all potential participants) in a specific market have somehow become aware of that price which is capable of clearing the market, and have correctly anticipated that that price would indeed prevail in this market. A price that "clears the market" means, in this mainstream sense of the term, one which ensures that all those who might, were they to be informed as to this prevailing price, be prepared to sell (buy), are in fact so informed and are in fact able to find buyers (sellers) willing to accept their offers to sell (buy) at this prevailing price. Mises's "plain state of rest" does not entail any such assumptions concerning the state of information. This plain state of rest "comes to pass," in the real world, "again and again" (Mises, 1966, p. 244). "At any instant all those transactions take place which the parties are ready to enter into at the realizable price." "When the stock market closes, the brokers have carried out all orders which could be executed at the market price." Clearly, such a state of rest (which, as Mises emphasizes, "is not an imaginary construction," but a state achieved again and again in the real world) refers to the completion of transactions between only those who are aware of the existing situation. The "supply and demand" which are continually in equilibrium in Mises's world, do not refer to the supply and demand schedules so basic to mainstream microeconomic theory. They refer simply to the circumstance that, in any situation, those potential transactors who have been aware of available mutually beneficial trade possibilities, will all certainly have moved to take advantage of these opportunities; once these opportunities have been grasped, market activity of course ceases, the plain state of rest has been attained.

To describe the price emerging from these exchange transactions as a "market-clearing price" (Salerno, 1993, p. 121) is therefore misleading.

Certainly the price permits all those who stand to gain by exchanging at this price and who are aware of this—to exchange to the point where no known remaining mutually gainful opportunities exist. But the term "market-clearing price" (a term not used by Mises) is used in standard economics to refer to the exhaustion of all mutually gainful exchange opportunities under the hypothetical conditions of (relevant) omniscience. Standard economics indeed notoriously proceeds, in applying supply and demand theory to the real world, to operate as if conditions of relevant omniscience can be taken as given. Mises is certainly not making any such assumption of omniscience. His market prices are certainly not "market-clearing prices" (in the usual sense of that term). There is, one is able to reassure the puzzled reader, therefore no contradiction in his exposition. Real-world market prices are not the equilibrium prices of standard economic theory. (Real-world prices relate to equilibrium only in a very narrow sense, a sense to which no attention at all is given in standard theory.) Real-world prices are indeed likely to be "false" prices, setting off entrepreneurial-competitive activity modifying the pattern of resource allocation. The real-world pattern of resource allocation at any given moment can be described as optimal only relative to existing information in fact possessed by entrepreneurial market participants. The tension in Mises is quite imaginary; it is perceived—quite understandably and reasonably perceived—only as a result of reading Mises through the spectacles acquired in studying mainstream economics.

But this resolution of the puzzle should itself surely raise a different puzzle of its own. It would appear, if one accepts the above interpretation of Mises, that Mises's references to what is achieved every day in the market must, while certainly true, strike any economist as being merely *trivially* true. The optimality achieved every day in the market is optimality only within the extremely narrow framework relevant to real-world conditions. All those aware of the opportunities for mutually gainful exchange that are in fact available, take advantage of these perceived opportunities. To recognize this truth may be an achievement for someone who had not previously understood the significance (and mutual gainfulness) of inter-personal exchange. But this has little to do with the central insight which all economists share, concerning the effectiveness of markets in tending to stimulate the exhaustion of *all possible* opportunities for mutually gainful exchange. For this we must of course proceed, with Mises, to recognize that the market prices at any date are surely "false" prices, prices which generate entrepreneurial activity likely to cause those false prices to change. Certainly Mises clearly understood, and clearly expounded, the competitive entrepreneurial process that continually tends to replace "false" prices by more "truthful" prices. But, then, one can only ask, what is the point of emphasizing the apparently trivial Misesian insights concerning what is actually achieved every day in the "plain state of rest"?

The purpose of this chapter is to argue that, in emphasizing these apparently trivial insights, Mises revealed his unique understanding of what is achieved in the capitalist system. To appreciate this, it will be helpful to go back to the pioneering vision of the founder of the Austrian tradition, to Carl Menger. (It is perhaps worth while recalling that Mises, referring to his first reading, in 1903, of Carl Menger's *Grundsätze,* remarked that "it was the reading of this book that made an 'economist' of me" [Mises, 1978, p. 33].)

THE VISION OF CARL MENGER[2]

Menger is usually recognized as one of the three pioneers of marginal utility economics, offering economists a theory of subjective value. But, in regard to a subjective theory of value, the claims made on behalf of Menger's originality are somewhat clouded. As Professor Streissler has shown (Streissler, 1990), there were German economists of the early nineteenth century, with whose works Menger was unquestionably familiar, whose value theory had incorporated subjective insights long before Menger. Yet Menger certainly believed that his *Grundsätze* was breaking entirely new ground. (Hayek has told us that Menger "is said to have once remarked that he wrote the *Grundsätze* in a state of morbid excitement" [Hayek, 1934].)

What appears to have happened was that Menger glimpsed, at least, a grand perspective on the functioning of the entire market system which contrasted radically with the still dominant Ricardian way of seeing that system. For the Ricardian vision, the size and rate of growth of aggregate output, and the pattern of its distribution among the factor classes which produce it, are inexorably determined, at least in the long run, by objective, physical realities. In the explanation of such determination there is no place for any roles for human resourcefulness, human valuation, human expectations, human discoveries. Menger, on the other hand, glimpsed a way to understand economic history in diametrically opposite terms. For this view, the physical and biological realities recede into the background; it is the impact of the actions of human beings which alone actively determines the course of human events. It was this revolutionary new vision which, we suggest, was responsible for the "morbid excitement" with which Menger wrote his book. And this was a vision that had certainly not been shared by the early nineteenth-century German pioneers in the subjective theory of value, to whom Streissler has referred.

It was Menger, rather than any forerunners, who (already in his 1871 book) recognized how it is the consumer valuation of output which tends to be reflected in the market prices of the relevant inputs—which Menger identified as "higher order goods"—making Menger a pathbreaker in the development of neoclassical marginal productivity theory. It was this insight which drew the attention of the profession to the truth that the importance of the means needed to achieve specific ends is governed entirely by the importance attached to those ends. This is not merely an insight demolishing cost theories of value; it is an insight which introduces a new understanding of economic causality throughout the economic system. Every act of production, every market transaction, is set in motion and wholly governed by consumer preferences. Armed with this radical, and quintessentially "Austrian," vision of Menger, we may return to Mises and his understanding of the capitalist process.

MISES AND THE DOCTRINE OF CONSUMER SOVEREIGNTY

The concept of "consumer sovereignty" entered into economic terminology, it appears, largely as a result of the work of the late William H. Hutt.[3] This concept became central to Mises's understanding of the market economy. We shall argue that, in emphasizing this centrality, Mises was simply pursuing the Mengerian vision which we have briefly discussed in the preceding section.

In *Human Action,* one section of chapter 15 ("The Market") is entitled "The Sovereignty of the Consumers." In that section (a mere two pages, in a 900-page treatise) Mises presented, we believe, his own vision of the capitalist process. Mises explains that while entrepreneur-producers directly control production and "are at the helm and steer the ship," they are not supreme; the "captain is the consumer." "Neither the entrepreneurs nor the farmers nor the capitalists determine what has to be produced. The consumers do that" (Mises, 1966, p. 270). "A wealthy man can preserve his wealth only by continuing to serve the consumers in the most efficient way." So that "the owners of the material factors of production and the entrepreneurs are virtually mandatories or trustees of the consumers" (ibid., p. 271). Mises finds only one instance where the wishes of the consumers can be flouted. We shall, later in this chapter, pay a good deal of attention to this exception to the general rule of consumer sovereignty.

In *Human Action* not much further attention is paid to the idea of consumer sovereignty, but there can be no doubt as to its centrality for Mises's understanding of the market economy. This writer vividly recalls Mises's continually repeating, in his lectures and seminar presentations, the assertion that it is by his decisions to buy or refrain from buying, that the consumer controls the pattern of production. A glance at the index to a volume of Mises's more popular and shorter pieces (Mises, 1990) reveals how frequently the idea of "consumer sovereignty" shaped his thinking, especially in his later years.

Now there is no doubt that, in emphasizing the supremacy of consumers in the market economy, to popular audiences, Mises was often going beyond his role of positive scientist; he was often appealing to widely shared judgments of value. "A free-market economy," Mises was in effect explaining to his audiences, "caters precisely to the people whom you, my audience, wish to endow with power, viz. the consuming public." A society's resources, no matter by whom they are owned, are inevitably placed at the command of those whom Mises's audiences would wish to be placed in command. Mises was certainly entitled to draw normative conclusions from his economics (so long as he refrained from claiming scientific status for the judgments of value on the basis of which those conclusions are drawn). But in fact for Mises the doctrine of consumer sovereignty was much more fundamental and significant than its being a normative application of positive economics. The doctrine of consumer sovereignty was, in its own right, an important part of positive economics; it was a scientific theorem marking the completion of Menger's vision. What happens in markets is, whether one deems this desirable or undesirable, that consumers shape the pattern of resource use, and the assignment of resource rewards, according to their preferences. The pattern of production we observe at any date, the outputs being produced, the methods of production being employed, and the rewards being given to the various owners of productively used resources, are those dictated by consumers. Entrepreneurs are powerfully motivated to take the most careful heed of consumer preferences, as these are anticipated and imagined by the shrewdest and most alert participants in the market. The consumer is indeed "the captain." This *may* be seen as a desirable feature of the market economy; but whether this is so seen or not, for Mises the significant scientific point is simply that this consumer supremacy does in fact prevail. In free markets it is the consumers whose preferences govern every act of production, and every transaction involving the purchase and sale of a unit of resource service.[4]

CONSUMER SOVEREIGNTY AND THE MUTUAL BENEFITS DERIVED FROM EXCHANGE

In order better to appreciate the meaning and significance of consumer sovereignty, it may be helpful to contrast the doctrine of consumer sovereignty, on the one hand, with the doctrine of mutual benefit derived from exchange, on the other. The market is often hailed as the arena in which all parties to freely made exchanges benefit (in their own *ex ante* best judgment); the market is the social framework permitting and stimulating all possible positive-sum exchange games. The recognition of this achievement of the market in this way, is certainly an important economic insight. It is indeed possible to interpret the entire market process, involving resource markets, processes of production, and product markets, as being simply an elaboration of the central circumstance that all parties to voluntary exchanges are beneficiaries of these exchanges. (There is a solid basis for the conjecture that Walras's more mature expositions of general equilibrium theory, including production, emerged simply as the logical extension of his earlier version of general equilibrium in the pure exchange economy.) But the doctrine of consumer sovereignty, taken in conjunction with what we have described as Menger's vision, permits us to see the overall character of the market process from an entirely different angle. What happens in the market economy is not merely that the owners of resource services and those eager to consume the products (able to be produced with these resource services) are, through the intermediation of entrepreneurial producers, led to mutually beneficial exchanges. What happens in the market economy is that the owners of resource services are led to sell those services to those producers whose production plans are best calculated to cater to consumer preferences. The preferences of consumers determine the uses to which resources are assigned. As we have cited from Mises, "the owners of the material factors of production and the entrepreneurs are virtual mandatories or trustees of the consumers." The market may certainly validly be seen as the arena in which the potential benefits from voluntary exchanges are extracted; it is, however, even more fundamentally, the arena in which the value scales of consumers come to govern the disposition of potential factors of production.

THE SIGNIFICANCE OF PRIVATE PROPERTY

For Mises, the doctrine of consumer sovereignty offers an insight into the social role fulfilled by the institution of private property. There is, as a matter of scientific fact, no conflict of interest between the owners of productive resources (whether land or labor power), on the one hand, and the consuming public on the other. The owner of a productive resource can derive economic benefit from his resource only to the extent that he places it at the service of the consuming public. As we have already cited from Mises, a "wealthy man can preserve his wealth only by continuing to serve consumers in the most efficient way." The doctrine of consumer sovereignty demonstrates the harmony of interests existing in a market economy between owners of resources and consumers. Recognizing this harmony of interests is merely another way of sharing Menger's vision. It is the circumstance that consumers dictate the allocation of resources, which in fact creates this harmony of interests. And of course it is the institution of private property which permits and stimulates this harmony of interests.

Because entrepreneurs compete in resource markets, inspired by the hope of winning pure profit by redirecting the deployment of resources in ways more satisfying to consumers, we are able to understand how indeed consumers control and ultimately direct the pattern of production, the organization of industry, and the allocation of resources among competing industries. But Mises pointed out one situation—the case which he called the "monopoly price" case—in which the doctrine of consumer sovereignty does not apply. "Monopoly prices are an infringement of the sway of the consumers" (Mises, 1966, p. 272). For this monopoly price situation, the institution of private property does not spell a harmony of interests between the resource owners and the consuming public. For that situation—and only for that situation—it might indeed be rational for consumers to invoke political power to modify the outcomes forthcoming from the unhampered market. It was Mises's merit (and a reflection of his intellectual integrity) to identify this case and accord it the scientific attention it deserves. Unfortunately, not all Mises's followers have properly appreciated the place which his theory of monopoly price plays in his overall understanding of the capitalist system.

MISES AND THE THEORY OF MONOPOLY PRICE[5]

The nature and place of monopoly theory in Mises's system differs radically from the part which monopoly theory plays in standard microeconomics. For standard economics a monopolistic market for a produced commodity differs from a (perfectly) competitive market primarily in that the monopolist producer faces a downward-sloping demand curve, so that the profit-maximizing decision by the monopolist producer permits him to charge a price which is higher than the marginal cost of his output. Monopoly theory is then a theory exploring the peculiarities of decision making by a *producer*; the consequences of monopoly decision making are assessed primarily in terms of the way such decision making may be held responsible for resource misallocation, in regard to the economy as a whole. For the Misesian theory of monopoly price, matters are quite different.

For Mises, monopoly is identified *at the level of resource ownership*—not, except as a derivative, at the level of the decisions made by producers. For Mises, the possible case of resource monopoly (where the entire supply of a scarce resource is controlled by a single resource owner) is of scientific and normative interest not in terms of possible "misallocation of resources" (a concept which is not clearly identified in the Misesian system). The case of a resource monopoly is of interest insofar as it may affect incentives in a manner *at variance with the doctrine of consumer sovereignty*. Depending upon the degree of elasticity of demand for the monopolized resource, it may be the case that its owner may extract greater revenue from the market by withholding (or even destroying) part of the resource stock which he owns than he could extract by placing all of it at the service of consumers. He might then charge a "monopoly price" which would enable him to gain by thus withholding part of his resource stock. If this is indeed the case, then we have an exception to the general rule of consumer sovereignty. We have an exception to the general rule that private ownership of resources results in a harmony of owners' interests with those of the consuming public. We have a case where it is in the interest of property owners, in effect, to deny consumers the productive capacity of the resources they own. For Mises, the austere, *wertfrei* scientist, such a case is not, by itself, "bad" or "inefficient." It is simply a case which, unlike any other possible situation, pits the interests of consumers against those of a property owner. It would not be irrational, in such a case, for consumers to explore political avenues through which to modify the outcomes that would emerge from the unhampered market.

Given the availability of substitute resources (i.e. given the likelihood that the demand curve for the resource may be sufficiently elastic to make it impossible to gain by withholding part of the resource supply from production), given the incentives for entrepreneurial innovations likely either to increase the supply of this resource, or to reduce the uniqueness of any particular monopolized resource, Mises did not believe that the case of monopoly price is an empirically important case.[6] But it remains an intriguing theoretical possibility. It is intriguing for Mises, one feels quite certain, primarily in its unique property of permitting production to be conducted in a pattern which no longer faithfully reflects the preferences of consumers. It represents the theoretical possibility that, as a result of an accident of the pattern of resource ownership, Menger's vision may be partly inaccurate; economic phenomena may, in an unhampered market, *not* be shaped exclusively and entirely by consumer demand; sovereignty over production may not reside entirely in the preferences of the consuming public, but in the ownership rights of one or more resource owners.

As with many theoretical exceptions to generally prevailing patterns, the case of monopoly price seems of importance, for the Misesian system, not so much in the intriguing possibility which it itself represents, as in the light which it throws on the more general pattern—that to which Menger's vision and the doctrine of consumer sovereignty do apply. Indeed, now that we understand the sweeping generality of the doctrine of consumer sovereignty, we can perhaps better understand certain aspects of Mises's system which, at the outset of this chapter, we found mystifying.

MISES, MARKET PRICES, AND CONSUMER SOVEREIGNTY

It will be recalled that Mises had made certain assertions concerning the actual market prices that prevail in real-world markets, which we found puzzling. Those assertions attributed apparent optimality properties to these prices, and to the transactions to which they give rise. We were able to establish, certainly, that Mises emphatically understood that the market prices on any given date are likely to be false prices, generating corrective entrepreneurial-competitive production activity. But we were left mystified regarding the sense in which the everyday market prices (and the transactions to which they give rise) can be pronounced the "correct" prices, prices consistent with an "equilibrium of demand and supply." Surely, we asked, the simple insight that in any market, exchanges benefit all parties to them (in their own best estimation)— and the related insight that, to the extent that potential beneficiaries are aware of the possible opportunities arising from exchange, they can surely be relied upon to take advantage of them—is too simple, almost too trivial, and too limited, to permit Mises to denounce any governmental interference as counterproductive. Perhaps the insights we have gained in the preceding sections of this chapter can help demystify Mises's position.

Once we have understood the central position of the doctrine of consumer sovereignty in Mises's overall system, we can surely sense and appreciate the deep respect Mises felt for the *actual* market prices of productive resources. Certainly these prices are likely to be "false" prices, in that they necessarily imperfectly anticipate the true future valuations of consumers for the various possible potential products (at the times when these products might conceivably be made available to consumers). Nonetheless these prices, and the transactions in which they emerge, are wholly governed—of course, ignoring now the special exception of the monopoly price case—by the preferences of consumers; these prices and these transactions fulfill Menger's vision, they express consumer sovereignty. Mises would of course not deny that, in the absence of omniscience, actual prices and actual plans for production, may only imperfectly reflect the patterns of intensity of consumers' preferences. But "sovereignty" need not imply that the wishes of the sovereign are instantaneously, successfully, carried out; it may surely mean that each act of those directly or indirectly acknowledging that sovereignty, is motivated by the incentive of fulfilling those wishes as far as human effort and human will can succeed in doing. Even the mistakes which may occur under pressure of this incentive, must also be attributed to the supremacy of the sovereign. Surely this was Mises's profound insight into the character of the capitalist market process:

at every moment the decisions made by entrepreneur-producers and resource owners, are directly or indirectly made under the powerful incentive to cater to the true pattern of consumer preferences. Each market price for a resource directly reflects the judgments of competing entrepreneurs as to the most valuable use—valuable as judged by anticipated consumer willingness to pay—to which that resource can be assigned. Each production plan that is initiated at any given moment expresses the judgments of competing entrepreneurs (acting in the light of the resource market prices of the moment, and in the light of their anticipations of the market prices for future products) as to the most effective ways of deploying productive resources in the service of satisfying consumer preferences.

The circumstance that, in the face of the utter uncertainty of the future (and in the face of the similarly imperfectly informed state of market participants concerning present economic conditions)—the production plans initiated at any given date are inevitably flawed, does not in the slightest qualify the assertions made at the conclusion of the preceding paragraph. The near-certainty that hindsight will reveal the "falsity" of present prices, and the "inefficiency" of present production plans, does not in the slightest degree cast a shadow on the validity of Menger's vision, or upon the reality of consumer supremacy, at all times. The truth remains that, at any given time, the market is effectively deploying the best current information commanded by market participants, and the most accurate and shrewdest entrepreneurial judgments concerning future market conditions. What drives and motivates such deployment, economic analysis reveals, is the incentive to win pure profit, through improving the faithfulness with which consumer preferences are respected in the patterns of production.

So that when Mises declares any intervention by government which might alter market prices (or other decisions that might have been made in an unhampered market) to be harmful, he does not imply that the prices (or other decisions) which would have emerged in an unhampered market on any given date are optimal (in the sense that they accurately reflect all the considerations which an omniscient observer would wish to have taken into account). What he means is that the existing conditions on an unhampered market express the most strenuous efforts on the part of the shrewdest entrepreneurial minds to identify and correct existing discrepancies (between what *might* be done to best satisfy consumer preferences, and what *is* being done). Not only are these strenuous efforts being made at all times, these efforts have been made in the past, and current market prices have been modified (from those of the past) to the extent that the past shrewd judgments of entrepreneurs revealed those earlier plans to have been "false."

When Mises emphasized the virtues of those real-world market prices and transactions which continually generate his "plain states of rest," he was not simply emphasizing the somewhat obvious, even trivial, insight that, in the best *ex ante* judgments of all market participants, their market exchanges on any given date make them better off. He was, instead, emphasizing the role being played by real-world prices and transactions, in the exercise of consumer sovereignty—recall our earlier contrast between (a) seeing the market, in a production economy, as merely the extension of insights relevant to the pure exchange economy, and (b) seeing such a market as the arena in which Menger's vision is actualized. For Mises, the supremacy of the consumer is not simply a tendency manifested in the ongoing entrepreneurial-competitive market process; it is a reality fulfilled at every moment. Certainly such supremacy is not to be confused with any hypothetically "perfect" allocation of resources to correspond to the pattern of consumer preferences. Where neoclassical welfare economics focused exclusively on such possible correspondence, Mises's more "dynamic," "process-oriented" mindset focused on a quite different aspect of markets. In seeing the market as *continually striving*, as it were, better to satisfy consumer preferences, Mises's articulated an understanding and appreciation of free markets which, most unfortunately, relatively few of his readers have themselves understood and appreciated.

NOTES

1. For Mises's discussion of the "evenly rotating economy," see Mises (1966, pp. 246ff.).

2. The ideas briefly presented in this section have been developed more fully by the writer in his editorial Introduction to volume one of Kirzner (1994).

3. See Hutt (1936, ch. 16); Hutt (1940). Hutt used the term "consumer sovereignty" fairly frequently in his papers of the mid-1930s, see e.g. Hutt (1935) (reprinted as chapter 12 of Pejovich and Klingaman, 1975).

4. The late Murray N. Rothbard has sharply attacked Hutt's notion of consumer sovereignty (Rothbard, 1962, pp. 560–66). (Rothbard does not refer to Mises's very frequent references to the consumer sovereignty doctrine.) However Rothbard concedes

that in a "formal" sense (in which the ultimate goals of producers are recognized as consumption goals) "consumer sovereignty, by definition, always, obtains" (Rothbard, 1962, p. 561). There is reason to believe that Rothbard's position is (regardless of its validity) not inconsistent with the interpretation of Mises being presented in this and subsequent sections of this chapter. However, there seems to be a link between Rothbard's critique of Hutt's notion of consumer sovereignty, and his critique of Mises's ideas on monopoly price. On the latter point see the writer's discussion in a later section of this chapter.

5. For further discussion of the Misesian theory of monopoly price (and a critique of some work of followers of Mises who have, in this writer's opinion, not adequately appreciated the Misesian theory), see Kirzner (1991).

6. Nor, it should be emphasized, is the case of monopoly price one that can be empirically identified and observed. Failure to use all the available supply of the monopolized resource may simply reflect the monopolist's entrepreneurial judgment that future consumer demand may be strong enough to justify postponing its use to the future. Even physical destruction of part of the supply *might* (admittedly far-fetchedly!) be the manner in which the monopolist is expressing his own consumer preferences . . .

REFERENCES

Hayek, Friedrich A. (1934) Introduction to *Collected Works of Carl Menger,* London: London School of Economics.

Hutt, William H. (1935) "The Nature of Aggressive Selling," *Economica.*

——— (1936) *Economists and the Public,* London: Jonathan Cape.

——— (1940) "The Concept of Consumers' Sovereignty," *Economic Journal* March.

Kirzner, Israel M. (1991) "The Driving Force of the Market: The Idea of 'Competition' in Contemporary Theory and in the Austrian Theory of the Market Process," in Richard M. Ebeling (ed.) *Austrian Economics, Perspectives on the Past and Prospects for the Future,* Hillsdale, MI: Hillsdale College Press, reprinted as chapter 12 in the present volume. [Reference is to the original source material.—Ed.]

Kirzner, Israel M., ed. (1994) *Classics in Austrian Economics,* 3 volumes, London: William Pickering and Chatto.

Mises, Ludwig von (1966) *Human Action, A Treatise on Economics* [1st edn, 1949], 3rd rev. edn, Chicago: Henry Regnery.

——— (1978) *Notes and Recollections,* South Holland, IL: Libertarian Press.

——— (1990) *Economic Freedom and Interventionism, An Anthology of Articles and Essays,* selected and edited by Bettina Bien Greaves, Irvington-on-Hudson, NY: Foundation for Economic Education.

Pejovich, Svetozar and Klingaman, David (1975) *Individual Freedom, Selected Works of William H. Hutt,* Westport, CT: Greenwood Press.

Rothbard, Murray N. (1962) *Man, Economy, and State, A Treatise on Economic Principles,* Princeton, NJ: Van Nostrand.

Salerno, Joseph T. (1993) "Mises and Hayek Dehomogenized," *Review of Austrian Economics* 6(2).

Streissler, Erich (1990) "The Influence of German Economics on the Work of Menger and Marshall," in Bruce Caldwell (ed.) *Carl Menger and His Legacy in Economics*, Durham, NC: Duke University Press, pp. 31–68.

HUMAN ACTION, FREEDOM, AND ECONOMIC SCIENCE

I

In pondering which topic to choose for a paper in a volume honoring Professor Hans Sennholz, a scholar who has devoted his long and fruitful career to the dissemination of the ideas of his teacher, Ludwig von Mises, with such distinction, my memory took me back to my first meeting, at New York University, with Hans in the mid-fifties. This was, in fact, in the Mises seminar held each Thursday evening in a palatial room in a townhouse on Washington Square North. It is this trip down memory lane which has, indirectly, indeed suggested the topic for this paper.

I was a very green young graduate student at the time I first met Hans, who had just completed his doctoral dissertation under Mises. It was a short time later (early 1956, I believe) that Mises suggested to me a topic for my own dissertation. I have often thought back to my sheer good fortune not only in being able to study under Mises, but, in particular, to have been guided by him from that early stage in my work, to think intensively about the foundations of economic science. What has brought me to the topic of this paper is my recent realization that it has taken me some thirty-five years to appreciate fully what I now believe to be the uniqueness of Mises's own position in the topic which he suggested for my research. Let me explain.

Mises suggested that I explore the changing views about individual behavior which economists had, since the time of Adam Smith, adopted in order for them to grasp the possibility of a science of economics. Given the apparent unpredictability of individual behavior it is intuitively difficult to account for the economic regularities which seem to occur. It was necessary somehow to "understand" individual behavior in a way consistent with the possibility of "scientific laws." The classical economists had seen economics as a science of wealth, made possible by the

From *A Man of Principle: Essays in Honor of Hans F. Sennholz*, ed. J. W. Robbins and M. Spangler (Grove City, Pa.: Grove City College Press, 1992), 241–48; available from Libertarian Press, Inc. (www.libertarianpress.com). Reprinted by permission of Mary Sennholz.

notion of selfish, materialistic, economic man. Neoclassical economics had escaped this view and (as ultimately made clear by Lionel Robbins) was able to see economics as an abstract science rooted in allocative, maximizing, economizing individual behavior. Mises saw his own system as going beyond the Robbinsian view, permitting us to see economic science as made possible by *human action,* the decisions made by purposeful, reasoning human beings intent on improving their situations. I learned a very great deal by pursuing this suggestion of Mises, a great deal of the history of economic doctrines, and a great deal concerning the epistemological foundations of economics. This research enabled me to complete a doctoral dissertation which matured, several years later, into my first book, *The Economic Point of View* (1960). I burden the reader with these autobiographical details in order to provide the background for the present paper. It is my present opinion that the concluding chapter in that book, the chapter discussing the Misesian system, does not do full justice to Mises's understanding of the role of human action in serving as the foundation for economic science.

In the following section, I briefly outline the relevant portion of my 1960 discussion of Mises's notion of human action and its implications, and contrast that discussion with my present understanding of the implications of Misesian human action. In section III, I place this deepened appreciation for "what Mises really meant,"[1] in the context of broader twentieth-century developments within the Austrian economics tradition. I also draw attention to the implications of this deepened understanding, for appreciating the role of individual freedom in inspiring the efficiencies of the market process.

II

The difference between my 1960 understanding of Misesian human action and my 1991 appreciation of it can be expressed as follows: In 1960 I had understood Misesian economics as proceeding by logically tracing through the consequences of interacting individual human decisions—each of which was governed by reason—in pursuit of respective individual purposes. It is this purposefulness of action which characterizes "conduct that is accompanied by the consciousness of volition, of something more than a bundle of reflexes responding to specific stimuli. The nature of these various stimuli and the directions towards which they variously tend to guide action are completely independent of the desires and will of the actor. . . . But because man possesses the power to reject one course of action for another . . . , the physical, physiological, and psychological sciences do not exhaust the facts of action that are capable of scientific explanation. . . . Sciences of human action will be distinct from other sciences in that the former begin where the latter end, *viz.* in the implications of the rationality that governs purposeful behavior."[2]

The possibility of a science of economics, explaining the emergence of market regularities out of the freely made decisions of autonomous individuals, rested not on any fictitious reduction of man to the classical caricature of selfish *homo oeconomicus* single-mindedly pursuing material wealth. Nor did it rest on the neoclassical view of man as lightning calculator of mathematical problems of utility maximization in the context of given ends and means. Instead the Misesian system (as interpreted in my 1960 chapter) rested simply on the "praxeological" insight that the action taken by a purposeful human being will be one reflecting his rationality, his reasoned assessment of the possibilities for and consequences of alternative attempts at improving his situation. (Optimal, economizing, allocation of given scarce means among competing given ends might well be one possible consequence of this rational assessment. But what renders a science of economics possible is this latter rationality, rather than the particular allocative pattern which has monopolized the attention of neoclassical economics.)

There is nothing in this 1960 discussion which draws attention to the role of entrepreneurial discovery in generating the systematic results which economic science is able to explain. And, from my perspective of 1991, it is this which seems the major inadequacy of the earlier treatment.

I should perhaps emphasize that the characteristic Austrian emphasis on market *processes* (as distinct from the exclusive neoclassical preoccupation with market states of equilibrium) was well known to me in 1960.[3] Although (as will be made clear in section III) I was not yet sufficiently aware of the cardinal role of entrepreneurial discovery in Mises's system, I certainly did appreciate the sense in which Mises saw the market as a *process* (possibly pointing in the direction of equilibrium). There is no discussion of market process in my 1960 chapter not because I was unaware of its central role in Mises's understanding of the operation of the market, but because (as I then thought) the process character of the market had no bearing on the definition of the "economic" side of social phenomena (which my 1960 book was devoted to explore). What made economic science possible, I understood Mises to argue, was the rationality, the purposefulness of human action. Market processes emerge in systematic fashion because of this rationality, of this purposefulness. The critics who had attacked the validity of economics because it depended upon the view of man as unrealistically selfish, or as mechanically maximizing, were wrong; economics does not depend (and, in Mises's eyes, never did really depend) on these caricatures. The theorems of economics depend only on the power of reason to guide purposeful behavior, that is all. It was thus not necessary to emphasize the process nature of markets in order to identify the unique "point of view" which economics expresses. So I believed in 1960.

What I wish now to emphasize is that, from my 1991 perspective, this earlier way of understanding Mises is inadequate. When Mises identified the concept of human action as the essential building block for a praxe-ological economic science, it is now clear to me that this implies far more than simply the importance of purposefulness for the analysis *of decisions made in given situations.* The concept of human action, it is now clear to me, is important in the Misesian system because of its fruitfulness in explaining how *economic agents discover changes that have occurred in their very market situations,* and generate, as a consequence, those systematic market processes which are so central to Misesian economics.

Critics of economics have, for close to two hundred years, criticized it for depending upon some variant of the idea of universal human self-ishness. In 1960 I understood the Misesian response to this criticism to consist simply in identifying the essential key to human behavior *in given situations* as purposefulness rather than selfishness. I now understand the proper Misesian response to this criticism to consist in showing how the purposefulness of human action (without any necessary selfish moti-vations) is the essential key to the discovery by agents that they are in fact *not* in the "given situations" which they had hitherto assumed to be relevant.

For my 1960 understanding, the entrepreneurial element in Mise-sian human action is not important for the distillation of an analytically unique economic point of view. For my present understanding matters appear rather differently. What sets Mises's conception of human action (as the foundation of economics) apart from the mainstream neoclassical conception of the rational, economizing decision (in that same role) is, as I now see, that, unlike the latter, the concept of human action illuminates directly those dynamic processes through which the market absorbs and responds to exogenous changes. When we challenge the erroneous belief that the efficiency of market outcomes depends upon selfishness, we are able to do so by showing how the flexibility and responsiveness of market adjustments is rooted, not necessarily in man's passion for material wealth (and certainly not in any programmed pattern of allocative maximization), but in man's entrepreneurial propensity to discover changes which can redound to his benefit (i.e., to the more successful attainment of his goals, *whatever* they may be). If we are able to recognize that possibility for understanding social phenomena which is not covered by the most complete imaginable application of the physical, physiological, and psychological sciences, we are inevitably drawn to recognize also that this possibility transcends the narrow scope of static decision making. That uniquely economic element which enables us, in Misesian fashion, to understand the economic rationale of the human decision, inevitably illuminates for us at the same time the manner in which that rationale extends to the dynamics of discovery in the context of change, and hence to the dynamic processes which are thus generated.

Whereas my 1960 exposition implied, in effect, that the entrepreneurial element in Misesian human action is not essential for the identification of what constitutes, for Mises, the economic point of view, I now believe this to be incorrect. A Misesian appreciation for the existence of a uniquely economic point of view rests, it now seems to me, squarely on that understanding of the discovery-potential in human action which constitutes its entrepreneurial aspect. Let me, in section III, now turn to place my new appreciation of "what Mises really meant," in the context of some of the more fundamental changes in the core of Austrian economics which have occurred during the past three quarters of a century.

III

During the nineteen-twenties the Austrian economists enjoyed considerable reputation within the profession. Economists visiting the Continent, whether from England or from the U.S., would almost invariably make it their business to visit Vienna. The subjectivist approach of the Austrians was widely recognized and respected as one of the key traditions in contemporary economic thinking. Yet it seems fair to state that the understanding which Austrians had of their own subjectivism and of the theory of markets which it was able to support was, from today's perspective, quite limited.

When Lionel (later Lord) Robbins wrote his *Nature and Significance of Economic Science* in 1932, there can be no doubt that he accurately reflected the Austrian thinking which he had learned from his visits to Vienna.[4] That thinking enabled Robbins to formulate the economic decision in narrowly allocative terms. And it was Robbins's formulation which led subsequent microeconomic thought to see the market not as an unfolding discovery process, but as an equilibrium network of perfectly dovetailing individual allocative decisions.[5] There was nothing in the post–World War II work of prominent Austrians such as Rosenstein-Rodan and Machlup—whose Austrianism was rather narrowly rooted in the doctrines dominant in Vienna in the twenties—to indicate that these developments were in any way inconsistent with Austrian doctrines. Yet the writings of Mises and Hayek (especially those subsequent to World War II) enable us to see these developments sparked by Robbins's 1932 book as gravely flawed.

From our present-day perspective we can see how Mises and Hayek were able to advance Austrian understanding of markets significantly beyond the limited subjectivism of the inter-war Austrian tradition. It becomes clear that Mises was, already in the 'thirties, if not earlier, articulating a view of market processes which emphasized human action as a driving force for change, and which saw market processes themselves as systematic processes propelled by human action. Hayek came to emphasize the role of knowledge and the discovery processes needed to overcome the gaps in knowledge attributable to the phenomenon of dispersed information.

Although Mises never did employ Hayek's terminology drawing attention to the discovery of existing but dispersed information, there is every reason to interpret Mises's entrepreneurial market process in terms of such mutual discovery by market participants. In my 1963 book, *Market Theory and the Price System,* I attempted to present a Misesian statement of the core body of price theory in precisely such terms. However I did not, at that time, see the importance of the *entrepreneurial* element in human action, for the generation of such market learning processes.

When, ten years later, I published *Competition and Entrepreneurship,* I certainly did understand the importance of this entrepreneurial element in human action. But I have not, until quite recently,[6] recognized how this element was integral not only to Mises's theory of the market process, but also to his perception of how it is only this element that makes at all possible a uniquely economic chain of causation in social phenomena, a chain which only economic science can explain.

Late twentieth-century Austrian economics has consistently paid at least lip service to the idea that economics is a science of human action. But we have perhaps not paid sufficient attention to what Mises meant by this insight. We can now see, I believe, that human action drives the market in a sense that is quite distinct from any of the implications of the maximizing rationality which governs Robbinsian equilibrium economics. Human action drives the market, more fundamentally, in that it expresses the changes in agents' awareness of their environment and of their visions of the future—changes which are inspired by their "entrepreneurial" alertness to the dynamic world in which we live. This alertness is motivated by the purposefulness which defines and identifies conscious human action. If we are to understand the world in which we live—the world of disequilibrium as distinct from the analytical-model world of equilibrium—we must recognize how the decisions taken during any given span of time reflect this aspect of human action. It is the systematic market process of mutual discovery so generated, which constitutes the core of Misesian economics. Our understanding of what causes *these* facts of the market process is not exhausted by the fullest application of the physical, physiological and psychological sciences; for the fullest possible understanding we can draw, in addition, upon the explanatory power of the science of economics, the science of human action. The systematic changes in bids, offers, and completed transactions, which constitute the competitive market process, can be grasped by understanding how initial errors generate profitable opportunities which come to be perceived and exploited by alert, purposeful market participants. One cannot identify the economic side of life without drawing attention to this feature of human action and its implications for social processes.

It is worthy of notice that our deepened understanding of the manner in which human action inspires the market process and identifies the economic aspect of social phenomena affords us a correspondingly deeper appreciation for the role of individual freedom in Misesian economics. Individual freedom, quite apart from its ethical or philosophical appeal, is important, of course, for all schools of microeconomics, as a prerequisite for the beneficial operation of the market system. But for a science of human action this observation means more than the simple insight that free individuals can be relied upon to squeeze maximum benefits from any given situation. For the science of human action, free-dom is the circumstance which permits and inspires market participants *to become aware* of beneficial (or other) *changes* in their circumstances. An environment in which human freedom is limited, in which profitably exploited opportunities invoke confiscatory social reactions, is an envi-ronment in which beneficial changes may never be noticed in the first place. An understanding of Misesian economics thus permits us to see directly how it points unerringly to the social usefulness of political insti-tutions which guarantee individual liberties and the security of individual rights to life and property.

NOTES AND REFERENCES

1. Although Mises wrote a commendatory Foreword to my 1960 book, and never did suggest that I had failed to grasp his position, I do not see this as inconsistent with the thesis that my earlier treatment was inadequate. The fact is that, despite my present inter-pretation of the Misesian system, it must be acknowledged that this interpretation of Mises's views argues for insights which Mises himself did *not* explicitly articulate. Possibly he took them as obvious; it is not then implausible that he took them as obviously implicit also in the more superficial exposition of Mises's position which I offered in 1960. Or it is possible that my present understanding of Mises's views incorporates insights which, even for Mises himself, were never more than implicit in his understanding of the workings of the market. Either way, there is no great difficulty in explaining why Mises did not critically identify what I now see as the inadequacies in my 1960 discussion.

2. Kirzner, Israel M., *The Economic Point of View* (Princeton, NJ: Van Nostrand, 1960), p. 151.

3. See also Kirzner, Israel M., *Market Theory and the Price System* (Princeton, NJ: Van Nostrand, 1963), pp. 22–31.

4. For further discussion of the matters dealt with in this section, see Kirzner, Israel M., "Ludwig von Mises and Friedrich von Hayek: The Modern Extension of Aus-trian Subjectivism," in Norbert Leser, editor, *Die Wiener Schule der Nationalökonomie* (Wien: Hermann Bohlau, 1986), together with the references cited in that paper.

5. On this see Walsh, Vivian C., *Introduction to Contemporary Microeconomics* (New York, NY: McGraw-Hill, 1970), p. 17.

6. For an expression of my recently learned insights, see Kirzner, Israel M., "Self-Interest and the New Bashing of Economics," *Critical Review* (Winter–Spring, 1990) Volume 4, numbers 1–2, especially pp. 33–39.

HUMAN ACTION, 1949: A DRAMATIC EPISODE IN INTELLECTUAL HISTORY

A great book, it has been remarked, is like a great castle. It can be viewed from many different angles, each offering a unique perspective. Viewing Ludwig von Mises's monumental work from the vantage of 2009 permits one to see with great clarity one fascinating aspect of the book—the sheer *drama* of its emergence at the time that it appeared. This is a theme on which I have touched more than once over the years. I am grateful for the present opportunity to articulate this theme in somewhat greater detail.

Some 13 years ago (in the May 1996 *Freeman,* which celebrated the first 50 years of public service splendidly contributed by the Foundation for Economic Education), I dwelt on the pivotal role played by FEE in upholding the flag of Austrian economics. I dwelt especially on the role it played (most importantly by providing Mises with a congenial "base") in nurturing the Austrian economics tradition during decades in which the professional reputation of the school was at its very lowest. That paper focused, in part, on the contribution of the Foundation to the subsequent revival of Austrian economics in this country. The present note complements that earlier piece by focusing on the altogether dramatic character of the long-run impact of this magnum opus of Mises, a work that anchored everything which Mises was to write under FEE auspices, and to which the Austrian economics revival is, unquestionably, to be attributed.

THE INTELLECTUAL DRAMA OF *HUMAN ACTION*

The term "drama" may seem out of place in regard to a serious tome on the foundations of a serious discipline. But *Human Action* is no ordinary work. It is a work which, at the time, was seen as written in starkly uncompromising fashion, articulating a particular worldview and a particular understanding of economics—at a time when that worldview and that understanding were thought to have been decisively nudged off the professional stage. The book came to be summarily dismissed, and subsequently ignored, as the last gasp of a dying intellectual tradition. But this judgment was grievously mistaken.

From *The Freeman* 59, 7 (September 2009): 8–11. Reprinted by permission.

Human Action was *not* a work merely presenting, once again, the ideas of an earlier tradition. The book in fact represented, we must point out, a dramatic *revision,* a dramatic *deepening* of the insights of the Austrian school. Precisely when the Austrian economics tradition was widely seen as virtually dead, as material only for treatises on the history of economic thought—precisely at that time that very tradition brilliantly produced a sparkling, fresh, fundamentally new interpretation of its central tenets. Six decades later we can see how Mises's revision and reinterpretation inspired a revival of serious academic and scholarly interest in Austrian economics. Seen from this perspective, the 1949 publication of *Human Action* must surely be recognized as a dramatic episode in the history of economics.

THE DECLINE OF AUSTRIAN ECONOMICS, 1932–1945

At the outset of the 1930s the Austrian school of economics was recognized on the continent, in the United Kingdom, and in the United States as an important component of contemporary academic economics. For young scholars from America visiting the European academies at that time, an invitation to present their work at a seminar at the University of Vienna was a highly valued professional achievement. In Britain, Lionel Robbins, the most prominent economist at the University of London, published his 1932 classic, *An Essay on the Nature and Significance of Economic Science,* replete with insights and citations the author had culled from the Austrian literature and from his visits to Vienna. In that same year Robbins invited the brilliant young Friedrich Hayek (a close associate and protégé of Mises) to join the London faculty in a prestigious professorship. And Hayek's appearance on the British academic scene had an almost dramatic impact on British economics discussion, especially in regard to capital and monetary theory.

Yet just a few short years later, it seemed, this success had evaporated. The advance of economic theory in the '30s (advances related in particular to the work of Piero Sraffa and John Maynard Keynes, to theories of imperfect and monopolistic competition, to the theories of socialist economics, and to sophisticated advances in mathematical economics) seemed to have left the Austrians far behind. They were seen to have been defeated by Keynes (in regard to macroeconomic issues), by Frank Knight (in regard to capital theory), and by Oskar Lange and by Abba Lerner (on the possibility of efficient socialist economic planning), and to have failed

to keep pace with the exciting developments in welfare theory, econometrics, and mathematical economics. The physical dispersal of the circle
of Vienna economists who had attended Mises's famed *privatseminar* as
a result of the political turmoil of the times certainly contributed to the
impression that the Vienna tradition was no longer a live component of
modern economic thought. (Mises himself had left Vienna for Geneva in
1934.) Although Mises published *Nationalökonomie* in Geneva in 1940
and Hayek published *The Pure Theory of Capital* in 1941, the economics
profession paid virtually no attention to these works. By the end of World
War II, with Mises a refugee in New York and without a regular academic
position, the outlook for the future of the Menger–Böhm-Bawerk tradition seemed bleak indeed.

Moreover, it can be argued, certain aspects of the developments in
mainstream economic theory during the '30s—despite their overall
thrust *away* from the path of Austrian theory—may well have seemed
to *erode* the case for a distinctive Austrian presence. In its early years the
Austrian school had gained its distinctiveness from its pioneering challenge to the dominance of the German Historical School. But by the
1930s, *that* war (on behalf of the legitimacy of abstract economic theory)
had been decisively won; all the major schools of European economic
thought were on the side of the Austrians in regard to the role of pure
theory. And in 1932 Mises himself had written to the effect that all "modern" schools of economic thought subscribe to the same set of economic
principles, albeit in different languages and with different modes of exposition. Mises himself, it seems clear, had (in 1932) not recognized the *gulf*
that (as would later become amply clear!) separated the dominant Anglo-
American mainstream from the economics that Mises himself identified
with the Austrian tradition. So a number of Mises's disciples (including,
perhaps, Fritz Machlup, Gottfried Haberler, and Paul Rosenstein-Rodan)
might be excused for thinking that what was important to the Austrian
tradition was by now (the '30s) well-accepted in mainstream economics.
There was no intellectual profit, such Austrians came to believe, to be
gained by insisting on the distinctiveness of the Austrian label.

THE SOCIALIST CALCULATION DEBATE
AND THE MISES-HAYEK REVOLUTION

Yet if the immediate post–World War II scene appeared so wholly inhospitable to a distinctive Austrian economics, both Mises and Hayek were

in fact working, independently but along parallel paths, toward a revolutionary reinterpretation of their intellectual heritage. (This note is, of course, focusing on Mises's classic work of 1949. But it would be a serious mistake to fail to note that the "drama" we have seen in the appearance of Mises's book had its parallel in the appearance of Hayek's 1948–49 volume of essays, *Individualism and Economic Order*. I have elsewhere discussed the complementarity between those two contributions in "Ludwig von Mises and Friedrich von Hayek: The Modern Extension of Austrian Subjectivism," republished as chapter 7 in my *The Meaning of Market Process: Essays in the Development of Modern Austrian Economics*.)

The "socialist economic calculation debate" that raged in the prewar decade had, it seems reasonable to believe, induced the revolutionary revisions in their understanding of markets. The uncritical acceptance by the economics profession of the Lange-Lerner thesis—that socialists can plan efficiently by modeling their plan after general equilibrium conditions (postulated by mainstream theorists as governing competitive market systems)—taught Mises and Hayek that their own understanding of how markets work differed *fundamentally* from that of their neoclassical colleagues. Mises, in particular, now realized that mainstream neoclassical theorists do *not* subscribe to the same understanding of the economic principles governing markets to which Austrian economists (or, at any rate, he) subscribe. Mises wrote *Human Action* to articulate with utmost conviction his *refusal* to accept that mainstream neoclassical interpretation of how markets work. *Human Action* was a defiant declaration of theoretic independence—a declaration spelling out explicitly what had hitherto (at least in Mises's view) been implicit in *earlier* neoclassical (and particularly in Austrian) market theory. (See Frank M. Machovec's *Perfect Competition and the Transformation of Economics*.)

This explicit articulation constituted a dramatic, revolutionary deepening and extension of existing Austrian theory. That it came to inspire the late-twentieth-century revival of Austrian economics, although ignored and overlooked when it was first published, is in large part what made the publication of *Human Action* an episode of intellectual drama.

MARKET PROCESS VERSUS MARKET EQUILIBRIUM

What the socialist economic-calculation debate taught Mises, I believe, is that it is necessary, in order to promote economic understanding of what the market system achieves, to replace expository emphasis on attainable market equilibrium patterns with an emphasis on the character of the *processes* of equilibration. (For an exhaustive exploration tending to support this assertion, see Don Lavoie's *Rivalry and Central Planning: The Socialist Calculation Debate Reconsidered*.)

This latter emphasis reveals the essentially *entrepreneurial* character of the market process and underscores the role of *dynamic competition* (as against the state of so-called "perfect competition") in this entrepreneurial process. (In Hayek's work a parallel shift of emphasis was being articulated: namely, a replacement of a world of imagined perfect mutual knowledge by a world in which the market "learning" process tends continually to expand the scope of mutual knowledge—subject, of course, to the continual disruptions generated by exogenous changes in demand patterns, resource availabilities, and so on.) The writers who believed that central planners *could* emulate market efficiency had overlooked, in Mises's view, the subtle processes of entrepreneurial *discovery,* through which alone one could postulate any systematic tendencies toward market equilibrium.

By focusing on the entrepreneurial process at work in markets unhampered by governmental obstacles to competitive entry, Mises offered much more than a reinterpretation of traditional price theory. His insights offered a brilliant new understanding of the meaning of market competition and thus also a revolutionary perspective on the theory of monopoly. Mises's understanding of the market process implied not only the rejection of mainstream orthodoxy in the theory of socialism, but also far-reaching implications for the theory of antitrust policy and, more generally, for the theory of government regulatory policy.

For many years this new emphasis in Misesian-Austrian economics was completely ignored. In the immediate post–World War II decade the focus of professional attention was not on the precise formulation of the foundations of microeconomics, but on the extent to which microeconomics must, in the real world, be superseded, as a practical matter, by Keynesian macroeconomic considerations. Moreover, the increasing sophistication of mathematical economics, and its applications in the elaboration of the ambitious Walrasian general-equilibrium theoretic enterprise, combined to make Mises's ideas seem old-fashioned, elementary, and even primitive. As is now well-known, these were decades (stretching from after the 1921 publication of Knight's *Risk, Uncertainty and Profit* until William Baumol's pioneering work almost half a century later in the resurrection of the entrepreneurial role) in which mainstream economic theory almost completely lost sight of the entrepreneur.

THE DRAMA OF THE AUSTRIAN REVIVAL

But Mises's great work was *not* destined to be buried forever under this deafening silence. By the 1960s and '70s younger students and scholars were beginning to discover Mises's work and to recognize the sparkling *freshness* of his ideas. The economics profession—or at least some of its more daring and independent-minded graduate students—were at the same time beginning to take note of and to acknowledge the stultifying irrelevance of much of what was being taught in mainstream graduate departments. The downfall of Keynesian economics during the latter decades of the century focused renewed attention on the foundation of microeconomics. In *Human Action* more and more young scholars redis-covered ideas that enabled them to make sense of the complex world that economic science is supposed to help us understand. The downfall of the Soviet Union focused attention on the profound truths about socialism to be extracted from the Misesian foundations. That downfall taught many that the mainstream of the profession, which had for decades defended the possibility of socialist economic efficiency and had contemptuously dismissed those who had challenged that possibility, was simply and ingloriously wrong.

The modest revival of interest in the Austrian economics tradition over the past four decades has highlighted, in my opinion, the drama inherent in the first appearance of *Human Action*. This work was the courageous manifesto of a scholar of incorruptible integrity who, close to the seventh decade of his life, contributed a brilliantly fresh articulation of econom-ics truths. That this work was ignored for decades and only subsequently won recognition (albeit modest), adds to the intellectual drama of this episode in the twentieth-century development of economic thought. Speculation concerning the *future* influence that may yet be exerted by this towering work only enhances the excitement sparked by this drama.

REFLECTIONS ON THE MISESIAN
LEGACY IN ECONOMICS

This chapter was first published as a paper by the *Review of Austrian Economics* in honor of the memory of Murray N. Rothbard. As I wrote it, my mind went back over 40 years, to the first time that I had met him. It was at the opening session of the Seminar in Economic Theory which Professor Mises conducted in the fall semester of 1954. That occasion was also my first meeting with Ludwig von Mises, and it is etched deeply in my memory. Two statements by Mises at that seminar meeting stand out in my recollection. One statement was his very opening substantive sentence that evening. "The market," Mises began, "is a process." (See also the statement in *Human Action* [1966, p. 257]: "The market is not a place, a thing, or a collective entity. The market is a process.")

Coming as I did from a rather spotty undergraduate training in economics (and mainly along Keynesian lines), Mises's statement, I recall, left me completely puzzled. I had thought of the market as a place, an arena for exchanges, as an abstract idea referring to voluntary exchange translations. I could not fathom what on earth could be meant by the observation that the market is a process. I now, in retrospect, consider that all my subsequent training and research in economics, both before and after obtaining my doctorate under Mises, has consisted in learning to appreciate what it was that Mises meant by this assertion.

The second statement by Mises which stands out in my memory from that September 1954 evening, is a reference that Mises made to Murray Rothbard. Murray had, it appeared, recently completed a paper which Mises found to be excellent. He briefly but warmly complimented Murray on that piece of work, and expressed the hope and the prediction that Murray would continue to produce a great deal of future work of similar excellence. The years since 1954 have amply borne out Mises's hope and his prediction. Murray Rothbard's output during these four decades has been prodigious. The breadth of his reading across so many disciplines

From Israel M. Kirzner, *The Driving Force of the Market: Essays in Austrian Economics* (New York and London: Routledge, 2000), 151–64: the original source is *Review of Austrian Economics* 9, 2 (1996): 143–54. Reprinted by permission.

has been breathtaking; his sheer energy in producing thousands of pages of published work has been stupendous. It is a privilege to contribute this paper to a memorial issue dedicated to the memory of Murray N. Rothbard.

This chapter will have to do with the first of the two statements made by Mises at that 1954 seminar session. I will be taking issue with a certain tendency, present in a number of recent expositions of Mises's work, to de-emphasize (or even flatly to deny) the centrality of the idea of the market as a process in the Misesian system. I consider clarification concerning the character of the Misesian system to be of critical importance for the future direction of modern Austrian economics, and for its ability to contribute fruitfully to the restoration of economic understanding for the economics profession and for intelligent lay people at large. And this matter is also, of course, of fundamental importance in projecting an accurate overall view of Mises's own contributions. While I shall, in my argument, be taking issue with a number of relevant statements by Rothbard, I trust that the reader will appreciate that the purpose of this paper is simply to further that very Misesian legacy to which Rothbard dedicated his entire life's work as an economist. It is as a memorial to Murray Rothbard's consistency in this regard, and his willingness to bear formidable costs to his professional career in order not to compromise the honesty of his expositions, that this chapter has been written. The purpose of any critical observations in this chapter (whether directed at Rothbard or at others) is certainly not to stir up strife within the Austrian camp; quite the reverse. I am convinced that a clear, shared understanding of Mises's central vision can bring together all those who appreciate the intellectual content of the Misesian legacy. To contribute an attempt in this direction, in honor of the memory of an outstanding exponent of that legacy, is the purpose of this chapter.

THE MISESIAN MARKET PROCESS

My own understanding of what Mises means when he describes the market as a process can be stated simply, as follows.

Mises saw the market process as a continually *corrective* process driven and constituted by active entrepreneurial grasping of pure profits.

> The essential fact is that it is the competition of profit-seeking entrepreneurs that does not tolerate the preservation of *false* prices of the

factors of production. The activities of the entrepreneurs are the element that would bring about the unrealizable state of the evenly rotating economy if no further changes were to occur.

(Mises, 1966, pp. 337–38; emphasis in the original)

The market process consists, that is, in the continual correction of false prices that occurs in the course of entrepreneurial competition. If exogenous changes were not to occur, this corrective process would eventually lead to a price structure for factors of production and consumer goods, in which all entrepreneurial profit has been squeezed out. In the real world, at any given moment, factors of production are able to be purchased at false prices, prices which permit entrepreneurs to capture pure entrepreneurial profits. False prices are false in that they incorrectly reflect the relative urgency of consumer demand for the various alternative possible products that can be created with these factors. It is this discoordination between what might be produced and what in fact is being produced, which offers alert entrepreneurs opportunities for pure gain.

What makes profit emerge is the fact that the entrepreneur who judges the future prices of the products more correctly than other people do buys some or all of the factors of production at prices which, seen from the point of view of the future state of the market, are too low.

(Mises [1951] 1962, p. 109)

Entrepreneurs "are the first to understand that there is a discrepancy between what is done and what could be done." Their activity brings about a systematic adjustment of factor prices. They "bid higher prices for some factors of production and lower the prices of other factors of production by restricting their demand for them." Their activity also generates price adjustments for consumer goods.

In supplying the market with those consumers' goods in the sale of which the highest profits can be earned, they create a tendency toward a fall in their prices. In restricting the output of those consumers' goods the production of which does not offer chances for reaping profit, they bring about a tendency toward a rise in their prices. All these transformations go on ceaselessly and could stop only if the unrealizable conditions of the evenly rotating economy and of static equilibrium were to be attained.

(Mises, 1966, p. 336)

·All this ceaseless sequence of corrective price adjustments constitutes Mises's entrepreneurial market process.

This Misesian corrective process from a false set of prices towards a set of fully mutually adjusted prices may be restated in the terms in which Hayek understood the market process to constitute a "discovery procedure" (Hayek [1968] 1978, ch. 12). "False" prices reflect the decisions of entrepreneurs who have not yet understood the correct implications of consumer preferences (present or future) for the relative values of resources today. The way in which entrepreneurial activity tends to correct such false prices is through their realization of the profit possibilities inherent in such false prices. Grasping these profit possibilities is the way in which entrepreneurs express their discoveries concerning the correct valuation of resources (and thus, in effect, concerning better ways in which resources can be deployed in serving the preferences of consumers). The tendency which this entrepreneurial process generates towards equilibration is thus one of gradually enhanced mutual anticipation on the part of market participants. In the theoretical limit, in the hypothetical state of equilibrium in which no entrepreneurs would earn profit or suffer losses, we would be able to say that "all people . . . anticipate correctly the future state of the market" (Mises [1951] 1962, p. 108). Although it was Hayek, rather than Mises, who extensively articulated the nature of the market equilibrating process as one of gradually enhanced mutual knowledge, there can be no doubt that an interpretation of the Misesian process in terms of enhanced mutual knowledge is a valid one. Disequilibrium prices are "false" prices; as entrepreneurial profit taking nudges prices towards their correct levels, entrepreneurs have been led to more accurate anticipations concerning relevant future market configurations.

What makes possible the entrepreneurially driven process of equilibration is active market competition. It is only the possibility of unrestricted entrepreneurial entry which permits more alert entrepreneurs to deploy their superior vision of the future in order to correct the misallocations of resources reflected in the false prices which characterize disequilibrium. It is the continual threat of such entry which tends to keep incumbent entrepreneurs alert and on their toes. The reason that Mises had little patience for the concept of perfect competition (see his approving reference to Hayek's pioneering essay on this matter, "The Meaning of Competition" [Mises, 1966, p. 278n]), was that this concept can relate only to an already attained state of equilibrium. It has nothing to do with, and can throw no light upon, the competitive forces which drive the entrepreneurial market process. In deepening his (and our) understanding of the competitive process as consisting in a discovery procedure, Hayek was articulating insights that are, at the very least, thoroughly consistent with Mises's own understanding of the dynamic entrepreneurial competition which, for Mises, constitutes the heart of this market process.

THE SHARED UNDERSTANDING OF MISES
AND HAYEK ON THE MARKET PROCESS

To draw attention, as we have in the preceding paragraphs, to the shared understanding that is apparent in Mises's and Hayek's treatment of the market process, is not to "homogenize" separate systems or "paradigms" of economic thought. Mises and Hayek are, to be sure, distinct thinkers with different views—sometimes fundamentally different views—on many issues in economic theory and method. There is a definite contribution to be made, towards properly understanding each of these two great Austrian economists, by drawing attention to the matters on which they disagree. But, we must insist, (a) the general character of the market process does *not* constitute such an area of disagreement; and (b) this area of shared understanding is so central to the work of both Mises and Hayek, that our awareness of their common position in this matter must definitively dispel any suggestion of the existence of a Misesian "paradigm," in regard to the market process, that is sharply to be distinguished from a Hayekian "paradigm." Yet such claims have recently been made.

MISES AND HAYEK DEHOMOGENIZED?

Professor Salerno has, in a number of recent papers (1990, 1991, 1993, 1994), initiated a line of intellectual historiography designed to drive a wedge between Mises's and Hayek's understanding of markets. Murray Rothbard and Jeffrey Herbener (Rothbard 1991, 1992, 1994; Herbener 1991) have hailed Salerno's thesis as providing definitive grounds for the rejection by all "Misesians" of what Salerno, Rothbard, and Herbener see as grave "Hayekian" errors.[1]

The asserted distinctions on the basis of which Salerno declares the existence of two paradigms, a Misesian and a Hayekian, can be summarized as follows: (a) Hayek was trained under Wieser, and this accounts for his failure to have absorbed the Mengerian insights which, through the teachings of Böhm-Bawerk, later matured into the Misesian position (Salerno, 1993, p. 114); (b) Hayek believed that "in order for prices to fulfill their knowledge-disseminating and plan-coordinating functions, the economy must subsist in a state of (what Salerno calls) 'proximal equilibrium,' wherein realized prices are always fairly accurate indicators of future prices" (p. 128); Mises, on the other hand, considered the concept of equilibrium as only a mental tool. It "is impossible to determine and meaningless to suggest that the real economy is closer to the FSR [final state of rest], and therefore manifests a superior coordination of plans and greater allocative efficiency, at one instant of time than it was at a previous instant" (p. 129). The social role fulfilled by prices does not depend on the attainment or near attainment of the FSR. This leads directly to the next point. (c) For Hayek, allocative efficiency consists in plan coordination among market participants. For Mises, on the other hand, the social efficiency achieved by the market consists (and is always perfectly attained) in the *ex ante* "appraisement and allocation of resources [by entrepreneurs] in strict accordance with anticipated consumer preferences" (p. 130). Salerno recognizes that, in regard to *ex post* efficiency, entrepreneurial errors are inevitable in a world of uncertainty and change. However, apparently the only systematic process which Salerno recognizes in Mises as tending to correct such *ex post* inefficiencies, is that in which less astute entrepreneurs come to be weeded out of the system through their repeated speculative failures and resulting losses (pp. 131ff.). (d) For Hayek the essence of the market process and of its social function, is in its overcoming of the "knowledge problem" arising out of dispersed knowledge "among the multitude of individual consumers and producers" (p. 115). It is this property of the market, and its absence in the socialist economy, which identified, for Hayek, the fundamental weakness of socialist planning. For Mises, on the other hand, Salerno and his colleagues claim, even if the socialist planners were miraculously endowed with perfect information, they would nonetheless be unable to "rationally calculate how to combine resources to render efficient production" (Herbener, 1991, p. 43).

It is, indeed, especially the interpretation of Mises's thesis concerning the impossibility of socialist economic calculation that has been perhaps the central focus of Salerno's "two-paradigm" thesis. After a number of pages in which Salerno (quite unsuccessfully, it must surely appear) seeks to refute Leland Yeager's definitive paper (Yeager, 1994) demonstrating that Mises's thesis does, after all, require that we attribute to Mises at least implicit recognition of Hayek's "knowledge problem," Salerno sums up as follows: "Thus market oriented PC [i.e., perfect competition] theorists, such as Hayek and Yeager, and neoclassical socialist GE [i.e., general equilibrium] theorists are brothers under the skin" (Salerno, 1994, p. 119).[2] Let us indeed, then, take up Salerno's treatment of the Misesian thesis; it will, I believe, permit us to confront Salerno's major points of contention. We shall, I further believe, be able in this way to place our finger not only on the source of the two-paradigm fallacy, but (at the same time), also on a significant element in Mises to which Salerno has properly drawn attention. The circumstances that Salerno's recognition of this element in Mises has, in our judgment, unfortunately misled him (and Rothbard) to see fundamental divergence where none exists, should not blind us to the value of this characteristically Misesian insight for Austrian economic understanding.

MISES AND THE CALCULATION PROBLEM

Salerno and Rothbard are fully justified in emphasizing the subtlety of the Misesian concept of economic calculation. With much of what they say in exposition of that concept, this writer is in full agreement. He objects only to the quite unwarranted conclusion which they draw from that exposition to the effect that the Misesian calculation problem has nothing whatever to do with Hayek's knowledge problem. A possible contribution to this unfortunate misunderstanding lies, I believe, in Hayek's earlier ambiguity concerning the nature of his knowledge problem. This writer has for a number of years (see Kirzner [1984] 1992, p. 149), pointed out that Hayek's brilliant 1945 paper, "The Use of Knowledge in Society," was seriously confused in making it appear that the function of prices in communicating knowledge was a function that is filled, in principle, also in the state of equilibrium. Salerno and Rothbard would be on firm ground if they objected, as this writer has objected, to such an equilibrium treatment of the place of knowledge and the communication function of prices. But the truth is (as becomes evident in Hayek's later work, see especially Hayek [1968] 1978) that Hayek's knowledge problem relates fundamentally to those states of affairs in which—precisely because of the knowledge problem—market agents are making plans which do not, in the fullest sense of the term, dovetail with each other.

As Salerno and Rothbard point out, calculation is needed in order to appraise the wisdom of prospective action. Without the tool of genuine money prices, economic agents would be reduced to comparing goods sacrificed and goods received, in the face of their obvious heterogeneity and incommensurability. Such an agent would be called upon, in effect (except in the simplest of Crusoe economies), to make decisions with his eyes closed; he would have no way of knowing whether his outcome represents profit or loss. Market prices provide the indispensable tool needed for calculation. Because the socialist society does not include resource markets, its central planners must operate without known resource values. Their decisions must be made, in effect, with eyes closed.

Under capitalism, entrepreneurs make their plans based on their entrepreneurial awareness of the resource prices they must pay in the more immediate future, and of the product prices they anticipate that they will be able to command in the more remote future. These anticipated prices provide the entrepreneur with cardinal numbers on the basis of which to appraise the profitability (or its absence) of prospective entrepreneurial activities. In the absence of resource prices under socialism, rational central planning is literally impossible, as Mises stated (and as Salerno and Rothbard quite correctly emphasize in their interpretation of Mises).

Where Salerno and Rothbard have (as demonstrated by Yeager) gone astray,[3] is in their refusal to recognize that this impossibility of rational calculation and action under socialism *can* illuminatingly be recognized as arising out of the limitations of the human planning mind—in other words, as consisting in a disastrous knowledge gap which, without market prices for resources, it is impossible to bridge. We may readily concede that Mises did not articulate his calculation problem in terms of knowledge; but this does not in the slightest imply that that problem cannot be seen to consist of a knowledge problem. Reasonable interpreters of Mises may disagree on whether (as this writer emphatically believes to be the case) Mises's calculation problem is indeed seen more clearly when its knowledge implications are made explicit. But there is no basis whatever for claiming that, in exposing these knowledge implications of the Misesian argument, one is distorting or falsifying that argument.

To be unable to calculate the worthwhileness of a prospective action taken in a market society, is, after all, to not know the importance to others of the goods and services one commits to that action, and the importance to others of the goods one will obtain from that action. It is quite true, that Mises pointed out (and Salerno and Rothbard cite this again and again) that the calculation problem would exist even for a socialist planning authority possessing on its desks and in its computer memories, the fullest technological information of the age, full information on available resource availabilities, and full (and somehow, unanimous) information of the social ranking of the importance of ends. This is because, even armed with such "knowledge" (or, perhaps, precisely because the authority would be engulfed by these floods of information), the members of the authority would still not know what they would need to know, in order to calculate. As Leland Yeager has explained, possessing all this information is not the same as having assimilated it, and having been able to deploy it (whether by computing the solution to simultaneous equation systems, or whatever) to discover the relative values of the relevant resources and products. The members of the authority would not know what one needs to know in order to calculate the worthwhileness of prospective decisions.

For Mises (as Salerno and Rothbard correctly point out) prices are not primarily signals economizing on the cost of communicating information.[4] Their social function consists in providing decision makers with meaningful cardinal numbers with which to calculate the worthwhileness of prospective actions. To be "meaningful" we do not require these cardinal numbers to be roughly equal to or close to relevant equilibrium values. We require only that, at each point in time, these cardinal numbers reflect the interplay of the decisions made by the keenest (as well as those less keen) of the entrepreneurial minds in the market economy. In all this, I am in complete agreement with Salerno and Rothbard.

But it is precisely here, I believe, that Salerno and Rothbard have, in properly drawing attention to an underemphasized element in Mises's position on economic calculation, been led into error. The element being here referred to is that, for Mises, even market prices that are very far from their equilibrium values perform a valuable role in enabling entrepreneurs to calculate. Let me emphasize even more starkly the aspect of this element in Mises which appears to have most impressed Salerno and Rothbard: even if we could imagine that the equilibrating market process has not yet succeeded in nudging disequilibrium prices at all towards equilibrium, these prices yet perform their social role in making possible economic calculation. It is apparently this aspect of the Misesian position which has taught Salerno and Rothbard that what makes calculation possible cannot be and is not that knowledge-enhancing process which, for Hayek and other Austrians, constitutes the process of market equilibration. It followed, for these two scholars, that the Misesian calculation problem under socialism cannot and must not be identified with the Hayekian knowledge problem (which tends to become solved during the course of the equilibrating market process). But there is no reason at all to arrive at such an understanding (or, rather, misunderstanding) of Mises's position.

FALSE PRICES AND LESS FALSE PRICES

As cited earlier, Mises certainly did recognize that disequilibrium market prices are, in a sense, "false prices": they reflect erroneous expectations (i.e., erroneous "knowledge") being held by entrepreneurs concerning the true preferences of consumers. It is the equilibrating force generated by the process of entrepreneurial competition, we saw, which for Mises tended to replace false prices by less false prices. We have every reason to believe that, when Mises sees market prices as effective tools for entrepreneurial calculation, his view of prices is, at the very least, rendered even more benign by his understanding of the market process in which earlier false prices have tended to have become replaced by less false prices. (Of course this tendency may be frustrated by entrepreneurial error in an uncertain, changing world. There is no guarantee that today's prices are necessarily less false than yesterday's. But this possibility does not eliminate the existence of a systematic process in which entrepreneurial profit-seeking activity identifies those false prices which promise pure profits, and, by grasping those profits, tends to replace them by prices which more accurately reflect the true values to consumers, of resources and products.)

Salerno and Rothbard are right to emphasize that for Mises the prices which prevail at any time fulfill their function of rendering economic calculation possible. This, we must insist, is not because all prices, at all times, are "market clearing prices," in any sense relevant for our evaluation of the social efficiency of the price system. After all, false prices reflect production plans which are, by definition, at variance with the true preferences of consumers. The Misesian insight that all prices, at all times, render economic calculation possible, arises out of two closely related circumstances: (a) at each instant in time, the price offers and bids, and thus also the realized prices, reflect the expectations of the most canny entrepreneurs in the market (so that what may, a day later, with the wisdom of hindsight, indeed be seen as having been false prices, were nonetheless, in terms of the most perceptive entrepreneurial assessment of the preceding day, at that time expressive of the most judicious readings—the best knowledge—of consumer preferences); (b) at each instant in time, current prices are the outcomes of processes of entrepreneurial profit-seeking corrections of still earlier false prices; at no time, in the real world, can we say that the corrective market process has not yet begun its work. At each instant, therefore, current market prices reflect the best conceivable estimates of relative consumer preferences. The calculations which entrepreneurs make by reference to such prices (and by reference to such expected future prices) are thus informed by the assessment of the shrewdest of entrepreneurs, operating under the powerful incentive of winning pure profits.

What we wish to stress is that the capacity of market prices to inspire calculative economic activity is based solidly on the extent to which prices do express correct assessments of (i.e., the relevant knowledge regarding) both current and future preferences of consumers, and the current and future production plans of other entrepreneurs. As Mises pointed out in his first statements on the calculation problem (see, e.g., Mises [1922] 1936, pp. 115–17), market prices are not perfect tools in this respect: but they are extraordinarily valuable tools nonetheless. Their value surely lies in the expression of the best available entrepreneurial knowledge concerning market conditions.

It is quite true that for Mises this "best available entrepreneurial knowledge" expressed in current market prices would be valuably useful for calculation purposes, even if one could imagine these prices not already to reflect the corrective entrepreneurial market process which tends to replace false prices with prices less false. But the circumstance that in fact current market prices reflect that corrective market process (and our awareness that Mises did indeed emphasize this circumstance in regard to market prices) should convince us that an appreciation of the role of market prices stated in terms of the "Hayekian" knowledge problem is simply a somewhat differently articulated appreciation for the calculative properties Mises taught us to understand to exist in those market prices.

SOME OBSERVATIONS ON THE MISESIAN LEGACY

Mises had a profound and subtle understanding of the market's operation. In that understanding, the character of the market as a process in
which mistaken entrepreneurial judgments tend to come to be replaced
by more accurate judgments (and thus one in which false prices are
replaced by less false prices), was a central feature: Hayek, too, had his
own understanding of the market's operation. In certain respects, particularly in its articulation of the role of knowledge and discovery, that understanding can be differentiated from that of Mises. But the centrality of the
knowledge-corrective character of the market process for both Mises and
Hayek cannot seriously be doubted. Whatever the differences between
a Hayekian articulation of the market process and a Misesian articulation, the centrality of the notion of the corrective process for both, is the
crucially important circumstance. It is this that should convince us that
any talk of a Hayekian "paradigm" which differs fundamentally from the
Misesian paradigm should be dismissed as not only reflecting a mistaken
doctrinal judgment, but as reflecting a mistaken judgment with poten-
tially catastrophic implications for the future of Austrian economics.

Austrians are a beleaguered minority in the economics profession
today. One of the core doctrinal issues separating Austrian economics
from the mainstream is that Austrians understand the entrepreneurial
character of the market process. We learned this from Mises. From Hayek
we learned additional, complementary insights. If we wish to preserve
and build upon the Misesian legacy, we must not generate confusion
(both among Austrians and their opponents) by exaggerating perceived
differences between Mises and Hayek, to the point where the centrally
shared insights of both are dangerously obscured.

NOTES

1. Because of Salerno's initiating and prominent role in the "two-paradigm" literature, this section refers primarily to his writings. However, similar statements can
typically also be found in the above cited papers of Rothbard and Herbener.

2. The biting sarcasm employed in this assertion is but a relatively mild example
of the rhetorical excesses appallingly to be found in the "two-paradigm" literature
against such writers as Hayek, Lachmann, and others charged with having diverged
from the asserted "Misesian paradigm." I take this opportunity strongly to protest
the use of verbal terrorism in Austrian economics. Even if (which is far from being
the case) the asserted criticisms of Hayek, Lachmann, and others were valid, there

would be absolutely no justification for the manner in which these great economists have been treated in the literature under discussion. The near-demonization of Hayek and Lachmann for alleged deviations from an asserted Misesian orthodoxy is a most distressing phenomenon. If Austrian economists (and the *Review of Austrian Economics*) are to be able to work constructively in the rough and tumble of the intellectual market place, anything approaching rhetorical brawling must once and for all be rejected.

3. This chapter concentrates critically only upon those aspects of Salerno's and Rothbard's papers which are directly relevant to our placing the market process at the center of Mises's system. We do not take up here any criticism of a number of related assertions contained in these papers (concerning: entrepreneurship, uncertainty, the future, alertness, discovery, and coordination) which this writer finds puzzling, contradictory, or otherwise based on possible misunderstanding.

4. This is the aspect of Hayek's 1945 paper which the mainstream literature (and now Salerno *et al.*) have seen as central to Hayek's position. This writer has long deplored according centrality to such a "communication" role, and has argued that Hayek's later work suggests that he, too, saw beyond such a narrow interpretation of the role of prices (see Kirzner [1984] 1992, ch. 8).

REFERENCES

Hayek, Friedrich A. (1978) "Competition as a Discovery Procedure," in *New Studies in Philosophy, Politics, Economics, and the History of Ideas*, Chicago: University of Chicago Press. This paper was delivered as a lecture in 1968.

Herbener, Jeffrey M. (1991) "Ludwig von Mises and the Austrian School of Economics," *Review of Austrian Economics* 5(2), pp. 33–50.

Kirzner, Israel M. (1984) "Prices, the Communication of Knowledge and the Discovery Process," in Kurt R. Leube and Albert H. Zlabinger (eds.) *The Political Economy of Freedom: Essays in Honor of F. A. Hayek*, Vienna: Philosophia Verlag. Reprinted in I. M. Kirzner (1992) *The Meaning of Market Process: Essays in the Development of Modern Austrian Economics*, London and New York: Routledge.

Mises, Ludwig von (1936) *Socialism: An Economic and Sociological Analysis*, trans. J. Kahane, London: Jonathan Cape; German original published in 1922.

———— [1951] (1962) "Profit and Loss," reprinted in *Planning for Freedom*, 2nd edn., South Holland, IL: Libertarian Press.

———— (1966) *Human Action: A Treatise on Economics*, 3rd rev. edn., Chicago: Contemporary Books.

Rothbard, Murray N. (1991) "The End of Socialism and the Calculation Debate Revisited," *Review of Austrian Economics* 5(2), pp. 51–76.

———— (1992) "The Present State of Austrian Economics," Working Paper of the Ludwig von Mises Institute.

———— (1994) Review of Bruce Caldwell and Stephan Boehm (eds.) *Austrian Economics: Tensions and New Directions, Southern Economic Journal*, October.

Salerno, Joseph T. (1990) "Ludwig von Mises as Social Rationalist," *Review of Austrian Economics* 4, pp. 26–54.

———— (1991) "Commentary: The Concept of Coordination in Austrian Macroeconomics," in Richard M. Ebeling (ed.) *Austrian Economics, Perspectives on the Past and Prospects for the Future,* Champions of Freedom Series, Vol. 17, Hillsdale, MI: Hillsdale College Press.

———— (1993) "Mises and Hayek Dehomogenized," *Review of Austrian Economics* 6(2), pp. 113–46.

———— (1994) "Reply to Leland B. Yeager on 'Mises and Hayek on Calculation and Knowledge,'" *Review of Austrian Economics* 7(2), pp. 111–25.

Yeager, Leland B. (1994) "Mises and Hayek on Calculation and Knowledge," *Review of Austrian Economics* 7(2), pp. 93–109.

TRIBUTE TO VON MISES: "ON THE MARKET"

In paying tribute to the memory of an inspiring teacher and towering scholar and thinker, it seems eminently appropriate to draw attention to the major intellectual "vision" which sparked and sustained the master's contributions to his science. To those who knew him, Ludwig Mises was, in the face of shocking neglect by so many of his contemporaries, a living exemplar of incorruptible intellectual integrity, a model of passionate, relentless scholarship and dedication. It will not be easy to forget these stern lessons which he so courageously personified. But what will surely live on even longer in future histories of economic thought will be those distinctive elements of Mises's extraordinary contribution which set it so clearly apart from the dominant economics of his age. It was into the enunciation of these elements that Mises poured a lifetime of what can almost be called intellectual martyrdom. It is for the brief exposition of one of these brilliantly seminal ideas—the perception of the market exclusively in process terms—that these lines are set down.

In the sweep of the development of economic ideas over the past two centuries, the concept held by the various thinkers concerning the market has been crucial. The pioneers of modern economics after 1870, reinvigorating the contributions of the earlier classical economists by the infusion of powerful new insights into the nature of demand, offered a view of the operation of the market society which was of enormous significance. Henceforth economic literacy could not fail to embrace the understanding of the way in which the free interaction of the decisions of owners of resources, of producers, and of consumers in the market systematically generates determinate patterns of prices, output quantities and qualities, methods of production, and resource allocation.

However, in the ferment of intellectual developments in economics during the twentieth century, this understanding came, in the work of the dominant schools, to be perceived within a mechanistic framework

From Israel M. Kirzner, *The Driving Force of the Market: Essays in Austrian Economics* (New York and London: Routledge, 2000), 275–77; the original source is "Tribute to von Mises," part IV, *National Review* (November 9, 1973): 1246, 1260. © 1973 by National Review, Inc. Reprinted by permission.

which did violence to the subtle insights a more profound awareness of the market is able to confer. The market came to be seen as a kind of computer, grinding our the equilibrium solution compatible with the basic data of the system—a task which presumes that the economic actors already possess perfect knowledge. The theory of the market came to mean the solving by the theorist of the computation problem. Moreover this theory came to be seen as equally well suited to the needs of societies choosing to allocate their resources by central direction; the socialist planner could, it came to be thought, simulate the success with which the market allocates resources by merely addressing himself to the very same computation problem which it was thought to be the function of market theory to solve.

It was this view of the market which Mises denied with every ounce of energy. It is no exaggeration to say that this denial was central to the major portion of Mises's disagreements with the various economic doctrines of his age. Future economists, when they come to accept, as in time they surely must, the validity of the Misesian critique of the faulty perception of the market, will find it necessary to re-examine many of the doctrines of contemporary economics with which Mises took issue. For Mises the market is not a computer grinding out equilibrium solutions to sets of simultaneous equations. Rather the market is a delicate *process* whereby, against the background of continually changing conditions, and with information available only in limited and piecemeal fashion, the decisions of market participants are, through their interplay in the market, brought into steadily more dovetailing adjustment. In this process the key roles are played by restless, active, ever alert entrepreneurship, and by its counterpart, the merciless, ceaseless, impartial court of active competition. Both these latter roles—completely absent in the dominant equilibrium versions of market theory—are crucial in the emergence of the kaleidoscopically changing patterns of market prices.

It was the "process" perception of markets and of market prices that led Mises unerringly to dismiss all attempts to recognize "non-market prices" as devices through which socialist planners might simulate the achievements of the market economy. The notion of non-market prices can have relevance only in a world of equilibrium situations; it bears no analytical or functional resemblance to the prices which emerge, during disequilibrium, in markets revealing the impact of entrepreneurial competition against a background of widespread ignorance.

It was the "process" perception of markets and of market prices that led Mises to deplore with such sharpness the dominance over economics achieved by mathematical techniques during his own lifetime. Such techniques, useful though they may be to the derivation of the conditions for equilibria of various kinds, must inevitably mask the more subtle processes of entrepreneurial change which (because they depend on essentially extra-economic flashes of awareness) do not permit analysis within the procrustean bed of maximization techniques.

And it was the "process" perception of markets and of market prices that led Mises to reject the various attempts by economists since the 1930s to build theories of the market based on notions of monopolistic or imperfect competition. Such models fail, Mises believed, because they reveal precisely the central weaknesses of the theories they seek to replace, viz., an exclusive concern with equilibrium, and a failure to understand the active entrepreneurial-competitive process.

No economist perceived more thoroughly and sadly than Mises how the rejection of his ideas was leading Western societies relentlessly down a path along which the free interplay of independent, individual decisions in the market was being steadily replaced by the centralization of more and more political and economic power in the hands of governments and their functionaries. If Western society ever achieves a reversal of this trend, if it ever learns to respect the decisions of free men interacting within a framework of rigorously maintained individual rights, it can only be as a result of Mises's vision and insight into the true character of the market society. Here indeed we have a monument to Mises the construction of which is well worth our diligence and our dedication.

PUBLISHED WORKS OF ISRAEL M. KIRZNER

Compiled by Peter J. Boettke, Frédéric E. Sautet, and Rosolino A. Candela

BOOKS

1960

The Economic Point of View. Princeton, N.J.: Van Nostrand, 1960.

Reprinted Kansas City, Mo.: Sheed and Ward, 1976.
Romanian edition, 1996.
Reprinted in The Collected Works of Israel M. Kirzner, ed. Peter J.
   Boettke and Frédéric Sautet. Indianapolis: Liberty Fund, 2009.

1963

Market Theory and the Price System. Princeton, N.J.: Van Nostrand, 1963.

Reprinted in The Collected Works of Israel M. Kirzner, ed. Peter J.
   Boettke and Frédéric Sautet. Indianapolis: Liberty Fund, 2011.

1966

An Essay on Capital. New York, N.Y.: August M. Kelley, 1966.

Reprinted in Peter J. Boettke and Frédéric Sautet, eds., *Essays on Capital
   and Interest: An Austrian Perspective*, 14–133. Indianapolis: Liberty
   Fund, 2012.

1973

Competition and Entrepreneurship. Chicago: University of Chicago Press,
   1973.

Spanish edition, 1975.
German edition, 1978.
Paperback (English) edition, Chicago: University of Chicago Press, 1978.
Japanese edition, 1985.
Portuguese edition, 1986.
Reprinted in The Collected Works of Israel M. Kirzner, ed. Peter J.
   Boettke and Frédéric Sautet. Indianapolis: Liberty Fund, 2013.

1979

Perception, Opportunity, and Profit: Studies in the Theory of Entrepreneurship.
   Chicago: University of Chicago Press, 1979.

Paperback edition, 1983.
German edition, 1988.

1982

Method, Process, and Austrian Economics: Essays in Honor of Ludwig von Mises. Lexington, Mass.: Lexington Books, 1982.

1985

Discovery and the Capitalist Process. Chicago: University of Chicago Press, 1985.

1986

Subjectivism, Intelligibility, and Economic Understanding: Essays in Honor of Ludwig M. Lachmann on His Eightieth Birthday. New York: New York University Press, 1986.

Views on Individualism: Presentations. St. Louis, Mo.: Saint Louis Humanities Forum, 1986.

1988

Unternehmer und Marktdynamik. Munich: Philosophia Verlag, 1988.

1989

Discovery, Capitalism, and Distributive Justice. Oxford: Basil Blackwell, 1989.

Spanish edition, 1995.
Reprinted in The Collected Works of Israel M. Kirzner, ed. Peter J. Boettke and Frédéric Sautet. Indianapolis: Liberty Fund, 2016.

1992

The Meaning of Market Process: Essays in the Development of Modern Austrian Economics. London and New York: Routledge, 1992.

1994

Classics in Austrian Economics: A Sampling in the History of a Tradition. 3 vols. London: William Pickering and Chatto, 1994.

1996

Essays on Capital and Interest: An Austrian Perspective. Aldershot, U.K., and Brookfield, Mass.: Edward Elgar, 1996.

Reprinted in The Collected Works of Israel M. Kirzner, ed. Peter J. Boettke and Frédéric Sautet. Indianapolis: Liberty Fund, 2012.

1997

How Markets Work: Disequilibrium, Entrepreneurship, and Discovery. IEA Hobart Paper 133. London: Coronet Books, 1997.

Italian translation, 2002.

Reprinted in Peter J. Boettke and Frédéric Sautet, eds., *Competition, Economic Planning, and the Knowledge Problem*, 257–322. Carmel, Ind.: Liberty Fund, 2018.

2000

The Driving Force of the Market: Essays in Austrian Economics. London and New York: Routledge, Foundations of the Market Economy, 2000.

2001

Ludwig von Mises: The Man and His Economics. Wilmington, Del.: ISI Books, 2001.

Reprinted in The Collected Works of Israel M. Kirzner, ed. Peter J. Boettke and Frédéric Sautet. Carmel, Ind.: Liberty Fund, 2019.

2015

Austrian Subjectivism and the Emergence of Entrepreneurship Theory. In The Collected Works of Israel M. Kirzner, ed. Peter J. Boettke and Frédéric Sautet. Indianapolis: Liberty Fund, 2015.

2018

The Essence of Entrepreneurship and Nature and Significance of Market Process. In The Collected Works of Israel M. Kirzner, ed. Peter J. Boettke and Frédéric Sautet. Carmel, Ind.: Liberty Fund, 2018.

2019

Reflections on Ethics, Freedom, Welfare Economics, Policy, and the Legacy of Austrian Economics. In The Collected Works of Israel M. Kirzner, ed. Peter J. Boettke and Frédéric Sautet. Carmel, Ind.: Liberty Fund, 2019.

ARTICLES AND CHAPTERS IN BOOKS

1962

"Rational Action and Economic Theory." *Journal of Political Economy* 70, no. 4 (August 1962): 380–85.

Reprinted in Stephen C. Littlechild, ed., *Austrian Economics* 1:481–86. Aldershot, U.K., and Brookfield, Mass.: Edward Elgar, 1990.

Reprinted in Peter J. Boettke and Frédéric Sautet, eds., *The Economic Point of View*, 211–20. Indianapolis: Liberty Fund, 2009.

1963

"On the Premises of Growth Economics." *New Individualist Review* 3, no. 1 (Summer 1963): 20–28.

> Reprinted in Peter J. Boettke and Frédéric Sautet, eds., *The Essence of Entrepreneurship and the Nature and Significance of Market Process*, 291–304. Carmel, Ind.: Liberty Fund, 2018.

"Rational Action and Economic Theory: Rejoinder." *Journal of Political Economy* 71, no. 1 (February 1963): 84–85.

> Reprinted in Peter J. Boettke and Frédéric Sautet, eds., *The Economic Point of View*, 225–27. Indianapolis: Liberty Fund, 2009.

1965

"What Economists Do." *Southern Economics Journal* 31, no. 3 (January 1965): 257–61.

> Reprinted in Peter J. Boettke and Frédéric Sautet, eds., *Reflections on Ethics, Freedom, Welfare Economics, Policy, and the Legacy of Austrian Economics*, 119–25. Carmel, Ind.: Liberty Fund, 2019.

1967

"Divergent Approaches in Libertarian Economic Thought." *Intercollegiate Review* 3 (January–February 1967): 101–8.

> Reprinted in Peter J. Boettke and Frédéric Sautet, eds., *Reflections on Ethics, Freedom, Welfare Economics, Policy, and the Legacy of Austrian Economics*, 18–30. Carmel, Ind.: Liberty Fund, 2019.

"Methodological Individualism, Market Equilibrium and Market Process." *Il politico* 32, no. 4 (December 1967): 787–99.

> Reprinted in Peter J. Boettke and Frédéric Sautet, eds., *Austrian Subjectivism and the Emergence of the Entrepreneurship Theory*, 175–89. Indianapolis: Liberty Fund, 2015.

1970

"The 'Power' Problem on Campus: An Economist's View." *Intercollegiate Review* 6 (Spring 1970): 99–103.

> Reprinted in *Freeman* 20, no. 8 (August 1970): 476–82.
> Reprinted in Peter J. Boettke and Frédéric Sautet, eds., *Reflections on Ethics, Freedom, Welfare Economics, Policy, and the Legacy of Austrian Economics*, 69–75. Carmel, Ind.: Liberty Fund, 2019.

1971

"Entrepreneurship and the Market Approach to Development." In F. A. Hayek, Henry Hazlitt, Leonard R. Read, Gustavo Velasco, and

F. A. Harper, eds., *Toward Liberty: Essays in Honor of Ludwig von Mises* 2:194–208. Menlo Park, Calif.: Institute for Humane Studies, 1971.

Published as "La función del empresario y el desarrollo economico" in *Tópicos de actualidad* 15, no. 298 (July 1973).

Reprinted in *Perception, Opportunity, and Profit: Studies in the Theory of Entrepreneurship*, 107–19. Chicago: University of Chicago Press, 1979.

Reprinted in Peter J. Boettke and Frédéric Sautet, eds., *The Essence of Entrepreneurship and the Nature and Significance of Market Process*, 310–22. Carmel, Ind.: Liberty Fund, 2018.

1972

"Advertising." *Freeman* 22, no. 9 (September 1972): 515–28.

Reprinted in Tibor R. Machan, ed., *The Libertarian Alternative: Essays in Social and Political Philosophy*, 478–91. Chicago: Nelson Hall, 1974.

Reprinted in Peter J. Boettke and Frédéric Sautet, eds., *Competition, Economic Planning, and the Knowledge Problem*, 232–45. Carmel, Ind.: Liberty Fund, 2018.

"Altruism, Social Responsibility, and the Market Economy." *Hillsdale Report* 11, no. 4 (1972): 1–6.

Reprinted in Peter J. Boettke and Frédéric Sautet, eds., *Reflections on Ethics, Freedom, Welfare Economics, Policy, and the Legacy of Austrian Economics*, 231–43. Carmel, Ind.: Liberty Fund, 2019.

1973

"Tribute to von Mises: On the Market." *National Review*, November 9, 1973, 1246, 1260.

Reprinted as "Ludwig von Mises, 1881–1973: On the Market" in *The Driving Force of the Market: Essays in Austrian Economics*, 275–77. London and New York: Routledge, Foundations of the Market Economy, 2000.

Reprinted as "Tribute to Von Mises: 'On the Market'" in Peter J. Boettke and Frédéric Sautet, eds., *Ludwig von Mises: The Man and His Economics*, 227–29. Carmel, Ind.: Liberty Fund, 2019.

1974

"Capital, Competition, and Capitalism." In *Champions of Freedom: The Ludwig von Mises Lecture Series*, Hillsdale, Mich.: Hillsdale College Press, 1974.

Reprinted in *Perception, Opportunity, and Profit: Studies in the Theory of Entrepreneurship*, 91–106. Chicago: University of Chicago Press, 1979.

Reprinted in Peter J. Boettke and Frédéric Sautet, eds., *Competition, Economic Planning, and the Knowledge Problem*, 3–17. Carmel, Ind.: Liberty Fund, 2018.

"Producer, Entrepreneur, and the Right to Property." *Reason Papers*, no. 1 (Fall 1974): 1–17.

Reprinted in Samuel L. Blumenfeld, ed., *Property in a Humane Economy*, 245–62. La Salle, Ill.: Open Court, 1974.
Reprinted in *Perception, Opportunity, and Profit: Studies in the Theory of Entrepreneurship*, 185–99. Chicago: University of Chicago Press, 1979.
Reprinted in Peter J. Boettke and Frédéric Sautet, eds., *Discovery, Capitalism, and Distributive Justice*, 173–87. Indianapolis: Liberty Fund, 2016.

"The Ugly Market: Why Capitalism Is Hated, Feared, and Despised." *Freeman* 24, no. 12 (December 1974): 724–36.

Reprinted in Mark W. Hendrickson, ed., *The Morality of Capitalism*, Irvington-on-Hudson, N.Y.: Foundation for Economic Education, 1992.
Reprinted in Parth J. Shah, ed., *Morality of Markets*, 69–82. New Delhi: Academic Foundation, 2004.
Reprinted in Peter J. Boettke and Frédéric Sautet, eds., *Reflections on Ethics, Freedom, Welfare Economics, Policy, and the Legacy of Austrian Economics*, 244–56. Carmel, Ind.: Liberty Fund, 2019.

1976

"Discussion." In Wassily Leontief and Herbert Stein, *The Economic System in an Age of Discontinuity: Long Range Planning or Market Reliance?* New York: New York University Press, 1976.

"Equilibrium versus Market Process." Published in Edwin G. Dolan, ed., *The Foundations of Modern Austrian Economics*, 115–25. Kansas City, Mo.: Sheed and Ward, 1976.

Reprinted in *Perception, Opportunity, and Profit: Studies in the Theory of Entrepreneurship*, 3–12. Chicago: University of Chicago Press, 1979.
Reprinted in Peter J. Boettke and Frédéric Sautet, eds., *The Essence of Entrepreneurship and the Nature and Significance of Market Process*, 125–33. Carmel, Ind.: Liberty Fund, 2018.

"Ludwig von Mises and the Theory of Capital and Interest." In Laurence S. Moss, ed., *The Economics of Ludwig von Mises: Toward a Critical Reappraisal*, 51–66. Kansas City, Mo.: Sheed and Ward, 1976.

Reprinted in *Perception, Opportunity, and Profit: Studies in the Theory of Entrepreneurship*, 76–87. Chicago: University of Chicago Press, 1979.
Reprinted in Stephen C. Littlechild, ed., *Austrian Economics* 2:93–107. Aldershot, U.K., and Brookfield, Mass.: Edward Elgar, 1990.

Reprinted in Richard Ebeling, ed., *Austrian Economics: A Reader,* 464–80. Champions of Freedom Series, vol. 18. Hillsdale, Mich.: Hillsdale College Press, 1991.

Reprinted in Peter J. Boettke and Frédéric Sautet, eds., *Essays on Capital and Interest: An Austrian Perspective,* 134–46. Indianapolis: Liberty Fund, 2012.

"The 1975 Nobel Memorial Prize in Economics: Some Uncomfortable Reflections." *Freeman* 26, no. 4 (April 1976): 206–11.

Reprinted in Peter J. Boettke and Frédéric Sautet, eds., *The Essence of Entrepreneurship and the Nature and Significance of Market Process,* 281–86. Carmel, Ind.: Liberty Fund, 2018.

"On the Method of Austrian Economics." In Edwin G. Dolan, ed., *The Foundations of Modern Austrian Economics,* 40–51. Kansas City, Mo.: Sheed and Ward, 1976.

Reprinted in Stephen C. Littlechild, ed., *Austrian Economics* 1:313–24. Aldershot, U.K., and Brookfield, Mass.: Edward Elgar, 1990.

Published in Spanish as "Sobre el método de la economia austriaca." *Revista libertas* (May 1990).

Published in Italian as "Sul metodo dell'economia austriaca." *Nuova civiltà delle macchine* 16, no. 3/4 (1998): 14–20.

Reprinted in Peter J. Boettke and Frédéric Sautet, eds., *Austrian Subjectivism and the Emergence of the Entrepreneurship Theory,* 1–10. Indianapolis: Liberty Fund, 2015.

"Philosophical and Ethical Implications of Austrian Economics." In Edwin G. Dolan, ed., *The Foundations of Modern Austrian Economics,* 75–88. Kansas City, Mo.: Sheed and Ward, 1976.

Reprinted as "Philosophical and Ethical Implications in 'Austrian' Economic Theory" in *Nuova civiltà delle macchine* 29, no. 1–2 (2011): 32–44.

Reprinted in Peter J. Boettke and Frédéric Sautet, eds., *Reflections on Ethics, Freedom, Welfare Economics, Policy, and the Legacy of Austrian Economics,* 87–98. Carmel, Ind.: Liberty Fund, 2019.

"The Theory of Capital." In Edwin G. Dolan, ed., *The Foundations of Modern Austrian Economics,* 133–44. Kansas City, Mo.: Sheed and Ward, 1976.

Reprinted in Peter J. Boettke and Frédéric Sautet, eds., *Essays on Capital and Interest: An Austrian Perspective,* 169–78. Indianapolis: Liberty Fund, 2012.

1978

"Economics and Error." In Louis M. Spadaro, ed., *New Directions in Austrian Economics,* 57–76. Kansas City, Mo.: Sheed, Andrews, and McMeel, 1978.

Reprinted in *Perception, Opportunity, and Profit: Studies in the Theory of Entrepreneurship,* 120–36. Chicago: University of Chicago Press, 1979.

Reprinted in Peter J. Boettke and Frédéric Sautet, eds., *The Essence of Entrepreneurship and the Nature and Significance of Market Process*, 248–63. Carmel, Ind.: Liberty Fund, 2018.

"The Entrepreneurial Role in Menger's System." *Atlantic Economic Journal* 6, no. 3 (September 1978): 31–45.

Reprinted in *Perception, Opportunity, and Profit: Studies in the Theory of Entrepreneurship*, 53–75. Chicago: University of Chicago Press, 1979.

Reprinted in Peter J. Boettke and Frédéric Sautet, eds., *Austrian Subjectivism and the Emergence of the Entrepreneurship Theory*, 151–74. Indianapolis: Liberty Fund, 2015.

"Entrepreneurship, Entitlement, and Economic Justice." *Eastern Economic Journal* 4, no. 1 (January 1978): 9–25.

Reprinted in *Perception, Opportunity, and Profit: Studies in the Theory of Entrepreneurship*, 200–224. Chicago: University of Chicago Press, 1979.

Reprinted in J. Paul, ed., *Reading Nozick: Essays on Anarchy, State, and Utopia*. Totowa, 383–412. N.J.: Rowman and Littlefield, 1981.

Reprinted in Peter Vallentyne and Hillel Steiner, eds., *Left Libertarianism and Its Critics: The Contemporary Debate*, 191–213. New York: Palgrave, 2000.

Reprinted in Peter J. Boettke and Frédéric Sautet, eds., *Discovery, Capitalism, and Distributive Justice*, 188–213. Indianapolis: Liberty Fund, 2016.

"Foreword" to new edition of Ludwig von Mises, *The Ultimate Foundation of Economic Science: An Essay on Method*, v–ix. Kansas City, Mo.: Sheed, Andrews, and McMeel, 1978.

"The Perils of Regulation: A Market-Process Approach." Occasional Paper. Miami, Fla.: Law and Economics Center, University of Miami School of Law, 1978.

Reprinted in *Discovery and the Capitalist Process*, 119–49. Chicago: University of Chicago Press, 1985.

Reprinted in Richard Ebeling, ed., *Austrian Economics: A Reader*, 618–54. Champions of Freedom Series, vol. 18. Hillsdale, Mich.: Hillsdale College Press, 1991.

Reprinted in Peter J. Boettke and Frédéric Sautet, eds., *Reflections on Ethics, Freedom, Welfare Economics, Policy, and the Legacy of Austrian Economics*, 418–45. Carmel, Ind.: Liberty Fund, 2019.

1979

"Alertness, Luck, and Entrepreneurial Profit." In *Perception, Opportunity, and Profit: Studies in the Theory of Entrepreneurship*, 154–81. Chicago: University of Chicago Press, 1979.

Reprinted in Peter J. Boettke and Frédéric Sautet, eds., *The Essence of Entrepreneurship and the Nature and Significance of Market Process*, 24–49. Carmel, Ind.: Liberty Fund, 2018.

"Classical Economics and the Entrepreneurial Role." In *Perception, Opportunity, and Profit: Studies in the Theory of Entrepreneurship*, 37–52. Chicago: University of Chicago Press, 1979.

Reprinted in Peter J. Boettke and Frédéric Sautet, eds., *Austrian Subjectivism and the Emergence of the Entrepreneurship Theory*, 123–38. Indianapolis: Liberty Fund, 2015.

"Entrepreneurship, Choice, and Freedom." In *Festgabe für F. A. von Hayek*, special issue of *ORDO: Jahrbuch für die Ordnung von Wirtschaft und Gesellschaft*, Band 30 (May 1979): 245–56.

Reprinted in *Perception, Opportunity, and Profit: Studies in the Theory of Entrepreneurship*, 225–39. Chicago: University of Chicago Press, 1979.

Reprinted in Peter J. Boettke and Frédéric Sautet, eds., *Reflections on Ethics, Freedom, Welfare Economics, Policy, and the Legacy of Austrian Economics*, 3–17. Carmel, Ind.: Liberty Fund, 2019.

"Has the Libertarian Movement Gone Kooky? A Spirited Exchange." *National Review*, August 3, 1979, 967.

"Hayek, Knowledge, and Market Processes." In *Perception, Opportunity, and Profit: Studies in the Theory of Entrepreneurship*, 13–33. Chicago: University of Chicago Press, 1979.

Reprinted in Peter J. Boettke and Frédéric Sautet, eds., *The Essence of Entrepreneurship and the Nature and Significance of Market Process*, 134–55. Carmel, Ind.: Liberty Fund, 2018.

"Knowing about Knowledge: A Subjectivist View of the Role of Information." In *Perception, Opportunity, and Profit: Studies in the Theory of Entrepreneurship*, 137–53. Chicago: University of Chicago Press, 1979.

Reprinted in Peter J. Boettke and Frédéric Sautet, eds., *Competition, Economic Planning, and the Knowledge Problem*, 206–21. Carmel, Ind.: Liberty Fund, 2018.

"X-Inefficiency, Error, and the Scope for Entrepreneurship." In Mario J. Rizzo, ed., *Time, Uncertainty, and Disequilibrium: Exploration of Austrian Themes*, 140–51. Lexington, Mass.: Lexington Books, 1979.

Reprinted as "Comment: X-Inefficiency, Error, and the Scope for Entrepreneurship" in Peter J. Boettke and Frédéric Sautet, eds., *The Essence of Entrepreneurship and the Nature and Significance of Market Process*, 264–76. Carmel, Ind.: Liberty Fund, 2018.

1980

"The 'Austrian' Perspective on the Crisis." *Public Interest* (special issue, 1980): 111–22.

> Reprinted in Daniel Bell and Irving Kristol, eds., *The Crisis in Economic Theory*, 111–22. New York: Basic Books, 1981.
> Published in Spanish as "La crisis desde la perspectiva 'austríaca.'" In *La crisis en la teoría económica*, 16–75. Buenos Aires: El Cronista Comercial, 1981.
> Published in French as "La perspective 'autrichienne' sur la crise." In *Crise et renouveau de la théorie économique*, 191–208. Paris: Bonnel/Publisud, 1986.
> Reprinted in Stephen C. Littlechild, ed., *Austrian Economics* 1:191–204. Aldershot, U.K., and Brookfield, Mass.: Edward Elgar, 1990.
> Reprinted in Peter J. Boettke and Frédéric Sautet, eds., *Reflections on Ethics, Freedom, Welfare Economics, Policy, and the Legacy of Austrian Economics*, 126–37. Carmel, Ind.: Liberty Fund, 2019.

"The Morality of Capitalist Success." C. A. Moorman Lecture Series. Canton, Mo.: Culver-Stockton College, 1980.

> Reprinted in Peter J. Boettke and Frédéric Sautet, eds., *Reflections on Ethics, Freedom, Welfare Economics, Policy, and the Legacy of Austrian Economics*, 272–85. Carmel, Ind.: Liberty Fund, 2019.

"The Primacy of Entrepreneurial Discovery." In Arthur Seldon, ed., *Prime Mover of Progress: The Entrepreneur in Capitalism and Socialism*, 3–28. IEA Readings 23. London: Institute of Economic Affairs, 1980.

> Published in German as "Die zentrale Bedeutung unternehmerischen Entdeckens." *Zeitschrift für Wirtschaftspolitik*, 32 Jahrgang, Heft 3 (1983).
> Reprinted in *Discovery and the Capitalist Process*, 15–39. Chicago: University of Chicago Press, 1985.
> Reprinted in Richard Ebeling, ed., *Austrian Economics: A Reader*, 304–33. Champions of Freedom Series, vol. 18. Hillsdale, Mich.: Hillsdale College Press, 1991.
> Reprinted in Peter J. Boettke and Frédéric Sautet, eds., *Reflections on Ethics, Freedom, Welfare Economics, Policy, and the Legacy of Austrian Economics*, 363–83. Carmel, Ind.: Liberty Fund, 2019.

1981

"Mises and the Renaissance of Austrian Economics." In John K. Andrews, ed., *Homage to Mises: The First Hundred Years*, 14–18. Hillsdale, Mich.: Hillsdale College Press, 1981.

> Reprinted in Stephen C. Littlechild, ed., *Austrian Economics* 1:113–20. Aldershot, U.K., and Brookfield, Mass.: Edward Elgar, 1990.

Reprinted in Peter J. Boettke and Frédéric Sautet, eds., *Ludwig von Mises: The Man and His Economics,* 137–43. Carmel, Ind.: Liberty Fund, 2019.

"Mises on Entrepreneurship." *Wirtschaftspolitische Blatter* 28, no. 4 (1981): 51–57.

Reprinted in Peter J. Boettke and Frédéric Sautet, eds., *Ludwig von Mises: The Man and His Economics,* 150–58. Carmel, Ind.: Liberty Fund, 2019.

"Why the Market Outclasses the State." *Economic Affairs* 1, no. 3 (April 1981): 181–83.

Reprinted in Peter J. Boettke and Frédéric Sautet, eds., *Reflections on Ethics, Freedom, Welfare Economics, Policy, and the Legacy of Austrian Economics,* 38–40. Carmel, Ind.: Liberty Fund, 2019.

1982

"Competition, Regulation, and the Market Process: An 'Austrian' Perspective." *Cato Institute Policy Analysis,* no. 18 (September 30, 1982).

Reprinted in Peter J. Boettke and Frédéric Sautet, eds., *Reflections on Ethics, Freedom, Welfare Economics, Policy, and the Legacy of Austrian Economics,* 483–93. Carmel, Ind.: Liberty Fund, 2019.

"Introduction." In Israel M. Kirzner, ed., *Method, Process, and Austrian Economics: Essays in Honor of Ludwig von Mises,* 1–5. Lexington, Mass.: Lexington Books, 1982.

Reprinted in Peter J. Boettke and Frédéric Sautet, eds., *Ludwig von Mises: The Man and His Economics,* 144–49. Carmel, Ind.: Liberty Fund, 2019.

"Lionel Robbins's *Nature and Significance,* Fifty Years Later." Working Paper 82-12. New York: C. V. Starr Center for Applied Economics, New York University, 1982.

Reprinted in Peter J. Boettke and Frédéric Sautet, eds., *Reflections on Ethics, Freedom, Welfare Economics, Policy, and the Legacy of Austrian Economics,* 138–53. Carmel, Ind.: Liberty Fund, 2019.

"The Theory of Entrepreneurship in Economic Growth." In Calvin A. Kent, Donald L. Sexton, and Karl H. Vesper, eds., *Encyclopedia of Entrepreneurship,* 272–76. Englewood Cliffs, N.J.: Prentice-Hall, 1982.

Reprinted in Peter J. Boettke and Frédéric Sautet, eds., *The Essence of Entrepreneurship and the Nature and Significance of Market Process,* 305–9. Carmel, Ind.: Liberty Fund, 2018.

"Uncertainty, Discovery, and Human Action: A Study of the Entrepreneurial Profile in the Misesian System." In Israel M. Kirzner, ed., *Method, Process, and Austrian Economics: Essays in Honor of Ludwig von Mises,* 139–59. Lexington, Mass.: Lexington Books, 1982.

Reprinted in *Discovery and the Capitalist Process,* 40–67. Chicago: University of Chicago Press, 1985.

Reprinted in Stephen C. Littlechild, ed., *Austrian Economics* 3:122–42. Aldershot, U.K., and Brookfield, Mass.: Edward Elgar, 1990.

Reprinted in Peter J. Boettke and Frédéric Sautet, eds., *Ludwig von Mises: The Man and His Economics*, 159–82. Carmel, Ind.: Liberty Fund, 2019.

1983

"Entrepreneurs and the Entrepreneurial Function: A Commentary." In J. Ronen, ed., *Entrepreneurship: Where Did It Come From, and Where Is It Going?*, 281–90. Lexington, Mass.: Lexington Books, 1983.

Reprinted in Peter J. Boettke and Frédéric Sautet, eds., *The Essence of Entrepreneurship and the Nature and Significance of Market Process*, 13–23. Carmel, Ind.: Liberty Fund, 2018.

"Entrepreneurship and the Future of Capitalism." In Jules Backman, ed., *Entrepreneurship and the Outlook for America*, 149–72. New York: Free Press, 1983.

Reprinted in *Discovery and the Capitalist Process*, 150–68. Chicago: University of Chicago Press, 1985.

Reprinted in Peter J. Boettke and Frédéric Sautet, eds., *The Essence of Entrepreneurship and the Nature and Significance of Market Process*, 82–97. Carmel, Ind.: Liberty Fund, 2018.

1984

"Economic Planning and the Knowledge Problem." *Cato Journal* 4, no. 2 (Fall 1984): 407–18.

Reprinted in *The Meaning of Market Process: Essays in the Development of Modern Austrian Economics*, 152–62. London and New York: Routledge, 1992.

Reprinted in Peter J. Boettke and Frédéric Sautet, eds., *Competition, Economic Planning, and the Knowledge Problem*, 75–86. Carmel, Ind.: Liberty Fund, 2018.

"The Entrepreneurial Process." In Calvin A. Kent, ed., *The Environment for Entrepreneurship*, 41–58. Lexington, Mass.: Lexington Books, 1984.

Reprinted in *Discovery and the Capitalist Process*, 68–92. Chicago: University of Chicago Press, 1985.

Reprinted in Peter J. Boettke and Frédéric Sautet, eds., *The Essence of Entrepreneurship and the Nature and Significance of Market Process*, 193–212. Carmel, Ind.: Liberty Fund, 2018.

"Incentives for Discovery." *Economic Affairs* 4, no. 2 (January 1984): 4.

Reprinted in Peter J. Boettke and Frédéric Sautet, eds., *Reflections on Ethics, Freedom, Welfare Economics, Policy, and the Legacy of Austrian Economics*, 481–82. Carmel, Ind.: Liberty Fund, 2019.

"The Open-Endedness of Knowledge: Its Role in the F.E.E. Formula."
Irvington-on-Hudson, N.Y.: Foundation for Economic Education
[pamphlet]. [1984 or 1985].

Reprinted in *Freeman* 36, no. 3 (March 1986): 85–90.
Reprinted in *Ideas on Liberty*, June 2003, 9–13.
Reprinted in Peter J. Boettke and Frédéric Sautet, eds., *Competition,*
Economic Planning, and the Knowledge Problem, 197–205. Carmel,
Ind.: Liberty Fund, 2018.

"Prices, the Communication of Knowledge, and the Discovery Process." In
Kurt R. Leube and Albert H. Zlabinger, eds., *The Political Economy of*
Freedom: Essays in Honor of F. A. Hayek, 193–206. Munich and Vienna:
Philosophia Verlag, 1984.

Reprinted in *The Meaning of Market Process: Essays in the Development of Modern*
Austrian Economics, 139–51. London and New York: Routledge, 1992.
Reprinted in Peter J. Boettke and Frédéric Sautet, eds., *Competition,*
Economic Planning, and the Knowledge Problem, 18–32. Carmel, Ind.:
Liberty Fund, 2018.

1985

"Comment on R. N. Langlois, 'From the Knowledge of Economics to the
Economics of Knowledge: Fritz Machlup on Methodology and on the
"Knowledge Society."'" *Research in the History of Economic Thought and*
Methodology 3 (1985): 237–41.

Reprinted in Peter J. Boettke and Frédéric Sautet, eds., *Competition,*
Economic Planning, and the Knowledge Problem, 228–31. Carmel, Ind.:
Liberty Fund, 2018.

"Entrepreneurship, Economics, and Economists." In *Discovery and the*
Capitalist Process, 1–14. Chicago: University of Chicago Press, 1985.

Reprinted in Peter J. Boettke and Frédéric Sautet, eds., *Austrian*
Subjectivism and the Emergence of the Entrepreneurship Theory, 139–50.
Indianapolis: Liberty Fund, 2015.

"Liberalism and Limited Government." *Freeman* 35, no. 11 (November 1985):
678–80.

Reprinted in Peter J. Boettke and Frédéric Sautet, eds., *Reflections on*
Ethics, Freedom, Welfare Economics, Policy, and the Legacy of Austrian
Economics, 41–43. Carmel, Ind.: Liberty Fund, 2019.

"Must Capitalism Yield to Socialism?" *Economic Affairs* 5, no. 3 (April–June
1985): 35–37.

Reprinted in Peter J. Boettke and Frédéric Sautet, eds., *Reflections on*
Ethics, Freedom, Welfare Economics, Policy, and the Legacy of Austrian
Economics, 31–37. Carmel, Ind.: Liberty Fund, 2019.

"Rejoinder." *Economic Affairs* 5, no. 2 (January 1985): 49.

> Reprinted as "Rejoinder [The Case for Free Markets]" in Peter J. Boettke and Frédéric Sautet, eds., *Reflections on Ethics, Freedom, Welfare Economics, Policy, and the Legacy of Austrian Economics*, 446–47. Carmel, Ind.: Liberty Fund, 2019.

"The Role of the Entrepreneur in the Economic System." Occasional Paper 10. Sydney, Australia: Centre for Independent Studies, 1985.

> Reprinted in Peter J. Boettke and Frédéric Sautet, eds., *The Essence of Entrepreneurship and the Nature and Significance of Market Process*, 113–21. Carmel, Ind.: Liberty Fund, 2018.

1986

"Another Look at the Subjectivism of Costs." In Israel M. Kirzner, ed., *Subjectivism, Intelligibility and Economic Understanding: Essays in Honor of Ludwig M. Lachmann on His Eightieth Birthday*, 140–56. New York: New York University Press, 1986.

> Reprinted in Peter J. Boettke and Frédéric Sautet, eds., *Austrian Subjectivism and the Emergence of the Entrepreneurship Theory*, 81–97. Indianapolis: Liberty Fund, 2015.

"Entrepreneurship and American Competitiveness." In Stuart M. Butler and William J. Dennis Jr., eds., *Entrepreneurship: The Key to Economic Growth*, 15–29. Washington, D.C., and San Mateo, Calif.: Heritage Foundation and National Federation of Independent Business, 1986.

> Reprinted in Peter J. Boettke and Frédéric Sautet, eds., *Reflections on Ethics, Freedom, Welfare Economics, Policy, and the Legacy of Austrian Economics*, 510–25. Carmel, Ind.: Liberty Fund, 2019.

"Individualistic Capitalism." In Donna C. Charron, ed., *Views on Individualism*, 5–27. St. Louis, Mo.: St. Louis Humanities Forum, 1986.

> Reprinted in Peter J. Boettke and Frédéric Sautet, eds., *Reflections on Ethics, Freedom, Welfare Economics, Policy, and the Legacy of Austrian Economics*, 44–61. Carmel, Ind.: Liberty Fund, 2019.

"Ludwig von Mises and Friedrich von Hayek: The Modern Extension of Austrian Subjectivism." In Norbert Leser, ed., *Die Wiener Schule der Nationalökonomie*, 133–55. Vienna, Cologne, and Graz: Herman Böhlaus Nachf, 1986.

> Reprinted in Stephen C. Littlechild, ed., *Austrian Economics* 1:342–65. Aldershot, U.K., and Brookfield, Mass.: Edward Elgar, 1990.
> Reprinted in *The Meaning of Market Process: Essays in the Development of Modern Austrian Economics*, 119–36. London: Routledge, 1992.

Reprinted in Peter J. Boettke and Frédéric Sautet, eds., *Austrian Subjectivism and the Emergence of the Entrepreneurship Theory*, 28–60. Indianapolis: Liberty Fund, 2015.

"Roundaboutness, Opportunity and Austrian Economics." In Martin J. Anderson, ed., *The Unfinished Agenda: Essays on the Political Economy of Governmental Policy in Honour of Arthur Seldon*, 93–103. London: Institute of Economic Affairs, 1986.

Reprinted in Peter J. Boettke and Frédéric Sautet, eds., *Austrian Subjectivism and the Emergence of the Entrepreneurship Theory*, 111–20. Indianapolis: Liberty Fund, 2015.

"Taxes and Discovery: An Entrepreneurial Perspective." In Dwight R. Lee, ed., *Taxation and the Deficit Economy: Fiscal Policy and Capital Formation in the United States*, 359–80. San Francisco: Pacific Research Institute for Public Policy, 1986.

Reprinted in *Discovery and the Capitalist Process*, 93–118. Chicago: University of Chicago Press, 1985.
Reprinted in Peter J. Boettke and Frédéric Sautet, eds., *Reflections on Ethics, Freedom, Welfare Economics, Policy, and the Legacy of Austrian Economics*, 397–417. Carmel, Ind.: Liberty Fund, 2019.

1987

"The Austrian School of Economics." In John Eatwell, Murray Milgate, and Peter Newman, eds., *The New Palgrave: A Dictionary of Economics*, 145–51. London: Macmillan, 1987.

Reprinted in *The Meaning of Market Process: Essays in the Development of Modern Austrian Economics*, 57–69. London: Routledge, 1992.
Reprinted in Peter J. Boettke and Frédéric Sautet, eds., *Reflections on Ethics, Freedom, Welfare Economics, Policy, and the Legacy of Austrian Economics*, 555–70. Carmel, Ind.: Liberty Fund, 2019.

"Economic Harmony." In John Eatwell, Murray Milgate, and Peter Newman, eds., *The New Palgrave: A Dictionary of Economics*. London: Macmillan, 1987.

Reprinted in John Eatwell, Murray Milgate, and Peter Newman, eds., *The Invisible Hand*, 94–98. London: Macmillan, 1989.
Reprinted in Peter J. Boettke and Frédéric Sautet, eds., *Reflections on Ethics, Freedom, Welfare Economics, Policy, and the Legacy of Austrian Economics*, 602–7. Carmel, Ind.: Liberty Fund, 2019.

"The Economics of Errant Entrepreneurs." *Freeman* 37, no. 8 (August 1987): 301–2.

Reprinted in Hans F. Sennholz, ed., *Free to Try*, 22–24. Irvington-on-Hudson, N.Y.: Foundation for Economic Education, 1995.

Reprinted in Peter J. Boettke and Frédéric Sautet, eds., *The Essence of Entrepreneurship and the Nature and Significance of Market Process,* 277–80. Carmel, Ind.: Liberty Fund, 2018.

"Friedrich August von Hayek." Coauthored with Roger Garrison. In John Eatwell, Murray Milgate, and Peter Newman, eds., *The New Palgrave: A Dictionary of Economics,* 609–14. London: Macmillan, 1987.

Reprinted in John Eatwell, Murray Milgate, and Peter Newman, eds., *The Invisible Hand,* 119–30. London: Macmillan, 1989.
Reprinted in Peter J. Boettke and Frédéric Sautet, eds., *Reflections on Ethics, Freedom, Welfare Economics, Policy, and the Legacy of Austrian Economics,* 571–86. Carmel, Ind.: Liberty Fund, 2019.

"Spontaneous Order and the Case for the Free Market." In *Ideas on Liberty: Essays in Honor of Paul L. Poirot,* 45–50. Irvington-on-Hudson, N.Y.: Foundation for Economic Education, 1987.

Reprinted in Peter J. Boettke and Frédéric Sautet, eds., *Reflections on Ethics, Freedom, Welfare Economics, Policy, and the Legacy of Austrian Economics,* 62–68. Carmel, Ind.: Liberty Fund, 2019.

"Unternehmer: Finder von Beruf." *Wirtschaftswoche,* January 9, 1987, 46. Translated from English version written expressly for the occasion.

1988

"Advertising in an Open-Ended Universe." Foreword to Robert B. Ekelund Jr. and Daniel S. Saurman, *Advertising and the Market Process,* xv–xxii. San Francisco: Pacific Research Institute for Public Policy, 1988.

Reprinted in Peter J. Boettke and Frédéric Sautet, eds., *Competition, Economic Planning, and the Knowledge Problem,* 246–53. Carmel, Ind.: Liberty Fund, 2018.

"The Economic Calculation Debate: Lessons for Austrians." *The Review of Austrian Economics* 2, no. 1 (December 1988): 1–18.

Reprinted in *The Meaning of Market Process: Essays in the Development of Modern Austrian Economics,* 100–118. London and New York: Routledge, 1992.
Reprinted in Peter J. Boettke and Frédéric Sautet, eds., *Competition, Economic Planning, and the Knowledge Problem,* 106–26. Carmel, Ind.: Liberty Fund, 2018.

"Some Ethical Implications for Capitalism of the Socialist Calculation Debate." *Social Philosophy and Policy* 6, no. 1 (1988): 165–82.

Reprinted in Peter J. Boettke and Frédéric Sautet, eds., *Reflections on Ethics, Freedom, Welfare Economics, Policy, and the Legacy of Austrian Economics,* 295–315. Carmel, Ind.: Liberty Fund, 2019.

"Welfare Economics: A Modern Austrian Perspective." In Walter Block and Llewellyn H. Rockwell Jr., eds., *Man, Economy and Liberty: Essays in Honor of Murray N. Rothbard*, 77–88. Auburn, Ala.: Ludwig von Mises Institute, 1988.

Reprinted in *The Meaning of Market Process: Essays in the Development of Modern Austrian Economics*, 180–92. London and New York: Routledge, 1992.
Reprinted in Peter J. Boettke and Frédéric Sautet, eds., *Reflections on Ethics, Freedom, Welfare Economics, Policy, and the Legacy of Austrian Economics*, 200–212. Carmel, Ind.: Liberty Fund, 2019.

1989

"The Use of Labels in Doctrinal History: Comment on Baird." *Cato Journal* 9, no. 1 (Spring/Summer 1989): 231–35.

Reprinted in Peter J. Boettke and Frédéric Sautet, eds., *Reflections on Ethics, Freedom, Welfare Economics, Policy, and the Legacy of Austrian Economics*, 620–25. Carmel, Ind.: Liberty Fund, 2019.

1990

"Carl Menger und die subjektivistische Tradition in der Ökonomie." In Wolfram Engels, Herbert Hax, Friedrich August von Hayek, and Horst Claus Recktenwald, eds., *Carl Mengers wegweisendes Werk*, 61–83. Düsseldorf: Verlag Wirtschaft und Finanzen, 1990.

Published in English as "Carl Menger and the Subjectivist Tradition." In *The Meaning of Market Process: Essays in the Development of Modern Austrian Economics*, 70–85. London and New York: Routledge, 1992.
Reprinted in Peter J. Boettke and Frédéric Sautet, eds., *Austrian Subjectivism and the Emergence of the Entrepreneurship Theory*, 11–27. Indianapolis: Liberty Fund, 2015.

"Commentary" on Stephan Boehm, "The Austrian Tradition: Schumpeter and Mises." In Klaus Hennings and Warren J. Samuels, eds., *Neoclassical Economic Theory, 1870–1930*, 242–49. Boston, Dordrecht, and London: Kluwer, 1990.

Reprinted as "The Austrian Tradition: Commentary by Israel M. Kirzner" in Peter J. Boettke and Frédéric Sautet, eds., *Reflections on Ethics, Freedom, Welfare Economics, Policy, and the Legacy of Austrian Economics*, 626–34. Carmel, Ind.: Liberty Fund, 2019.

"Discovery, Private Property, and the Theory of Justice in Capitalist Society." *Journal des économistes et des études humaines* 1, no. 3 (October 1990): 209–24.

Reprinted in *The Meaning of Market Process: Essays in the Development of Modern Austrian Economics*, 209–26. London and New York: Routledge, 1992.

Reprinted in Peter J. Boettke and Frédéric Sautet, eds., *Discovery, Capitalism, and Distributive Justice*, 214–32. Indianapolis: Liberty Fund, 2016.

"Discussant: Israel M. Kirzner." In K. Groenvelt, J. A. H. Maks, and J. Muysken, eds., *Economic Policy and the Market Process: Austrian and Mainstream Economics*, 76–84. Amsterdam: Elsevier, 1990.

Reprinted as "Comments on the Debate between Professors Leontief and Stein on National Economic Planning" in Peter J. Boettke and Frédéric Sautet, eds., *Competition, Economic Planning, and the Knowledge Problem*, 169–73. Carmel, Ind.: Liberty Fund, 2018.

"Knowledge Problems and Their Solutions: Some Relevant Distinctions." *Cultural Dynamics* 3, no. 1 (1990): 32–48.

Reprinted in *The Meaning of Market Process: Essays in the Development of Modern Austrian Economics*, 163–79. London and New York: Routledge, 1992.

Reprinted in Peter J. Boettke and Frédéric Sautet, eds., *Competition, Economic Planning, and the Knowledge Problem*, 87–105. Carmel, Ind.: Liberty Fund, 2018.

"The Market Process: An Austrian View." In K. Groenveld, J. A. H. Maks, and J. Muysken, eds., *Economic Policy and the Market Process: Austrian and Mainstream Economics*, 23–39. Amsterdam: North Holland, 1990.

Reprinted in Peter J. Boettke and Frédéric Sautet, eds., *The Essence of Entrepreneurship and the Nature and Significance of Market Process*, 231–47. Carmel, Ind.: Liberty Fund, 2018.

"The Meaning of Market Process." In Alfred Bosch, Peter Koslowski, and Reinhold Veit, eds., *General Equilibrium or Market Process: Neoclassical and Austrian Theories of Economics*, 61–76. Tübingen: J. C. B. Mohr, 1990.

Reprinted in *The Meaning of Market Process: Essays in the Development of Modern Austrian Economics*, 38–54. London and New York: Routledge, 1992.

Reprinted in Peter J. Boettke and David L. Prychitko, eds., *Market Process Theories* 2:599–614. The International Library of Critical Writings in Economics 91. Cheltenham, U.K.: Edward Elgar, 1998.

Reprinted in Peter J. Boettke and Frédéric Sautet, eds., *The Essence of Entrepreneurship and the Nature and Significance of Market Process*, 213–30. Carmel, Ind.: Liberty Fund, 2018.

"Menger, Classical Liberalism, and the Austrian School of Economics." *History of Political Economy* 22, annual supplement (1990): 93–106.

Reprinted in Bruce Caldwell, ed., *Carl Menger and His Legacy in Economics*, 93–106. Durham, N.C., and London: Duke University Press, 1990.

Reprinted in *The Meaning of Market Process: Essays in the Development of Modern Austrian Economics*, 86–99. London and New York: Routledge, 1992.

Reprinted in Peter J. Boettke and Frédéric Sautet, eds., *Reflections on Ethics, Freedom, Welfare Economics, Policy, and the Legacy of Austrian Economics*, 526–41. Carmel, Ind.: Liberty Fund, 2019.

"Self-interest and the New Bashing of Economics: A Fresh Opportunity in the Perennial Debate?" *Critical Review* 4, no. 1–2 (1990): 27–40.

Reprinted in *The Meaning of Market Process: Essays in the Development of Modern Austrian Economics*, 195–208. London and New York: Routledge, 1992.

Reprinted in *Journal des économistes et des études humaines* 14, no. 1 (2004): 111–24.

Reprinted in Peter J. Boettke and Frédéric Sautet, eds., *Reflections on Ethics, Freedom, Welfare Economics, Policy, and the Legacy of Austrian Economics*, 99–113. Carmel, Ind.: Liberty Fund, 2019.

1991

"The Driving Force of the Market: The Idea of 'Competition' in Contemporary Economic Theory and in the Austrian Theory of the Market Process." In Richard M. Ebeling, ed., *Austrian Economics: Perspectives on the Past and Prospects for the Future*, 139–60. Champions of Freedom Series, vol. 17. Hillsdale, Mich.: Hillsdale College Press, 1991.

Reprinted in David L. Prychitko, ed., *Why Economists Disagree: An Introduction to the Alternative Schools of Thought*, 37–52. Albany, N.Y.: State University of New York Press, 1998.

Reprinted in *The Driving Force of the Market: Essays in Austrian Economics*, 222–38. London and New York: Routledge, Foundations of the Market Economy, 2000.

Reprinted in Peter J. Boettke and Frédéric Sautet, eds., *Competition, Economic Planning, and the Knowledge Problem*, 50–66. Carmel, Ind.: Liberty Fund, 2018.

"Friedrich A. Hayek, 1899–1992." *Critical Review* 5, no. 4 (1991): 585–92.

Reprinted in *The Driving Force of the Market: Essays in Austrian Economics*, 278–85. London and New York: Routledge, Foundations of the Market Economy, 2000.

"Ludwig M. Lachmann, 1906–1990." *Institute Scholar* 10, no. 2–3 (Winter 1991): 6–7.

Published in French in *Journal des économistes et des études humaines* 2, no. 2–3 (June–September 1991): 193–97.

Reprinted in *The Driving Force of the Market: Essays in Austrian Economics*, 286–89. London and New York: Routledge, Foundations of the Market Economy, 2000.

Reprinted as "Ludwig M. Lachmann, 1906–1990 [Obituary]" in Peter J. Boettke and Frédéric Sautet, eds., *Reflections on Ethics, Freedom, Welfare Economics, Policy, and the Legacy of Austrian Economics*, 587–90. Carmel, Ind.: Liberty Fund, 2019.

1992

"Austrian Economics and the Theory of Entrepreneurship: Israel M. Kirzner Interviewed by Stephan Boehm on 2 May 1989." *Review of Political Economy* 4, no. 1 (1992): 95–110.

Reprinted in Peter J. Boettke and Frédéric Sautet, eds., *Reflections on Ethics, Freedom, Welfare Economics, Policy, and the Legacy of Austrian Economics*, 689–707. Carmel, Ind.: Liberty Fund, 2019.

"Commentary: Entrepreneurship, Uncertainty, and Austrian Economics." In Bruce J. Caldwell and Stephen Boehm, eds., *Austrian Economics: Tensions and New Directions*, 85–102. Boston and Dordrecht: Kluwer Academic Publishers, 1992.

Reprinted in Peter J. Boettke and Frédéric Sautet, eds., *The Essence of Entrepreneurship and the Nature and Significance of Market Process*, 342–60. Carmel, Ind.: Liberty Fund, 2018.

"Human Action, Freedom, and Economic Science." In John W. Robbins and Mark Spangler, eds., *A Man of Principle: Essays in Honor of Hans F. Sennholz*, 241–49. Grove City, Pa.: Grove City College Press, 1992.

Reprinted in Peter J. Boettke and Frédéric Sautet, eds., *Ludwig von Mises: The Man and His Economics*, 199–206. Carmel, Ind.: Liberty Fund, 2019.

"Market Process Theory: In Defense of the Austrian Middle Ground." In *The Meaning of Market Process: Essays in the Development of Modern Austrian Economics*, 3–37. London and New York: Routledge, 1992.

Reprinted in Peter J. Boettke and Frédéric Sautet, eds., *The Essence of Entrepreneurship and the Nature and Significance of Market Process*, 156–92. Carmel, Ind.: Liberty Fund, 2018.

"Subjectivism, Freedom, and Economic Law: Ludwig Lachmann Memorial Lecture." *South African Journal of Economics* 60, no. 1 (March 1992): 24–33.

Reprinted in *The Driving Force of the Market: Essays in Austrian Economics*, 54–73. London and New York: Routledge, Foundations of the Market Economy, 2000.

Reprinted in Peter J. Boettke and Frédéric Sautet, eds., *Austrian Subjectivism and the Emergence of the Entrepreneurship Theory*, 61–80. Indianapolis: Liberty Fund, 2015.

1993

"The Morality of Pure Profit: The Logic and Illogic of a Popular Phobia."
Journal des économistes et des études humaines 4, no. 2–3 (June–
September 1993): 315–28.

Published in Italian as "Il profitto e la sua etica: Logica e illogica di una
fobia diffusa." *Biblioteca della libertá* 29, no. 124 (January–March
1994): 41–57.

Reprinted in Peter J. Boettke and Frédéric Sautet, eds., *Reflections on
Ethics, Freedom, Welfare Economics, Policy, and the Legacy of Austrian
Economics*, 316–31. Carmel, Ind.: Liberty Fund, 2019.

"The Pure Time-Preference Theory of Interest: An Attempt at Clarification."
In Jeffrey M. Herbener, ed., *The Meaning of Ludwig von Mises:
Contributions in Economics, Sociology, Epistemology, and Political
Philosophy*, 166–92. Dordrecht and Norwell, Mass.: Kluwer Academic
Publishers, 1993.

Reprinted in Peter J. Boettke and Frédéric Sautet, eds., *Essays on Capital
and Interest: An Austrian Perspective*, 147–68. Indianapolis: Liberty
Fund, 2012.

1994

"The Entrepreneur in Economic Theory." In Erik Dahmén, Leslie Hannah,
and Israel M. Kirzner, *The Dynamics of Entrepreneurship*, 45–61.
Crafoord Lectures No. 5. Malmö, Sweden: Lund University Press,
Institute of Economic Research, 1994.

Reprinted in Peter J. Boettke and Frédéric Sautet, eds., *The Essence of
Entrepreneurship and the Nature and Significance of Market Process*,
98–112. Carmel, Ind.: Liberty Fund, 2018.

"Entrepreneurship." In Peter J. Boettke, ed., *The Elgar Companion to Austrian
Economics*, 103–10. Aldershot, U.K., and Brookfield, Vt.: Edward Elgar,
1994.

Reprinted in Peter J. Boettke and Frédéric Sautet, eds., *The Essence of
Entrepreneurship and the Nature and Significance of Market Process*, 3–12.
Carmel, Ind.: Liberty Fund, 2018.

"The Ethics of Competition." In Horst Siebert, ed., *The Ethical Foundations of
the Market Economy*, 101–14. Tübingen: J. C. B. Mohr, 1994.

Reprinted in *The Driving Force of the Market: Essays in Austrian Economics*,
88–102. London and New York: Routledge, Foundations of the Market
Economy, 2000.

Reprinted in Peter J. Boettke and Frédéric Sautet, eds., *Reflections on
Ethics, Freedom, Welfare Economics, Policy, and the Legacy of Austrian
Economics*, 257–71. Carmel, Ind.: Liberty Fund, 2019.

"Introduction." In Israel M. Kirzner, ed., *Classics in Austrian Economics: A Sampling in the History of a Tradition*, 1:ix–xxx. London: William Pickering, 1994.

> Reprinted in Peter J. Boettke and Frédéric Sautet, eds., *Reflections on Ethics, Freedom, Welfare Economics, Policy, and the Legacy of Austrian Economics*, 635–57. Carmel, Ind.: Liberty Fund, 2019.

"Introduction." In Israel M. Kirzner, ed., *Classics in Austrian Economics: A Sampling in the History of a Tradition*, 2:vii–xx. London: William Pickering, 1994.

> Reprinted in Peter J. Boettke and Frédéric Sautet, eds., *Reflections on Ethics, Freedom, Welfare Economics, Policy, and the Legacy of Austrian Economics*, 658–72. Carmel, Ind.: Liberty Fund, 2019.

"Introduction." In Israel M. Kirzner, ed., *Classics in Austrian Economics: A Sampling in the History of a Tradition*, 3:vii–xvii. London: William Pickering, 1994.

> Reprinted in Peter J. Boettke and Frédéric Sautet, eds., *Reflections on Ethics, Freedom, Welfare Economics, Policy, and the Legacy of Austrian Economics*, 673–85. Carmel, Ind.: Liberty Fund, 2019.

"The Limits of the Market: The Real and the Imagined." In Wernhard Möschel, Manfred Streit, and Ulrich Witt, eds., *Marktwirtschaft und Rechtsordnung: Festschrift zum 70. Geburtstag von Prof. Dr. Erich Hoppmann*, 101–10. Baden-Baden: Nomos, 1994.

> Reprinted in *The Driving Force of the Market: Essays in Austrian Economics*, 77–87. London and New York: Routledge, Foundations of the Market Economy, 2000.
> Reprinted in Peter J. Boettke and Frédéric Sautet, eds., *Reflections on Ethics, Freedom, Welfare Economics, Policy, and the Legacy of Austrian Economics*, 384–94. Carmel, Ind.: Liberty Fund, 2019.

"A Tale of Two Worlds: Comment on Shmanske." In Peter J. Boettke, Israel M. Kirzner, and Mario J. Rizzo, eds., *Advances in Austrian Economics*, 1:223–26. Greenwich, Conn., and London: JAI Press, 1994.

> Reprinted in Peter J. Boettke and Frédéric Sautet, eds., *The Essence of Entrepreneurship and the Nature and Significance of Market Process*, 389–93. Carmel, Ind.: Liberty Fund, 2018.

"Value-Freedom." In Peter J. Boettke, ed., *The Elgar Companion to Austrian Economics*, 313–19. Aldershot, U.K., and Brookfield, Vt.: Edward Elgar, 1994.

> Reprinted in Peter J. Boettke and Frédéric Sautet, eds., *Reflections on Ethics, Freedom, Welfare Economics, Policy, and the Legacy of Austrian Economics*, 79–86. Carmel, Ind.: Liberty Fund, 2019.

1995

"Hayeks Theorie der Koordination von Märkten." In *Vademecum zu einem Klassiker der Marktkoordination.* [To accompany the facsimile republication of Hayek's *Preise und Produktion.*] Düsseldorf: Verlag Wirtschaft und Finanzen, 1995.

Published in English as "Hayek's Theory of the Coordination of Markets: A Commentary to Accompany the Facsimile Edition of Hayek's *Preise und Produktion.*" In Peter J. Boettke and Frédéric Sautet, eds., *Competition, Economic Planning, and the Knowledge Problem,* 174–93. Carmel, Ind.: Liberty Fund, 2018.

"The Nature of Profits: Some Economic Insights and Their Ethical Implications." In Robin Cowan and Mario J. Rizzo, eds., *Profits and Morality,* 22–47. Chicago: University of Chicago Press, 1995.

Reprinted in *The Driving Force of the Market: Essays in Austrian Economics,* 103–31. London and New York: Routledge, Foundations of the Market Economy, 2000.
Reprinted in Peter J. Boettke and Frédéric Sautet, eds., *Reflections on Ethics, Freedom, Welfare Economics, Policy, and the Legacy of Austrian Economics,* 332–60. Carmel, Ind.: Liberty Fund, 2019.

"The Subjectivism of Austrian Economics." In Gerrit Meijer, ed., *New Perspectives on Austrian Economics,* 11–22. London and New York: Routledge, 1995.

Reprinted in *The Driving Force of the Market: Essays in Austrian Economics,* 41–53. London and New York: Routledge, Foundations of the Market Economy, 2000.
Reprinted in Peter J. Boettke and Frédéric Sautet, eds., *Austrian Subjectivism and the Emergence of the Entrepreneurship Theory,* 48–60. Indianapolis: Liberty Fund, 2015.

1996

"Fifty Years of FEE—Fifty Years of Progress in Austrian Economics." *Freeman* 46, no. 5 (May 1996): 283–89.

Reprinted in Peter J. Boettke and Frédéric Sautet, eds., *Reflections on Ethics, Freedom, Welfare Economics, Policy, and the Legacy of Austrian Economics,* 591–601. Carmel, Ind.: Liberty Fund, 2019.

"Government Regulation and the Market Discovery Process." In Kurt R. Leube, ed., *Die Österreichische Schule der Nationalökonomie.* Texte-Band 2, *Von Hayek bis White,* Wien: Manz, 1996.

"Reflections on the Misesian Legacy in Economics." *Review of Austrian Economics* 9, no. 2 (September 1996): 143–54.

Reprinted in *The Driving Force of the Market: Essays in Austrian Economics,* 151–64. London and New York: Routledge, Foundations of the Market Economy, 2000.

Reprinted in Peter J. Boettke and Frédéric Sautet, eds., *Ludwig von Mises: The Man and His Economics*, 213–26. Carmel, Ind.: Liberty Fund, 2019.

1997

"Austrian Economics and Mainstream Economics, 1930–1950: A Study in Doctrinal Complementarity and Substitutability." In Kurt R. Leube, Angelo Petroni, and James S. Sadowsky, eds., *An Austrian in France: Festschrift in Honour of Jacques Garello*, 189–202. Turin, Italy: La Rosa Editrice, 1997.

Reprinted in Peter J. Boettke and Frédéric Sautet, eds., *Reflections on Ethics, Freedom, Welfare Economics, Policy, and the Legacy of Austrian Economics*, 608–19. Carmel, Ind.: Liberty Fund, 2019.

"The Crisis of Vision in Modern Economic Thought: An Austrian Economist's Perspective." *Advances in Austrian Economics* 4 (1997): 149–54.

"Entrepreneurial Discovery and Competitive Market: An Austrian Approach." *Journal of Economic Literature* 35, no. 1 (March 1997): 60–85.

Reprinted in *The Driving Force of the Market: Essays in Austrian Economics*, 3–40. London and New York: Routledge, Foundations of the Market Economy, 2000.
Reprinted in Dean A. Shepherd and Denis A. Grégoire, eds., *Entrepreneurial Opportunities*, The International Library of Entrepreneurship 25. Cheltenham, U.K., and Northampton, Mass.: Edward Elgar, 2012.
Reprinted as "Entrepreneurial Discovery and the Competitive Market Process: An Austrian Approach" in Peter J. Boettke and Frédéric Sautet, eds., *Competition, Economic Planning, and the Knowledge Problem*, 323–60. Carmel, Ind.: Liberty Fund, 2018.

"The Kirznerian Way: An Interview with Israel M. Kirzner." *Austrian Economics Newsletter* 17, no. 1 (Spring 1997): 1–8.

Reprinted as "The Kirznerian Way: An Interview with Israel M. Kirzner" in Peter J. Boettke and Frédéric Sautet, eds., *Reflections on Ethics, Freedom, Welfare Economics, Policy, and the Legacy of Austrian Economics*, 708–24. Carmel, Ind.: Liberty Fund, 2019.

1998

"Austrian Economics, the Coordination Criterion and Classical Liberalism." *Journal des économistes et des études humaines* 8, no. 2/3 (June/ September 1998): 187–200.

Reprinted in Peter J. Boettke and Frédéric Sautet, eds., *Reflections on Ethics, Freedom, Welfare Economics, Policy, and the Legacy of Austrian Economics*, 213–28. Carmel, Ind.: Liberty Fund, 2019.

"Coordination as a Criterion for Economic 'Goodness.'" *Constitutional Political Economy* 9, no. 4 (December 1998): 289–301.

Reprinted in *The Driving Force of the Market: Essays in Austrian Economics*, 132–48. London and New York: Routledge, Foundations of the Market Economy, 2000.
Reprinted in Peter J. Boettke and Frédéric Sautet, eds., *Reflections on Ethics, Freedom, Welfare Economics, Policy, and the Legacy of Austrian Economics*, 183–99. Carmel, Ind.: Liberty Fund, 2019.

"The Nature and Significance of Economic Education." *Freeman* 48, no. 10 (October 1998): 582–86.

Published in Spanish as "La naturaleza e importancia de la educación económica." Translated by Nadia Olivetto and Matías Spelta. *Revista digital orden espontáneo*, no. 9 (July 2010): 8–14.
Reprinted in Peter J. Boettke and Frédéric Sautet, eds., *Reflections on Ethics, Freedom, Welfare Economics, Policy, and the Legacy of Austrian Economics*, 545–52. Carmel, Ind.: Liberty Fund, 2019.

1999

"Concurrence et processus de marché: Duelques depères doctrinaux." In Jackie Krafft, ed., *Le processus de concurrence*. Paris: Editions Economica, 1999.

Published in English as "Competition and the Market Process: Some Doctrinal Milestones." In *The Driving Force of the Market: Essays in Austrian Economics*, 205–21. London and New York: Routledge, Foundations of the Market Economy, 2000.
Reprinted in Peter J. Boettke and Frédéric Sautet, eds., *Competition, Economic Planning, and the Knowledge Problem*, 33–49. Carmel, Ind.: Liberty Fund, 2018.

"Creativity and/or Alertness: A Reconsideration of the Schumpeterian Entrepreneur." *Review of Austrian Economics* 11, no. 1–2 (January 1999): 5–17.

Reprinted in *The Driving Force of the Market: Essays in Austrian Economics*, 239–57. London and New York: Routledge, Foundations of the Market Economy, 2000.
Reprinted in Peter J. Boettke and Frédéric Sautet, eds., *The Essence of Entrepreneurship and the Nature and Significance of Market Process*, 50–68. Carmel, Ind.: Liberty Fund, 2018.

"Hedgehog or Fox? Hayek and the Idea of Plan-Coordination." *Journal des économistes et des études humaines* 9, no. 2/3 (June/September 1999): 217–37.

Reprinted in *The Driving Force of the Market: Essays in Austrian Economics*, 180–202. London and New York: Routledge, Foundations of the Market Economy, 2000.

Reprinted in Peter J. Boettke and Frédéric Sautet, eds., *Competition, Economic Planning, and the Knowledge Problem,* 127–49. Carmel, Ind.: Liberty Fund, 2018.

"Los objetivos de la política "anti-trust": Una crítica." *Información comercial española,* no. 775 (December 1998–January 1999): 67–78.

Published as "The Goals of Antitrust: A Critique" in Peter J. Boettke and Frédéric Sautet, eds., *Reflections on Ethics, Freedom, Welfare Economics, Policy, and the Legacy of Austrian Economics,* 494–509. Carmel, Ind.: Liberty Fund, 2019.

"Mises and His Understanding of the Capitalist System." *Cato Journal* 19, no. 2 (1999): 215–28.

Reprinted in *The Driving Force of the Market: Essays in Austrian Economics,* 165–79. London and New York: Routledge, Foundations of the Market Economy, 2000.

Reprinted in Peter J. Boettke and Frédéric Sautet, eds., *Ludwig von Mises: The Man and His Economics,* 183–98. Carmel, Ind.: Liberty Fund, 2019.

"Philip Wicksteed: The British Austrian." In Randall G. Holcombe, ed., *15 Great Austrian Economists,* 101–12. Auburn, Ala.: Ludwig von Mises Institute, 1999.

Reprinted in Peter J. Boettke and Frédéric Sautet, eds., *Austrian Subjectivism and the Emergence of the Entrepreneurship Theory,* 98–110. Indianapolis: Liberty Fund, 2015.

"Rationality, Entrepreneurship and Economic Imperialism." In Sheila C. Dow and Peter E. Earl, eds., *Economic Organisation and Economic Knowledge: Essays in Honour of Brian Loasby* 1:1–13. Cheltenham, U.K., and Northampton, Mass.: Edward Elgar, 1999.

Reprinted in *The Driving Force of the Market: Essays in Austrian Economics,* 258–71. London and New York: Routledge, Foundations of the Market Economy, 2000.

Reprinted in Peter J. Boettke and Frédéric Sautet, eds., *Reflections on Ethics, Freedom, Welfare Economics, Policy, and the Legacy of Austrian Economics,* 154–67. Carmel, Ind.: Liberty Fund, 2019.

"Report on a Treatise." *Review of Austrian Economics* 12, no. 1 (June 1999): 81–94.

2000

"Entrepreneurial Discovery and the Law of Supply and Demand." *Freeman* 50, no. 2 (February 2000): 17–19.

Reprinted in Peter J. Boettke and Frédéric Sautet, eds., *The Essence of Entrepreneurship and the Nature and Significance of Market Process,* 401–4. Carmel, Ind.: Liberty Fund, 2018.

"Foreword" to Frédéric E. Sautet, *An Entrepreneurial Theory of the Firm*, xiii–xiv. London and New York: Routledge, 2000.

"Human Nature and the Character of Economic Science: The Historical Background of the Misesian Perspective." *Harvard Review of Philosophy* 8 (2000): 14–23.

"The Irresistible Force of Market Competition." *Freeman* 50, no. 3 (March 2000): 11–14.

> Reprinted in Peter J. Boettke and Frédéric Sautet, eds., *Competition, Economic Planning, and the Knowledge Problem*, 67–71. Carmel, Ind.: Liberty Fund, 2018.

"The Law of Supply and Demand." *Freeman* 50, no. 1 (January 2000): 19–21.

> Reprinted in Peter J. Boettke and Frédéric Sautet, eds., *The Essence of Entrepreneurship and the Nature and Significance of Market Process*, 397–400. Carmel, Ind.: Liberty Fund, 2018.

"Misesian Economics and the Path to Prosperity." In Richard M. Ebeling, ed., *Human Action: A 50-Year Tribute*, 227–34. Champions of Freedom Series, vol. 27. Hillsdale, Mich.: Hillsdale College Press, 2000.

"A Puzzle and Its Solution: Rejoinder to Professor Ahiakpor." *Freeman* 50, no. 7 (July 2000): 25–26.

> Reprinted in Peter J. Boettke and Frédéric Sautet, eds., *The Essence of Entrepreneurship and the Nature and Significance of Market Process*, 408–10. Carmel, Ind.: Liberty Fund, 2018.

"Toward an Austrian Critique of Governmental Economic Policy." *Freeman* 50, no. 4 (April 2000): 16–18.

> Reprinted in Peter J. Boettke and Frédéric Sautet, eds., *Reflections on Ethics, Freedom, Welfare Economics, Policy, and the Legacy of Austrian Economics*, 477–80. Carmel, Ind.: Liberty Fund, 2019.

2001

"Any Schmuck Can Consume: A Response." *Economic Affairs* 21, no. 1 (March 2001): 47.

"Two Cheers for Klein's Plea." *Eastern Economic Journal* 27, no. 2 (Spring 2001): 211–14.

2002

"Comment on 'A Critique of Kirzner's Finders-Keepers Defence of Profit.'" *Review of Austrian Economics* 15, no. 1 (January 2002): 91–94.

> Reprinted in Peter J. Boettke and Frédéric Sautet, eds., *Discovery, Capitalism, and Distributive Justice*, 255–60. Indianapolis: Liberty Fund, 2016.

2003

"The Open-Endedness of Knowledge." *Freeman* 53, no. 6 (June 2003): 9–13.

2004

"Economic Science and the Morality of Capitalism." In Dennis O'Keeffe, ed., *Economy and Virtue: Essays on the Theme of Markets and Morality*, 88–100. London: The Institute of Economic Affairs, 2004.

Reprinted in Peter J. Boettke and Frédéric Sautet, eds., *Reflections on Ethics, Freedom, Welfare Economics, Policy, and the Legacy of Austrian Economics*, 286–94. Carmel, Ind.: Liberty Fund, 2019.

2005

"Human Attitudes and Economic Growth." *Cato Journal* 25, no. 3 (Fall 2005): 465–69.

Reprinted in Peter J. Boettke and Frédéric Sautet, eds., *Reflections on Ethics, Freedom, Welfare Economics, Policy, and the Legacy of Austrian Economics*, 114–18. Carmel, Ind.: Liberty Fund, 2019.

"Information-Knowledge and Action-Knowledge." *Econ Journal Watch* 2, no. 1 (April 2005): 75–81.

Reprinted in Peter J. Boettke and Frédéric Sautet, eds., *Competition, Economic Planning, and the Knowledge Problem*, 222–27. Carmel, Ind.: Liberty Fund, 2018.

2006

"The Anatomy of Economic Advice: Part I." *Freeman* 56, no. 6 (July/August 2006): 28–33.

Reprinted in Peter J. Boettke and Frédéric Sautet, eds., *Reflections on Ethics, Freedom, Welfare Economics, Policy, and the Legacy of Austrian Economics*, 448–57. Carmel, Ind.: Liberty Fund, 2019.

"The Anatomy of Economic Advice: Part II." *Freeman* 56, no. 7 (September 2006): 14–19.

Reprinted in Peter J. Boettke and Frédéric Sautet, eds., *Reflections on Ethics, Freedom, Welfare Economics, Policy, and the Legacy of Austrian Economics*, 458–66. Carmel, Ind.: Liberty Fund, 2019.

"The Anatomy of Economic Advice: Part III." *Freeman* 56, no. 8 (October 2006): 17–22.

Reprinted in Peter J. Boettke and Frédéric Sautet, eds., *Reflections on Ethics, Freedom, Welfare Economics, Policy, and the Legacy of Austrian Economics*, 467–76. Carmel, Ind.: Liberty Fund, 2019.

"Calculation, Competition and Entrepreneurship." In Jack High, ed., *Humane Economics: Essays in Honor of Don Lavoie,* 29–46. Cheltenham, U.K., and Northampton, Mass.: Edward Elgar, 2006.

Reprinted in Peter J. Boettke and Frédéric Sautet, eds., *Competition, Economic Planning, and the Knowledge Problem,* 150–68. Carmel, Ind.: Liberty Fund, 2018.

"Hayek and Economic Ignorance: Reply to Friedman." *Critical Review* 18, no. 4 (2006): 411–15.

Reprinted in Peter J. Boettke and Frédéric Sautet, eds., *The Essence of Entrepreneurship and the Nature and Significance of Market Process,* 287–90. Carmel, Ind.: Liberty Fund, 2018.

Lifetime Achievement Award Acceptance Speech. Society for the Development of Austrian Economics. Charleston, S.C., November 2006.

"The Nature and Role of Entrepreneurship in Markets: Implications for Policy." With Frédéric Sautet. Mercatus Policy Series, Policy Primer No. 4. Arlington, Va.: Mercatus Center at George Mason University, 2006.

2008

"The Alert and Creative Entrepreneur: A Clarification." IFN Working Paper 760. Stockholm: Research Institute of Industrial Economics, 2008.

Reprinted in *Small Business Economics* 32, no. 2 (2009): 145–52.
Reprinted in Peter J. Boettke and Frédéric Sautet, eds., *The Essence of Entrepreneurship and the Nature and Significance of Market Process,* 69–81. Carmel, Ind.: Liberty Fund, 2018.

"Socialist Calculation Debate." In Ronald Hamowy, ed., *The Encyclopedia of Libertarianism,* 476–79. Thousand Oaks, Calif.: Sage, 2008.

2009

"*Human Action,* 1949: A Dramatic Episode in Intellectual History." *Freeman* 59, no. 7 (September 2009): 8–11.

Published in Spanish as "*La acción humana,* 1949: Un episodio dramático en la historia intelectual." *Revista digital orden espontáneo,* no. 6 (November 2009): 1–6.
Reprinted in Peter J. Boettke and Frédéric Sautet, eds., *Ludwig von Mises: The Man and His Economics,* 207–12. Carmel, Ind.: Liberty Fund, 2019.

2010

"The Meaning of 'Economic Goodness': Critical Comments on Klein and Briggeman." *Journal of Private Enterprise* 25, no. 2 (Spring 2010): 55–85.

"The 2010 June and Edgar Memorial Lecture: The Economics of Greed or the Economics of Purpose." *Annual Proceedings of the Wealth and Well-Being of Nations* 3 (2010–11); 17–29.

Reprinted as "The Economics of Greed or the Economics of Purpose" in Peter J. Boettke and Frédéric Sautet, eds., *Reflections on Ethics, Freedom, Welfare Economics, Policy, and the Legacy of Austrian Economics*, 168–80. Carmel, Ind.: Liberty Fund, 2019.

2014

"Buchanan and the Austrians: A Tale of Two Bridges." *Review of Austrian Economics* 27, no. 2 (June 2014): 119–28.

"Remarks on Receiving the Lifetime Achievement Award from the Fund for the Study of Spontaneous Order." *Review of Austrian Economics* 27, no. 3 (September 2014): 225–27.

2017

"The Entrepreneurial Market Process—An Exposition." *Southern Economic Journal* 83, no. 4 (April 2017): 855–68.

2018

"A Conversation with Israel Kirzner, July 2006, by Peter J. Boettke and Frédéric Sautet." In Peter J. Boettke and Frédéric Sautet, eds., *Reflections on Ethics, Freedom, Welfare Economics, Policy, and the Legacy of Austrian Economics*, 725–61. Carmel, Ind.: Liberty Fund, 2019.

"Entrepreneurial Inspiration." *Review of Austrian Economics*. Published electronically January 22, 2018. https://doi.org/10.1007/s11138-017-0413-0.

"The Ethics of Pure Entrepreneurship: An Austrian Economics Perspective." *Review of Austrian Economics*. Published electronically January 23, 2018. https://doi.org/10.1007/s11138-017-0412-1.

BOOK REVIEWS

Henry W. Briefs. *Three Views of Method in Economics. Journal of Political Economy* 71, no. 6 (December 1963): 614–15.

R. L. Smyth, ed. *Essays in Economic Methods. Journal of Political Economy* 72, no. 1 (February 1964): 97–98.

G. L. S. Shackle. *The Nature of Economic Thought: Selected Papers, 1955–1964. Journal of Business* 40, no. 2 (April 1967): 209–10.

"On Man-made Tightropes." Review of Jacques Rueff, *Balance of Payments. National Review*, February 27, 1968, 194.

Donald Dewey. *The Theory of Imperfect Competition: A Radical Reconstruction. Journal of Business* 43, no. 4 (October 1970): 489–90.

Henry Manne, ed. *Economic Policy and the Regulation of Corporate Securities.* *Journal of Business* 44, no. 4 (October 1971): 467–68.

Yale Brozen, ed. *Advertising and Society. Reason Magazine,* November 1975.

John R. Hicks. *Capital and Time: A Neo-Austrian Theory. Libertarian Review,* November 1975.

John R. Hicks and W. Weber, eds. *Carl Menger and the Austrian School of Economics. Libertarian Review,* November 1975.

J. W. Markham. *Conglomerate Enterprise and Public Policy;* J. F. Winslow, *Conglomerate Unlimited: The Failure of Regulation. American Political Science Review* 71, no. 1 (March 1977): 359–60.

John K. Galbraith. *The Age of Uncertainty. Libertarian Review,* September 1977.

Ludwig von Mises. *On the Manipulation of Money and Credit. Reason Magazine,* April 1979.

Frank A. Fetter. *Capital, Interest and Rent: Essays in the Theory of Distribution.* Edited by Murray N. Rothbard. *Austrian Economics Newsletter* 2, no. 3 (Spring 1980): 8–9.

Benjamin M. Friedman, ed. *New Challenges to the Role of Profit: The Third Series of the John Diebold Lectures at Harvard University. Public Choice* 35, no. 5 (1980): 633–35.

"Enter the New Economists." Review of Henri Lepage, *Tomorrow, Capitalism: The Economics of Economic Freedom. Inquiry,* September 1982, 34–36.

"Does Anyone Listen to Economists?" Review of George J. Stigler, *The Economist as Preacher and Other Essays. Inquiry: A Libertarian Review,* April 1983: 38–40. Reprinted as "Economists and the Correction of Error." In Daniel B. Klein, ed., *What Do Economists Contribute?,* 125–31. New York: New York University Press, 1999.

Daniel H. Hausman. *Capital, Profits and Prices: An Essay in the Philosophy of Economics. International Philosophical Quarterly* 23, no. 2 (June 1983): 220–22.

Robert F. Hébert and Albert N. Link. *The Entrepreneur, Mainstream Views and Radical Critiques. Southern Economic Journal* 50, no. 2 (October 1983): 611–12.

Helmut Frisch, ed. *Schumpeterian Economics. Journal of Economic Literature* 21, no. 4 (December 1983): 1501–2.

Mark Blaug. *The Methodology of Economics, or How Economists Explain. Austrian Economics Newsletter,* Spring 1984, 5–7.

"How Heroic Are Entrepreneurs?" Review of George Gilder, *The Spirit of Enterprise. Reason,* April 1985, 54–55.

Gerald O'Driscoll Jr. and Mario J. Rizzo. *The Economics of Time and Ignorance. Market Process* 3, no. 2 (Fall 1985): 1–4. Reprinted in Peter J. Boettke and David L. Prychitko, eds., *The Market Process: Essays in Contemporary Austrian Economics*, 38–44. Aldershot, U.K.: Edward Elgar, 1994.

"Beyond the Bliss of Equilibrium." Review of Albert O. Hirschman, *Rival Views of Market Society and Other Recent Essays*. *Reason*, August/September 1987, 72–73.

T. Alexander Smith. *Time and Public Policy*. *Freeman* 39, no. 8 (August 1989): 325–27.

Martin Currie and Ian Steedman. *Wrestling with Time: Problems in Economic Theory*. *Southern Economic Journal* 57, no. 3 (January 1991): 874–75.

Mark Skousen. *The Structure of Production*. *Journal of Economic Literature* 29, no. 4 (December 1991): 1761–63.

Roy E. Cordato. *Welfare Economics and Externalities in an Open-Ended Universe: A Modern Austrian Perspective*. *Cato Journal* 13, no. 1 (Spring/Summer 1993): 143–49.

Bettina Bien Greaves and Robert W. McGee. *Mises: An Annotated Bibliography: A Comprehensive Listing of Books and Articles by and about Ludwig von Mises*. *Freeman* 43, no. 11 (November 1993): 453–55.

Stavros Ioannides. *The Market, Competition and Democracy: A Critique of Neo-Austrian Economics*. *Freeman* 44, no. 1 (January 1994): 44–46.

David Ramsay Steele. *From Marx to Mises: Post-Capitalist Society and the Challenge of Economic Calculation*. *Economic Affairs* 14, no. 3 (April 1994): 46–48.

Brigitte Berger, ed. *The Culture of Entrepreneurship*. *Advances in Austrian Economics* 1 (1994): 327–30.

Stephen Kresge and Leif Wenar, eds. *Hayek on Hayek: An Autobiographical Dialogue*. *Economic Affairs* 15, no. 2 (March 1995): 57–58.

Jack Biner and Rudy Van Zijp, eds. *Hayek, Co-ordination and Evolution: His Legacy in Philosophy, Politics, Economics and the History of Ideas*. *Southern Economic Journal* 61, no. 4 (April 1995): 1243–44.

Christian Schmidt, ed. *Uncertainty in Economic Thought*. *Southern Economic Journal* 64, no. 1 (July 1997): 347–48.

Klaus H. Hennings. *The Austrian Theory of Value and Capital: Studies in the Life and Work of Eugen von Böhm-Bawerk*. *Economic Affairs* 17, no. 4 (December 1997): 62–63.

Steven G. Medema and Warren J. Samuels, eds. *A History of Economic Thought: The LSE Lectures by Lionel Robbins*. *Freeman* 52, no. 1 (January 2002): 60–62.

Alan Ebenstein. *Hayek's Journey: The Mind of Friedrich Hayek*. *NYU Journal of Law & Liberty* 1, no. 0 (2005): 300–303.

INDEX TO THE COLLECTED WORKS

ABBREVIATIONS

AS: Austrian Subjectivism and the Emergence of Entrepreneurship Theory
C&E: Competition and Entrepreneurship
CEP: Competition, Economic Planning, and the Knowledge Problem
DCDJ: Discovery, Capitalism, and Distributive Justice
ECI: Essays on Capital and Interest
EE: The Essence of Entrepreneurship and the Nature and Significance of Market Process
EPV: The Economic Point of View
LvM: Ludwig von Mises: The Man and His Economics
MTPS: Market Theory and the Price System
RE: Reflections on Ethics, Freedom, Welfare Economics, Policy, and the Legacy of Austrian Economics

AS: Austrian Subjectivism . . .; C&E: Competition and Entrepreneurship; CEP: Competition, Economic Planning . . .; DCDJ: Discovery, Capitalism, and Distributive Justice; ECI: Essays on Capital and Interest; EE: Essence of Entrepreneurship . . .; EPV: Economic Point of View; LvM: Ludwig von Mises; MTPS: Market Theory and the Price System; RE: Reflections on Ethics . . .

AS: Austrian Subjectivism . . .; C&E: Competition and Entrepreneurship; CEP: Competition, Economic Planning . . .; DCDJ: Discovery, Capitalism, and Distributive Justice; ECI: Essays on Capital and Interest; EE: Essence of Entrepreneurship . . .; EPV: Economic Point of View; LvM: Ludwig von Mises; MTPS: Market Theory and the Price System; RE: Reflections on Ethics . . .

AS: Austrian Subjectivism . . .; C&E: Competition and Entrepreneurship; CEP: Competition, Economic Planning . . .; DCDJ: Discovery, Capitalism, and Distributive Justice; ECI: Essays on Capital and Interest; EE: Essence of Entrepreneurship . . .; EPV: Economic Point of View; LvM: Ludwig von Mises; MTPS: Market Theory and the Price System; RE: Reflections on Ethics . . .

AS: Austrian Subjectivism . . .; C&E: Competition and Entrepreneurship; CEP: Competition, Economic Planning . . .; DCDJ: Discovery, Capitalism, and Distributive Justice; ECI: Essays on Capital and Interest; EE: Essence of Entrepreneurship . . .; EPV: Economic Point of View; LvM: Ludwig von Mises; MTPS: Market Theory and the Price System; RE: Reflections on Ethics . . .

compared, C&E:72–73, 100–105; terminology consequences, C&E:71–72; waste arguments, C&E:188–89. *See also* monopoly

complementarity, capital goods, ECI:27–28, 122, 173

complementarity characteristic, production factors, MTPS:162, 163

complementary goods, MTPS:55–56, 107–8, 110–11

Comte, Auguste, EPV:41, 93

congealed waiting, capital as, ECI:89–91

conscious being, presumption of, EPV:38

constant income concept, ECI:71–72

constant wants, assumption of, EPV:176–80

The Constitution of Liberty (Hayek), CEP:88, 134, LvM:123

consultant administrators and pamphleteers, EPV:21, 23

consumer activity: dynamic nature, MTPS:108–11; from resource owners, MTPS:43–44, 68n1; role in market system model, MTPS:16–17, 19–23, 41–42

consumer needs/decisions: in central planning systems, AS:16–17, 51; in determinate market framework, AS:65–67; focus of, AS:186; Menger's arguments, AS:12–18, 24, 26n3, 49; in radical subjectivism, AS:53–54, 56–57

consumer preferences: in capitalism, RE:246, 249, 277; control of economy, RE:533–35; mistaken,

RE:536; molding, RE:740–41; rankings, RE:491. *See also* subjectivism (RE)

consumers (C&E): in cost categories debate, C&E:117–20; entrepreneurship of, C&E:10–13, 32; as market process element, C&E:4–5, 7–10; as orthodox price theory element, C&E:3–4; and producer entrepreneurship, C&E:14–15, 18–20. *See also* advertising (C&E)

consumers-only model, competition element: overview, MTPS:113–15, 142–46; graphic representations, MTPS:147–52; imperfect knowledge conditions, MTPS:120–25, 132–38; monopoly effects, MTPS:138–42; multi-period market, MTPS:336–37; multiple-commodity market, MTPS:125–38; perfect knowledge conditions, MTPS:116–20, 130–31; resource-constrained model compared, MTPS:257–59, 261–62; single-commodity market, MTPS:115–25, 147–52

consumer sovereignty doctrine, ECI:5–6, 7, LvM:76–78, 82–83, 115–16, 188–92, 194–96, 197nn3–4, RE:474, 475–76, 533–38

consumption: in capital measurement problem, ECI:105–6, 121, 130–31; in income definitions, ECI:69–71, 72; production simultaneity, ECI:78–80; standards of living, RE:274, 284, 293; theory of, EPV:106–7; time structure, RE:562

AS: Austrian Subjectivism . . .; C&E: Competition and Entrepreneurship; CEP: Competition, Economic Planning . . .; DCDJ: Discovery, Capitalism, and Distributive Justice; ECI: Essays on Capital and Interest; EE: Essence of Entrepreneurship . . .; EPV: Economic Point of View; LvM: Ludwig von Mises; MTPS: Market Theory and the Price System; RE: Reflections on Ethics . . .

AS: Austrian Subjectivism . . .; C&E: Competition and Entrepreneurship; CEP: Competition, Economic Planning . . .; DCDJ: Discovery, Capitalism, and Distributive Justice; ECI: Essays on Capital and Interest; EE: Essence of Entrepreneurship . . .; EPV: Economic Point of View; LvM: Ludwig von Mises; MTPS: Market Theory and the Price System; RE: Reflections on Ethics . . .

AS: Austrian Subjectivism . . .; C&E: Competition and Entrepreneurship; CEP: Competition,
Economic Planning . . .; DCDJ: Discovery, Capitalism, and Distributive Justice; ECI: Essays on
Capital and Interest; EE: Essence of Entrepreneurship . . .; EPV: Economic Point of View; LvM:
Ludwig von Mises; MTPS: Market Theory and the Price System; RE: Reflections on Ethics . . .

AS: Austrian Subjectivism . . .; C&E: Competition and Entrepreneurship; CEP: Competition, Economic Planning . . .; DCDJ: Discovery, Capitalism, and Distributive Justice; ECI: Essays on Capital and Interest; EE: Essence of Entrepreneurship . . .; EPV: Economic Point of View; LvM: Ludwig von Mises; MTPS: Market Theory and the Price System; RE: Reflections on Ethics . . .

AS: Austrian Subjectivism . . .; C&E: Competition and Entrepreneurship; CEP: Competition, Economic Planning . . .; DCDJ: Discovery, Capitalism, and Distributive Justice; ECI: Essays on Capital and Interest; EE: Essence of Entrepreneurship . . .; EPV: Economic Point of View; LvM: Ludwig von Mises; MTPS: Market Theory and the Price System; RE: Reflections on Ethics . . .

AS: Austrian Subjectivism . . .; C&E: Competition and Entrepreneurship; CEP: Competition, Economic Planning . . .; DCDJ: Discovery, Capitalism, and Distributive Justice; ECI: Essays on Capital and Interest; EE: Essence of Entrepreneurship . . .; EPV: Economic Point of View; LvM: Ludwig von Mises; MTPS: Market Theory and the Price System; RE: Reflections on Ethics . . .

AS: Austrian Subjectivism . . .; C&E: Competition and Entrepreneurship; CEP: Competition, Economic Planning . . .; DCDJ: Discovery, Capitalism, and Distributive Justice; ECI: Essays on Capital and Interest; EE: Essence of Entrepreneurship . . .; EPV: Economic Point of View; LvM: Ludwig von Mises; MTPS: Market Theory and the Price System; RE: Reflections on Ethics . . .

AS: Austrian Subjectivism . . .; C&E: Competition and Entrepreneurship; CEP: Competition, Economic Planning . . .; DCDJ: Discovery, Capitalism, and Distributive Justice; ECI: Essays on Capital and Interest; EE: Essence of Entrepreneurship . . .; EPV: Economic Point of View; LvM: Ludwig von Mises; MTPS: Market Theory and the Price System; RE: Reflections on Ethics . . .

AS: Austrian Subjectivism . . .; C&E: Competition and Entrepreneurship; CEP: Competition, Economic Planning . . .; DCDJ: Discovery, Capitalism, and Distributive Justice; ECI: Essays on Capital and Interest; EE: Essence of Entrepreneurship . . .; EPV: Economic Point of View; LvM: Ludwig von Mises; MTPS: Market Theory and the Price System; RE: Reflections on Ethics . . .

AS: Austrian Subjectivism . . .; C&E: Competition and Entrepreneurship; CEP: Competition, Economic Planning . . .; DCDJ: Discovery, Capitalism, and Distributive Justice; ECI: Essays on Capital and Interest; EE: Essence of Entrepreneurship . . .; EPV: Economic Point of View; LvM: Ludwig von Mises; MTPS: Market Theory and the Price System; RE: Reflections on Ethics . . .

AS: Austrian Subjectivism . . .; C&E: Competition and Entrepreneurship; CEP: Competition, Economic Planning . . .; DCDJ: Discovery, Capitalism, and Distributive Justice; ECI: Essays on Capital and Interest; EE: Essence of Entrepreneurship . . .; EPV: Economic Point of View; LvM: Ludwig von Mises; MTPS: Market Theory and the Price System; RE: Reflections on Ethics . . .

AS: Austrian Subjectivism . . .; C&E: Competition and Entrepreneurship; CEP: Competition, Economic Planning . . .; DCDJ: Discovery, Capitalism, and Distributive Justice; ECI: Essays on Capital and Interest; EE: Essence of Entrepreneurship . . .; EPV: Economic Point of View; LvM: Ludwig von Mises; MTPS: Market Theory and the Price System; RE: Reflections on Ethics . . .

AS: Austrian Subjectivism . . .; C&E: Competition and Entrepreneurship; CEP: Competition, Economic Planning . . .; DCDJ: Discovery, Capitalism, and Distributive Justice; ECI: Essays on Capital and Interest; EE: Essence of Entrepreneurship . . .; EPV: Economic Point of View; LvM: Ludwig von Mises; MTPS: Market Theory and the Price System; RE: Reflections on Ethics . . .

AS: Austrian Subjectivism . . .; C&E: Competition and Entrepreneurship; CEP: Competition, Economic Planning . . .; DCDJ: Discovery, Capitalism, and Distributive Justice; ECI: Essays on Capital and Interest; EE: Essence of Entrepreneurship . . .; EPV: Economic Point of View; LvM: Ludwig von Mises; MTPS: Market Theory and the Price System; RE: Reflections on Ethics . . .

equilibrium conditions, MTPS:127–31; imperfect-knowledge scenario, MTPS:132–38; monopoly effects, MTPS:138–42; perfect-knowledge scenario, MTPS:130–31; resource-constrained model compared, MTPS:257–59, 261–62

multiple ends, in economizing theory, EPV:138–42

mutual benefit principle, consumer sovereignty contrasted, LvM:190–92

Myrdal, Gunnar, DCDJ:178, 183, EPV:7, 25, LvM:65, RE:89–91, 213, 451–52, 453, 529, 538, 539, 692

mysticism accusations, capital concepts, ECI:63–64, 170–71

naive profit theory, C&E:61–63

Nation, State and Economy (Mises), LvM:12

National Association of Manufacturers (NAM), LvM:21

National Bureau of Economic Research, LvM:21

Nationalökonomie (Mises), EPV:165, LvM:39, 44, 102, 209

Das Nationalökonomie (Schumpeter), EPV:73

natural-law philosophers, EPV:24–25

natural resources: discovery of, DCDJ:143, 148–49, 161–62, 199, 226–27; property rights to, DCDJ:133, 136–41, 149–53, 154. *See also* land; original acquisition from nature

natural sciences, eighteenth century, EPV:27

nature, struggle of man and, EPV:43–45

The Nature and Significance of Economic Science (Robbins) CEP:265, EPV:114, 143–44, LvM:32–33, 38, 208, RE:80–81, 129, 138–42, 144–47, 148–51, 560, 593, 611, 638, 644, 661, 663–64

Nazism, LvM:11–12, 16, 125–26

necessaries, science of, EPV:33–39

Nelson, R. R., EE:331

Nelson, Richard R., CEP:124

neoclassical economics (EPV), EPV:208, 210

neoclassical economics (LvM): and entrepreneurship, LvM:157; and free market defense, LvM:127–29; and government interventions, LvM:138–39; interest theory, LvM:107–8; price theory, LvM:73–74; social efficiency problem, LvM:113–14. *See also* economizing behavior (LvM); equilibrium state (LvM)

neoclassical economics (RE): Austrian School and, RE:126–27, 128–29, 130–37, 548, 608–9, 716–17; entrepreneurship, RE:365–66; foundations, RE:127–29, 453; influence, RE:547; in interwar period, RE:128, 547, 611–16, 662–64; market functions, RE:386; microeconomics, RE:141–42, 146, 597; price theory, RE:302; social efficiency, RE:304. *See also* equilibrium; Marshallian economics

AS: Austrian Subjectivism . . .; C&E: Competition and Entrepreneurship; CEP: Competition, Economic Planning . . .; DCDJ: Discovery, Capitalism, and Distributive Justice; ECI: Essays on Capital and Interest; EE: Essence of Entrepreneurship . . .; EPV: Economic Point of View; LvM: Ludwig von Mises; MTPS: Market Theory and the Price System; RE: Reflections on Ethics . . .

AS: Austrian Subjectivism . . .; C&E: Competition and Entrepreneurship; CEP: Competition,
Economic Planning . . .; DCDJ: Discovery, Capitalism, and Distributive Justice; ECI: Essays on
Capital and Interest; EE: Essence of Entrepreneurship . . .; EPV: Economic Point of View; LvM:
Ludwig von Mises; MTPS: Market Theory and the Price System; RE: Reflections on Ethics . . .

AS: Austrian Subjectivism . . .; C&E: Competition and Entrepreneurship; CEP: Competition, Economic Planning . . .; DCDJ: Discovery, Capitalism, and Distributive Justice; ECI: Essays on Capital and Interest; EE: Essence of Entrepreneurship . . .; EPV: Economic Point of View; LvM: Ludwig von Mises; MTPS: Market Theory and the Price System; RE: Reflections on Ethics . . .

AS: Austrian Subjectivism . . .; C&E: Competition and Entrepreneurship; CEP: Competition, Economic Planning . . .; DCDJ: Discovery, Capitalism, and Distributive Justice; ECI: Essays on Capital and Interest; EE: Essence of Entrepreneurship . . .; EPV: Economic Point of View; LvM: Ludwig von Mises; MTPS: Market Theory and the Price System; RE: Reflections on Ethics . . .

AS: Austrian Subjectivism . . .; C&E: Competition and Entrepreneurship; CEP: Competition, Economic Planning . . .; DCDJ: Discovery, Capitalism, and Distributive Justice; ECI: Essays on Capital and Interest; EE: Essence of Entrepreneurship . . .; EPV: Economic Point of View; LvM: Ludwig von Mises; MTPS: Market Theory and the Price System; RE: Reflections on Ethics . . .

AS: Austrian Subjectivism . . .; C&E: Competition and Entrepreneurship; CEP: Competition, Economic Planning . . .; DCDJ: Discovery, Capitalism, and Distributive Justice; ECI: Essays on Capital and Interest; EE: Essence of Entrepreneurship . . .; EPV: Economic Point of View; LvM: Ludwig von Mises; MTPS: Market Theory and the Price System; RE: Reflections on Ethics . . .

AS: Austrian Subjectivism . . .; C&E: Competition and Entrepreneurship; CEP: Competition, Economic Planning . . .; DCDJ: Discovery, Capitalism, and Distributive Justice; ECI: Essays on Capital and Interest; EE: Essence of Entrepreneurship . . .; EPV: Economic Point of View; LvM: Ludwig von Mises; MTPS: Market Theory and the Price System; RE: Reflections on Ethics . . .

AS: Austrian Subjectivism . . .; C&E: Competition and Entrepreneurship; CEP: Competition, Economic Planning . . .; DCDJ: Discovery, Capitalism, and Distributive Justice; ECI: Essays on Capital and Interest; EE: Essence of Entrepreneurship . . .; EPV: Economic Point of View; LvM: Ludwig von Mises; MTPS: Market Theory and the Price System; RE: Reflections on Ethics . . .

AS: Austrian Subjectivism . . .; C&E: Competition and Entrepreneurship; CEP: Competition, Economic Planning . . .; DCDJ: Discovery, Capitalism, and Distributive Justice; ECI: Essays on Capital and Interest; EE: Essence of Entrepreneurship . . .; EPV: Economic Point of View; LvM: Ludwig von Mises; MTPS: Market Theory and the Price System; RE: Reflections on Ethics . . .

AS: Austrian Subjectivism . . .; C&E: Competition and Entrepreneurship; CEP: Competition, Economic Planning . . .; DCDJ: Discovery, Capitalism, and Distributive Justice; ECI: Essays on Capital and Interest; EE: Essence of Entrepreneurship . . .; EPV: Economic Point of View; LvM: Ludwig von Mises; MTPS: Market Theory and the Price System; RE: Reflections on Ethics . . .

This book is set in Scala and Scala Sans, created
by the Dutch designer Martin Majoor in the 1990s.

This book is printed on paper that is acid-free and
meets the requirements of the American National
Standard for Permanence of Paper for Printed Library
Materials, z39.48-1992. ∞

Book design by Richard Hendel, Chapel Hill, North Carolina
Typography by Apex CoVantage, Madison, Wisconsin
Index to this volume and to the Collected Works by
Sherry L. Smith, Bend, Oregon
Printed and bound by Thomson-Shore, Inc., Dexter, Michigan